Debating Foreign Policy in the Renaissance

Speeches on War and Peace by Francesco Guicciardini

Edited by
Marco Cesa

EDINBURGH
University Press

To the memory of Stanley H. Hoffmann

Edinburgh University Press is one of the leading university presses in the UK. We publish academic books and journals in our selected subject areas across the humanities and social sciences, combining cutting-edge scholarship with high editorial and production values to produce academic works of lasting importance. For more information visit our website: edinburghuniversitypress.com

© Marco Cesa, 2017

Edinburgh University Press Ltd
The Tun – Holyrood Road, 12(2f) Jackson's Entry, Edinburgh EH8 8PJ

Typeset in 11/13 Sabon by
Servis Filmsetting Ltd, Stockport, Cheshire

A CIP record for this book is available from the British Library

ISBN 978 1 4744 1504 0 (hardback)
ISBN 978 1 4744 1505 7 (webready PDF)
ISBN 978 1 4744 1506 4 (epub)

The right of Marco Cesa to be identified as the editor of this work has been asserted in accordance with the Copyright, Designs and Patents Act 1988, and the Copyright and Related Rights Regulations 2003 (SI No. 2498).

Contents

Note on Sources and Texts

The six pairs of speeches from *The History of Italy* have been taken from the 3rd edition of the translation by Austin Parke Goddard (London: Z. Stuart, 1763). The excerpts have been checked against two Italian editions (*Opere*, ed. by E. Scarano, Turin: Utet, vols II and III, 1981; and *Storia d'Italia*, ed. by S. Seidel Menchi, Turin: Einaudi, 1971) and revised accordingly, in both substance and style. I have translated the remaining five pairs from their only available Italian edition (*Le cose fiorentine*, ed. by R. Ridolfi, Florence: Olschki, 1945, reprinted in 1983; and *Opere*, vol. VIII: *Scritti politici e Ricordi*, ed. by R. Palmarocchi, Bari: Laterza, 1933). The speeches have been arranged in chronological order according to the time of the events they address – an order that does not always coincide with the time of their composition; the pairs of speeches in Chapters 9 and 10 were written before all the others, in 1525.

Introduction*

Francesco Guicciardini (1483–1540) is primarily known for his writings on history and Florentine politics. From the sixteenth to the nineteenth century, his major work, *The History of Italy*, was translated six times into French, three times into English and Spanish, and once into Dutch and German, not to mention his *Maxims and Reflections* – a series of meditations grown out of his personal experiences – that had an even wider circulation. In a nutshell, it is no exaggeration to argue that Guicciardini's work deeply affected the European intellectual and political elites throughout the modern age.

Much of what Guicciardini says as a historian and a participant in the ongoing debate on Florentine political institutions inevitably deals with issues of international politics and foreign policy: *The History of Italy* is, in fact, the history of the relations between the Italian states and the European powers of the day, and the weight of the external world can be perceived in other important writings too. Yet, although we know quite a lot about Guicciardini the historian, his dark and pessimistic views on human affairs and his own brand of 'republicanism', precious little has been written about his perspective on international politics and foreign policy.[1] As a modest way to begin to shed some light on this side of Guicciardini's thought, I have chosen to focus not so much on his entire production – which, if one includes the public and private correspondence, is monumental –

* I would like to thank the friends and colleagues who have helped me with the translation of the texts contained in this volume. Francesco Bausi's generous and competent assistance has been decisive to my understanding of several sentences of Guicciardini's complex prose and a number of words in his vocabulary. Mark Gilbert, John Harper and, above all, Jennifer Varney have been kind enough to revise my English patiently. Needless to say, I remain the only person responsible for any errors or imperfections. While the full details of the secondary literature – in square brackets – are provided in the References section at the end of the Introduction, the relevant information relating to Guicciardini's works can be found in the endnotes.

but only on the part of it that seems immediately relevant to our purposes.

Guicciardini frequently engages in the analysis of political situations through pairs of opposing speeches, one in favour and one against any given policy on any given issue. Now, most of these pairs deal with foreign policy. As a whole, they constitute a remarkable collection of debates on war, peace, alliance and the like – in short, key issues in international affairs. Action takes place in various contexts: different Florentine institutions, the Venetian senate, the French royal council, the papal *Curia*, the imperial council. The structure of the debates is always straightforward: the first speaker argues that X is the right policy and Y the wrong one; the second speaker argues the opposite. Thus, each criticises the policy advice of the other, and each supports what the other opposes. Going beyond the rhetorical canons of humanist historiography, those speeches not only are incisive, elegant and compelling, but they are interesting for other reasons too. First, the criteria that are put forward to evaluate this or that strategy are the classical benchmarks in foreign policy: security, profit, reputation. Second, the speeches contain concepts, such as the balance of power and what will later be known as the 'security dilemma', that have been taken up and developed by contemporary international relations theory. In other words, the speeches can be seen as sophisticated analytical pieces that not only are structured around themes that, arguably, have always constituted the backbone of foreign policy debates, but are also illuminated by insights that still shape scholarly work in international politics.

I have thus collected all the pairs of speeches that deal with foreign policy decisions. Six come from *The History of Italy*, three from *Le cose fiorentine*, Guicciardini's incomplete work that only came to light in 1945, and two from miscellaneous papers. By and large, these speeches are either little known, or not known at all, to the general public nowadays; the last unabridged English translation of *The History of Italy* was published in the eighteenth century, and subsequent translations have left most of the speeches out. As for *Le cose fiorentine* and the miscellaneous writings, they have never been rendered into English. The Italianists and the students of the Renaissance are, of course, familiar with Guicciardini. This book is aimed at those who do not know him or know him just a little. In order not to discourage them, I have deliberately left out a number of issues that elicit the interest of the specialists only. Conversely, I have tried to give as many details as possible about the main historical events that the speeches address, so that the reader is enabled to appreciate both the content and the meaning of the debates better.

Guicciardini's Life and Times

Throughout the span of his life, Guicciardini was a first-hand witness to, and an active participant in, the events that would result in both the transformation of the ancient Florentine republic into an absolute princedom and the subjugation of most of Italy to foreigners.[2] Born in Florence on 6 March 1483, he belonged to one of the oldest and most prestigious families in town: his ancestors had been holding public positions since the beginning of the fourteenth century, and his closer relatives were supporters of the Medici, who had been ruling the city for most of the fifteenth century. After receiving the humanist education that was customary at the time – Latin, some Greek and the ancient historians: above all, Thucydides, Xenophon, Livy and Tacitus – he obtained a degree in law in 1505, and began a career as a lawyer. Meanwhile, the Medici regime had come to a temporary end in 1494, and the Florentine republic went through a long period of institutional reforms and political struggles, at the end of which the popular government found itself more and more at odds with the oligarchic party, with which the young Guicciardini identified himself. Between 1508 and 1509 he wrote – or began to write – his first works, most notably *The History of Florence*.[3] It should be pointed out from the outset that none of his writings was ever intended for an audience larger than his own family or even himself, with the major exception of *The History of Italy*, which he wrote in the last years of his life. Writing about politics – above all, Florentine institutions – and history – family and Florentine history – was an activity in which he indulged in his spare time, probably in an attempt to clarify matters to himself in particular: the habit of the reflective mind of a most practical man who was naturally inclined to address the various issues under investigation in the most detailed and careful manner, in a written format, and in the secrecy of his study room.

In 1511 Guicciardini was appointed ambassador to Spain and upon his departure he must have received the official instructions from Niccolò Machiavelli, who was at the time the Secretary of the Ten of War – the Florentine magistracy in charge of external and military affairs. Although the available evidence of a solid personal relationship between the two great Florentines covers only the last years of Machiavelli's life (1521-7), the two men had certainly met much earlier, and they must have been on good terms, despite their different political views and positions,[4] if as early as 1509 Machiavelli would end a letter to Francesco's brother, Luigi, with these words: 'If you write your Messer Francesco, tell him that I send the gang my regards.'[5] The almost two years that Guicciardini spent in Spain contributed much to his intellectual development. Not only was he deeply affected by his personal acquaintance with Ferdinand of Aragon, the 'circumspect and parsimonious, sagacious and dissimulating' [Ridolfi 1960/7, p. 44] King of Spain, but also he wrote, among other things, the first nucleus of his *Maxims and Reflections*[6] and a piece called *On How to Order the Popular Government*, better known as *Discorso di Logrogno*.[7] As the Florentine popular government had marginalised the oligarchic movement, the latter split into two main camps, one concentrating its efforts on overthrowing the regime and keeping in touch with the Medici who had been exiled, the other supporting a reform of the current arrangement centred upon the creation of a senate that would finally assign a relevant role to the optimates – the 'leading citizens', the 'wise', the 'men of worth' – while keeping the other republican institutions alive. Guicciardini belonged to this second camp. Equally critical of the previous Medici government that had minimised the political role of the few, and of the popular government built upon the many, he was also aware that the re-establishment of the oligarchic regime that had ruled the city at the beginning of the fifteenth century was unrealistic, for Florence was by now used to popular institutions. Besides, he also believed that a 'mixed' constitution modelled around the Venetian experience had some merits of its own in terms of stability, in so far as it would guarantee a fair representation of all the major social and political groups.

Guicciardini was still in Spain when the Florentine popular government collapsed under the weight of the Spanish and papal armies and the Medici were restored to power (August to September 1512). Upon his return to Florence in 1514, he resorted to his profession of lawyer and was appointed to some important public posts. Meanwhile, in 1513, Giovanni de' Medici, Lorenzo the Magnificent's son, had been elected pope as Leo X. In 1516 he nominated Guicciardini Governor of Modena. This was the beginning of a career as a papal top official under two Medici pontiffs – Leo X (1513–21) and Clement VII (1523–34) – that would last, with some intermissions, until 1534: Governor of Modena and Reggio (1517), President of Romagna (1524), Governor of Bologna (1531). Thus, after serving under a popular government that he did not like, Guicciardini ended up working for the Medici, despite his at best lukewarm sympathy for them. But this should not come as a surprise. He belonged to the narrow power elite that, by experience and family tradition, would retain its authority under any kind of political regime. For the Florentine oligarchs, in addition, it was essential to cooperate with the Medici in order not to be completely excluded from the management of political affairs and prevent any absolutist temptation of the ruling family that would destroy even the appearance of republican institutions [Martelli and Bausi 1996, pp. 325–6]. Throughout all of his life, Guicciardini remained convinced that the optimates should play a fundamental role in government. Such views would find a mature expression in the *Dialogue on the Government of Florence*, a work begun in 1521 and completed a few years later, when he was President of Romagna.[8]

As a papal officer, his main activities were largely confined to the administration of the cities and dominions under his responsibility, a function that he performed with rigour and impartiality. However, he was also involved in foreign policy and military affairs. Since the beginning of the century, Italy had become the main battlefield in an ongoing confrontation between Spain and France, which had resulted in the Spanish seizure of the Kingdom of Naples and the French occupation of the Duchy of Milan. The Spanish–French rivalry entered a new phase when Francis I became king of France in 1515, and Charles V king of Spain in 1516 and Holy Roman Emperor in 1519. In 1521 Leo X signed an alliance with the Emperor in order to expel the French from the Duchy of Milan and expand the dominions of the State of the Church. Guicciardini took part in the successful campaign that followed as Commissioner General to the papal army and in 1522 defended Parma from a French comeback. Then, the imperial forces inflicted a ruinous defeat upon the French at Pavia, and took Francis I prisoner (24 February 1525). As Charles seemed on the verge of establishing his control over all of Italy, Guicciardini became more and more involved in foreign policy, concerned as he was about the unchecked growth of imperial power. In fact, he was called to Rome to serve as an advisor to Clement VII, had a substantial influence on the Pope's decision to adhere to an anti-imperial alliance (League of Cognac, 22 May 1526), and participated in the war as Lieutenant General to the papal army. His role was, of course, political and administrative, not military: he was the representative of the Pope at the allied headquarters. The result of the campaign was catastrophic: without even trying to engage the enemy in battle, the allies managed to let it move undisturbed across Northern and Central Italy until the Landsknechts stormed and sacked Rome in May 1527. Charles's position in Italy was now unchallengeable.

One of the immediate implications of the occupation of Rome was the collapse of the Medici regime in Florence and the restoration of republican institutions. Guicciardini went back home, and for a while entertained the hope that a 'mixed' constitution might finally be established. Yet his long association with the Medici made him suspect in the eyes of the most radical exponents of the new regime, and he soon fell into disgrace. Accused of extortion, he had to face a trial from which he emerged innocent – as a public official, he was indeed incorruptible. But, embittered as he was with the popular party that had finally seized power, he eventually left Florence, and reached the Pope. Clement was at this time negotiating the terms of a general agreement with Charles, with an eye fixed on Florence, from which his family had been expelled. To Guicciardini, it was advisable that the republican government should find a compromise with Clement; the city would be in no position to challenge the Pope if he made peace with the Emperor. Thus, he engaged in a mediating effort between the Pontiff and the Florentines and succeeded in obtaining favourable conditions for the city. As a reward, he would be accused of machinations against the republic and sentenced as a rebel in absentia in the spring of 1530. Clement and Charles did sign, in June 1529, a peace treaty, which contemplated, among other things, the restoration of the Medici in Florence. Accordingly, the imperial forces began to lay siege to the city shortly afterwards. In November, the Pope and the Emperor met in Bologna to discuss the final arrangement of Italian affairs. Guicciardini was there: 'While Florence was besieged, its country districts devastated by the armies [. . .] he saw triumphant a foreign Emperor whom he had wished to drive out of Italy, and who was now virtually the ruler of Italy and the world' [Ridolfi 1960/7, p. 202].

The years between 1527 and 1530 must thus be seen as a period of profound disillusionment for Guicciardini, characterised as they were by a double failure: the disaster in foreign policy was coupled with the definitive abandonment of any interest in a 'mixed' constitution, for the popular party had proved so stubborn that any form of cooperation with it was by now impossible. His intellectual attitude, as we shall see later, was always practically oriented. In other words, he had no patience for abstract discussions on some ideal form of government; rather, he was interested in what could realistically be done in Florence, under the given circumstances. Now that the cleavage between the popular party and the optimates was simply too wide and deep to be ever filled, the only thing that could be done was to cope with the inevitable Medici regime as best one could. Throughout the same time span he wrote a number of works: three fictitious orations on his own personal situation,[9] another history of Florence – *Le cose fiorentine* – which he left incomplete,[10] the second and third versions of his *Maxims and Reflections*, and the *Considerations on the 'Discourses' of Machiavelli*.[11]

As Florence was eventually forced to surrender, in August 1530, Guicciardini was charged by Clement to punish the leaders of the republican government. Alessandro de' Medici, Clement's nephew (or possibly son), would be soon created duke by the Emperor, thereby putting a formal end to the secular republican institutions of the city. In 1531 the Pope appointed Guicciardini as Governor of Bologna – his last papal post. Here, he hosted a second meeting of the Pope and the Emperor, and from there he accompanied Clement to meet the King of France in Marseilles. After the Pope's death, in 1534, he went back to Florence and served as a chief advisor to Duke Alessandro. It is significant that, even now, he attempted to dissuade the Medici from establishing an absolute princedom. It was at this time that he began to write a historical work on the Italian events of 1525–6, the *Commentaries on the Lieutenancy*, that he would later incorporate into *The History of Italy*. When Alessandro was assassinated in January 1537, Guicciardini supported the election of Cosimo de' Medici, who was only eighteen, possibly with the hope of exerting some influence over him. But the young Duke soon moved towards assuming complete power, with the endorsement of the Emperor, and Guicciardini, although appointed to formally important public offices, was relegated to a marginal role. He thus retired to his villa near Florence and spent the last three years of his life writing what is considered his masterpiece, *The History of Italy*, dealing with Italian events from 1494 to 1534, within a broad European context.[12] He died on 22 May 1540.

Guicciardini on International Politics

Although Florentine domestic affairs and institutional arrangements were the main focus of Guicciardini's writings until the last years of his life, as a statesman and a historian of his own times he could not possibly ignore international politics and foreign policy. The sense of uncertainty, of the unpredictability of the future, so typical of his thought, reflected, at least in part, the extreme instability that he observed in the external world. Florence went through a regime change four times during his life, and each time under the impact of external events. To repeat, these were: the collapse of the Medici government and the re-establishment of republican institutions, as a result of the 1494 French invasion of Italy; the Medici restoration of 1512 by the Spanish army; the republican regime of 1527, after the sack of Rome, which put a temporary end to the Medici rule; and the definitive Medici restoration in 1530, this time thanks to imperial arms. In light of all this, one can easily see why Guicciardini could not help taking international politics into consideration even if his primary interests lay in domestic affairs. After all, one of the typical issues that characterised Florentine political thinking as a whole, in those troubled decades, was the contrast between the domestic realm, where justice and serenity may be achieved, and the outside world, in which force – and not the law – rules [Pocock 1975, pp. 114–17].

As early as 1512, in the *Discorso di Logrogno*, Guicciardini had come to the conclusion that, in their external relations, states are nothing but violence, 'occasionally masked by a pretence of decency', and that those 'who live unarmed are hard put to overcome others, and hard put to defend themselves'. Accordingly, defence is considered 'the most important matter of all', when it comes to the design of any constitutional arrangement, for the simple reason that even the best domestic institutions 'would be of little use if the city were subject to being overcome by force'.[13] Ten years later, in the *Dialogue*, he expresses the same views even more assertively. External affairs constitute the realm on which internal affairs depend – which is a quite remarkable observation for a work whose main focus is the domestic realm and how it should be organised. Even if Florence were content with her freedom and a small dominion – that is, even if Florence left the others alone – she would not be left alone by others. Hence, the city 'must either be powerful enough to oppress others or she must be oppressed by others'. And again, foreign and security affairs are more important than domestic affairs: should Florence lose her dominion, she would be subjugated, and her domestic institutions, no matter how good they might be, would be of no use; if, on the other hand, the city is not well ordered but can defend herself against her external enemies, it 'suffers, but does not die'.[14] In short, to Guicciardini, the external world is violent and dangerous, international politics is the domain of force, and the typical attitude of states, in their mutual relations, is shaped by a constant concern and fear of each other: 'nothing is, by nature, more apprehensive than states';[15] 'jealousy is only too natural for states.'[16]

But there is more. One of the reasons why Guicciardini's aristocratic conception of government assigns a predominant role to the optimates is to be found in the external world. Whereas Machiavelli reconciles the pursuit of domestic virtue and the imperative need to survive among violent states through his notion of citizen–warrior, Guicciardini follows a different path [Pocock 1975, pp. 132–45 and 237–8]. To him, the few are characterised by two main traits that differentiate them from the many: that is, a great-hearted inclination to achieve public glory – a positively connoted ambition that drives leading men to aspire to political positions because of their desire to excel in the management of public affairs; and 'prudence', a key term in Guicciardini's vocabulary, which is directly related to international politics. Prudence refers to the ability to decide and act while keeping an eye on the future, a deep

knowledge of world affairs with which those who have had extraordinary opportunities of acquiring it are endowed. It is, above all, external
policy that requires prudence, for international affairs may vary by the
day, and taking care of them cannot be but a matter of conjecture. This
is why self-defence and expansion – the two main activities in the external realm – demand exceptional diligence and industry. Now, a popular
government displays a number of traits that are at odds with those
requirements. The many 'don't think, don't concentrate, don't see, and
understand nothing until things are reduced to the point where they
are obvious to everyone':[17] that is, until it is too late. Providing against
dangers usually calls for money, trouble and difficulty – all things that
people dislike.[18] A popular government does not possess the means
and the ability to recognise the deceptions of the other powers.[19] The
many are slow in their decisions, which entails the risk of wasting the
opportunity; they may well wage war when it is necessary, but are unfit
to make it when it would be useful. Alliances, which are so often necessary, are effective only if they have gone through long and steady pre-
paratory talks and consultations among the same men – but in popular
governments those in office vary frequently and rapidly.[20] Due to their
slowness and irresolution, the many often tend to remain neutral, in
case of war – and neutrality is, generally speaking, a poor policy.[21] And,
on top of it all, a popular government manages to become involved
in unnecessary and dangerous undertakings, for its lack of prudence
predisposes it to miscalculate and believe that a difficult enterprise is,
in fact, easy.[22] To conclude, the extent of information and deliberation, which are so necessary in dealing with unexpected and sudden
events that may unravel fast and get out of control, is not compatible
with a popular government, for a large assembly cannot possess the
kind of knowledge – both intuitive and deliberative – that is needed to
grasp power politics. It does not come as a surprise, then, that foreign
policy is explicitly attributed to the senate, the pivot of Guicciardini's
constitutional design, in both major works that deal with institutional
reforms.[23]

   This perspective, in which domestic affairs are often seen through
the lens of a dangerous external world, is at play also when it comes to
the thorny issue of a civic militia, the controversial reform introduced
in the Florentine republic in 1506, thanks to Machiavelli's efforts – and
a recurrent theme in his major writings – only to be immediately abol-
ished by the restored Medici government. Guicciardini initially takes
a neutral stand towards a citizen army;[24] then, in 1512, he endorses
this idea, along with the acceptance of other institutions of the popular government – provided a senate endowed with substantial powers

be established – taking up Machiavellian arguments: the unreliability of mercenaries and the connection between 'good laws' and 'good arms' – that is, between sound political institutions and solid armed forces.[25] But ten year later, he adopts a clear anti-Machiavellian tone on the issue.[26] Although Florence made a very bad decision when it first decided to rely on mercenaries, any attempt to restore an army of her own now would be just as bad. The Roman example, so cherished by Machiavelli, is discarded and the crucial relations that it entailed between the form of government and the military system are revised. The latter was not a consequence of the former, as Machiavelli claimed, but it simply contributed to its success in allowing the Romans to be so powerful as to afford to neglect diplomacy in their external relations. Rome was not well ordered at all, internally:

> if they [the Romans] had fought with mercenary arms and had consequently needed to make use of the things unarmed cities need to use, that is diligence and care, minute scrutiny of everything, hard work and secret preparations, have no doubt about it: living at home as they did, they would have been ruined in a few years.[27]

Florence cannot imitate the Roman example unless all the other Roman conditions and qualities are there. The city was disarmed by the heads of the various factions fighting against each other long before the Medici took power; now it is no longer accustomed to bear arms and it is too late to remedy the matter. And since Florence cannot possibly hope to exert decisive military power abroad, the only means of which she can avail herself in the external world is diplomacy – an art that the many cannot understand, as we have seen above. Any disarmed city, in fact, cannot but rely on diplomacy; therefore, any disarmed city must have a form of government in which only the few can manage foreign policy. Precisely because Florence is disarmed, foreign policy is the most important field of government, which requires steady vigilance and prudence – the latter one of the qualities that denote the few. Guicciardini never says that Florence *should not* have an army of her own, and nor does he argue that a citizen army must be avoided because it would entail a popular government. He says, rather, that Florence *cannot* be armed, due to historical (and not ideological) reasons that make the matter highly problematic [Sasso 1984, pp. 80–99; Pocock 1975, pp. 239–52].[28]

   If the problem of Florentine institutional reform absorbed much of Guicciardini's attention until 1527, in a manner preventing him from focusing on foreign policy alone, after 1530 the tables were turned and the international dimension became paramount. By then, it was plain for all to see that the Florentine predicament was nothing but one aspect of the general Italian crisis, a crisis that had been triggered by the first French invasion of 1494 and that the weakness of the Italian states vis-à-vis the European great powers had made more and more manifest. In other words, by 1530 Guicciardini had come to the conclusion that Florence could not possibly achieve any stable domestic arrangement unless she took into account the broader international context. One of the reasons for his deep hostility to the radical government that ruled the Florentine republic from 1529 to 1530 was that its intransigent anti-Medici attitude and policies would inevitably facilitate an agreement between Clement VII and Charles V at the expense of the city. And when the expected Medici restoration took place under the Emperor's aegis, no further change would be possible without his permission. In fact, any internal upheaval would only increase the pressure from the outside, leading to foreign occupation and the loss of the last appearance of independence. Hence, the consolidation of the new Medici government – no matter how Guicciardini may have personally disliked a princedom – became important for reasons related to the external world, and the very notion of 'liberty', so central in many of his writings, was transformed. Until then, liberty had had mostly an internal connotation: in his early works, it referred to participation in the life of the state and the exercise of civic rights; later, as he wrote the *Dialogue*, 'liberty' was replaced by 'justice' – that is, personal security guaranteed by a set of fair laws; but now any reference to the domestic setting disappeared, and 'liberty' was mentioned and stressed only in relation to international politics – that is, as independence vis-à-vis the foreign powers [Albertini 1955/70, pp. 225–46].

It is now possible to point out a few more specific themes that constitute further evidence of the relevance of international politics in Guicciardini's thought. To begin with, all states being based upon violence, the connection between war and the state is deep and solid: war is made by states, and the state is what is at stake in war. Similarly, thinking about preserving the state entails thinking about war and arms, and the state itself, from this angle, is defined by a set of war-waging attributes: in his usurpation of the Duchy of Milan, Lodovico Sforza 'by little and little rendered himself master of the fortresses, army, treasure and all the foundations of the state'[29] [Fournel and Zancarini 2009, pp. 275–84]. Although he says that war can be necessary and, at times, even 'most useful',[30] Guicciardini never glorifies it [Bonadeo 1981]; in addition, he is certainly not a military thinker – it is significant that out of the 221 *Maxims and Reflections*, only a handful deal with military issues.[31] Yet, war is a constant presence in his writings. We have just seen what repercussions the violent external world has upon domestic affairs: prudence is especially required in the management of war;[32] *The History of Italy* is structured around a never-ending series of wars; even his first work, *The History of Florence*, despite its almost exclusive attention to Florentine affairs, sees in the 1494 French invasion a triggering event that changed states, the way of governing them, and the way of waging war itself;[33] and war is explicitly characterised as the field of human activity in which fortune plays the largest role.[34]

Similarly, the notion of balance of power emerges in his first work, is further refined when he is ambassador to Spain, inspires his policy recommendations against Charles V from 1525 to 1527, and comes up over and over again in his later writings. In *The History of Florence*, Guicciardini describes the pre-1494 Italian state system as being composed of five major powers – Milan, Venice, Florence, the State of the Church, and Naples – each of which pays steady attention to what the others are doing, lest any of them should increase its power so much as to frighten the rest.[35] In the summer of 1513, in a set of private letters to the Florentine ambassador to Rome, Guicciardini repeatedly expresses his views on the ongoing struggle between France, expelled from the Duchy of Milan the year before but still posing a threat, and Spain, by then firmly established in the Kingdom of Naples: as England is about to engage France beyond the Alps, Spain might be tempted to exploit this opportunity to expand her control further over Italy. Thus,

> although I would be pleased to see the King of France involved in a long war against England, I would not want to see him decline so much that Spain should no longer take him into consideration, for the excessive power of Spain would bring the same inconveniences as those which the excessive power of France entailed.[36]

Twelve years later, after the battle of Pavia and the decisive French defeat, Guicciardini is deeply concerned about the preponderance of the Spanish–imperial forces in Italy, for Charles V's power inevitably implies 'servitude' for the surviving Italian states. This theme surfaces over and over again from his letters, throughout 1525, as he first recommends temporising with the Emperor – any energetic reaction is out of the question, for the moment; suggests encouraging the French to hold on; and then, little by little, formulates the policy of a general anti-imperial coalition with the most threatened states [Jodogne 2002]. Finally, the same notion of balance of power shapes once more Guicciardini's account of the happy years that preceded the first French invasion of 1494, in *The History of Italy*. Lorenzo the Magnificent's foreign policy here receives unconditional approbation in memorable words that are worth repeating:

> Realising that it would be most dangerous to the Florentine republic and to himself if any of the major states should further increase their power, he carefully saw to it that the Italian affairs should be maintained in a state of balance, not leaning more towards one side than the other. This could not be achieved without preserving the peace and without being most diligently on the watch against every accident, even the slightest.[37]

Although the general idea is very similar to the one put forward in *The History of Florence*, two observations are in order. First, it must be noticed that peace is not the consequence of the balance, but one of the conditions under which such a balance can hold. The balance of power results in security, not peace; peace is necessary for the balance to work. Once the Italian balance has been destroyed by foreign armies, it cannot be restored because the incentives for peace are no longer there; the way to fight a foreign power is with the help of another foreign power.[38] Taking up the idea he put forward twenty years earlier, Guicciardini says that once Spain and France had established themselves in the Kingdom of Naples and the Duchy of Milan, respectively, it would have been a wiser policy to leave things as they stood, for at least the two foreign powers would have counterbalanced each other.[39] Instead, what follows is a long series of wars, and not only are Naples and Milan lost forever, but all the other Italian states fall into direct or indirect subjection and are absorbed by the new European balance [Phillips 1977, pp. 132–4; Albertini 1955/70, pp. 243–4]. Second – and related to this – in *The History of Italy* the balance of power assumes a new dimension, as it is projected from the Italian peninsula to the European continent. The King of Spain, the Holy Roman Emperor, the King of France and the King of England make their moves while keeping an eye on each other, try to prevent each other from growing too much in terms of power and territorial extension, and resort to force to defend their position. Each attempts to expand his own dominions and influence; each attempts to keep the others from doing so.

This European perspective does deserve to be stressed, for it is evidence in itself of the importance that Guicciardini attributed to international affairs. With *The History of Italy* Guicciardini is the first to break with territorial historiography and the established tradition according to which the historical narrative must be centred on a single state. Causal connections between events are extended on a continental scale and the inclusion of developments in Germany, France, England and Spain in the analysis of Italian affairs is 'instrumental in making men of his own time as well as of later times conscious of the existence of an interconnected state-system' [Gilbert 1965, p. 295]. This, coupled with his exclusive interest in political affairs, leads to an accurate discussion of international politics structured around the reciprocal dependence among states, the relations between domestic and foreign affairs, and the repercussions of military operations on politics and vice versa [Fueter 1911/63, pp. 91–3].

Rationalism, Relativism and Political Realism

Guicciardini categorically denies the usefulness of generalisations for practical purposes – a point on which he takes issue with Machiavelli – for circumstances vary to such a degree as to make general rules irrelevant when it comes to taking a decision; nor can wisdom be learned in books.[40] Yet, even those who call him an 'empiricist' concede that he was forced to take the theoretical problems of politics into considerations [Fueter 1911/63, pp. 86–8], and others point out that he certainly had general ideas about politics and human nature [Chabod 1933], that his insistence on experience did not result in the rejection of any conceptual structure [Pocock 1975, p. 220], and that he shared with Machiavelli – and his views on rules – more than one is usually ready to admit [Sasso 1984, pp. 1–4].

Guicciardini does believe in the repetitiveness of history, a view that is expressed in a letter to Machiavelli himself, in the *Dialogue*, in his *Maxims* and in one of the speeches of the present collection.[41] But he always insists on exceptions too, and on the need to differentiate between substance and appearance, between what looks similar and what is similar – a most demanding exercise that books cannot teach, for it requires natural gifts and experience. For a statesman often involved in delicate, if not dangerous, situations, it would be nice to find a guide for action in rules grounded in similarities between events; but reality is often so complex and contradictory that dealing with it entails much more than applying rules. Different times require different attitudes, for the same action that succeeds when it is undertaken at the right moment fails when it is undertaken at the wrong one;[42] 'it sometimes happens that fools do greater things than wise men';[43] and the future is so deceptive 'that very often even the wisest of men is fooled when he tries to predict it'.[44] In short, history may well repeat itself, but the differences – both seeming and, occasionally, even substantial – between situations are so many that uncertainty ends up permeating the human condition, including, of course, politics and political action. Within the broad circle of the repetitiveness of things, change is pervasive and yet difficult to recognise, especially in public affairs, 'for these, because of their bulk, move much more slowly and are subject to many more accidents' than private matters.[45] The value of history, therefore, must be seen not in a set of examples and models to be imitated – as the standard humanist view suggested – but in the source of experiences that it provides, thereby enriching our knowledge. Guicciardini is constantly engaged in the investigation of reality and is acutely aware of the relative nature of any design, calculation, judgement. The extreme variety of circumstances entails a profound sense of insecurity, of the precariousness of any situation, of the world's imperviousness to knowledge, as 'human affairs are as subject to change and fluctuation as the waters of the sea, agitated by the winds.'[46]

We should never forget, however, that Guicciardini is above all a statesman, and that to him action is paramount. While relying on the benefit of time may be a wise policy when you are in dire straits, if a fair opportunity presents itself you have to decide and act quickly, or else you will waste it, and who knows if and when it will ever return.[47] This implies a willingness to accept risks, for things can never be entirely safe.[48] Take two equally wise men – he says – one brave, the other timid. Both recognise the dangers ahead. But while the timid one expects the worst and refrains from action, the brave one believes that some dangers can be dodged by industry and some will fade away by chance. This is why the latter more than the former deserves to be called wise, for he 'knows the extent of a danger and fears it only as much as he should'.[49] In this assessment, prudence is paramount. According to the humanist tradition, prudence is acquired through experience and knowledge, and it entails not only circumspection but also the ability to recognise an opportunity [Santoro 1978, pp. 356–8]. It pertains to prudence to weigh every detail carefully, including the smallest ones. Prudence is related to the sense of what is feasible and possible on the one hand, and to a sound evaluation of the dangers on the other, and manifests itself in knowing how to adjust to necessity, now waiting for the right time to come, now taking risks, if this is indispensable. The opposite of being led by prudence is to be induced to act by brashness, hatred, covetousness, ill-conceived ambition, excessive fear – irrational impulses that are often ruinous. Next to prudence, discretion too plays a fundamental role. This is an innate quality that can rarely be acquired,[50] and that can be defined as intuition, the perception of invisible things, the *coup d'œil* cast over the hidden details that differentiate two seemingly similar situations [Gagneux 1970, pp. 258–61].

And yet, neither prudence nor discretion may be enough. The former would elicit the adoption of different courses of action, according to the circumstances, but this is more easily said than done, for man finds it hard, if not impossible, to resist his natural inclinations and the way they predispose him to be impetuous or timid, independently of the situation. In addition, differences are infinite in number and degree, and even discretion can be of only partial help. No matter how prudent and endowed with discretion one may be, one cannot take into consideration all the possibilities:

> Often – perhaps even the majority of times – events will take a [. . .] course that has not been foreseen and to which your decision is not tailored. Therefore, make your decisions [. . .] remembering that things can easily happen that should not have happened. Unless forced by necessity, do not restrict yourself.[51]

Conversely, sometimes a general overview of the situation is enough to come to a sound decision, while too careful an assessment of all the details of the case under investigation might lead to a decisional paralysis.[52] Even prudence and discretion, therefore, reveal all their limits. Although it is always advisable to proceed in a circumspect manner, we should not consider all the obstacles ahead as insurmountable, and 'it is only by working at things that they become easy: and in the process of working, difficulties disappear of their own accord.'[53] This does not mean that prudence and discretion can be disposed of, but it simply reflects the awareness that there is no way to make uncertainty and insecurity fade away.

All this is nicely illustrated by one of the most recurrent themes in Guicciardini's speeches. Speakers very often resort to a call for action based upon the notion that one should not give up a present and certain good out of fear of some future and dubious evil,[54] that a vain concern is just as harmful as overconfidence,[55] that it is a mistake to believe that all the possible dangers will actually materialise[56] – and the Pope is blamed for being so timid as to abandon 'himself to certain death rather than wanting to run the danger of dying'.[57] Such a systematic attack on exaggerated fears could easily be taken for a 'rule'. And yet, it is associated with both good and bad decisions. Nor should this come as a surprise, for the 'rule' does not count much, in itself. What truly matters is the prudence and the discretion of those who apply it: that is, their ability to assess the situation at hand in the most adequate way, to understand whether the dangers that have been evoked are real or groundless. In addition, the way circumstances may unfold, once a decision has been made, is beyond the control of even the most prudent man – which further deprives the 'rule' of any absolute meaning.

Guicciardini formulates and refines many of these views in the last phase of his life. In his earlier years, he seems to have had more faith in prudence as a guide to rational action.[58] It is throughout the 1520s that he is forced to deal more and more frequently with the unexpected and the 'fluctuation of human affairs'. In the *Dialogue*, the 'power of fortune' is explicitly acknowledged,[59] and the role of prudence – which is still there – is now more modest. The complete miscarriage of a carefully drafted policy, in 1527, and the calamity of the sack of Rome will give the last push. Fortune now becomes decisive, and the random alternation of success and failure is looked at as the norm. The anti-imperial policy supported by Guicciardini was blessed with all the conditions that would allow anyone to hope for victory and all the prudent men approved of it: the Pope could rely on the Venetians, the French and possibly the King of England, while not only was the enemy weak, in terms of troops and financial resources, but it was also finding itself isolated in a most hostile environment.[60] In light of all this, the ruinous outcome of the war becomes irrefutable evidence of the gap between any rational judgement and expectation, on the one hand, and what actually comes to pass, on the other. Thus, like many of his contemporaries [Gilbert 1965, pp. 268–70], Guicciardini assigns a fundamental role to fortune – and this is why not even the best and the brightest can ever be sure to succeed in their undertakings.[61] What is fortune? At times, the very situation at hand; at times, the set of human circumstances as a whole; at times, the broad context in which an individual, or a group, or a state is called to make a decision; at times, destiny and fate; at times, good luck and bad luck. It is, above all, the statesman who has to deal with fortune, in his attempt to reconcile the need to anticipate the result of his decision and the awareness of how impossible a task this is. Such an effort conveys a sense of impotence and, in particular, tragedy that constitutes a substantial part of Guicciardini's thought as a whole, for it is by his own action that the statesman ends up bringing about a result that is the opposite of what he intended [Gagneux 1970, pp. 249–51]. In *The History of Italy*, even the uncontested final winner, Charles V, makes egregious mistakes and is not able to obtain full satisfaction from his triumph.

As a result of all this, prediction may not be possible, but a rational explanation is. In the opening lines of *The History of Italy*, Guicciardini puts forward his well-known diagnosis of the calamities that have befallen the Italian states: fortune and the imprudent decisions made by the rulers have been the main causes of trouble. The two are immediately juxtaposed in a single strand – 'Such princes never allow themselves lei-sure to reflect on the instability of fortune'[62]– for a good reason: many – although not all – of the circumstances that go under the name of for-tune are the result of individual actions. An individual's action interacts with another individual's action and with the external circumstances at large. The result is a chaotic criss-crossing of errors and events that constitutes the fabric of the historical narrative [Scarano 1981, p. 42]. Thus, history is indeed a human-made process, although its outcomes, far from being linear, are often unintentional. But individual actions are only the surface. The huge gap between what is publicly said and what is actually done leads Guicciardini to focus on the motives that induced the main actors to behave as they did. Hence, a deep psychological analysis becomes the chief means by which he explains decisions and actions.[63] It is by looking inside the mind of the rulers that the causal connections can be revealed, what at first looked incomprehensible becomes intelli-gible, and reality is at least partially rationalised. On several occasions the investigation is left open, in so far as Guicciardini offers the reader an ample scope of motives, a long list of considerations that must have been on the individual ruler's mind. In these cases, though, intentions are often arranged in some hierarchical order, in which the last one is usually the most important [Cutinelli-Rèndina 2009, pp. 209–10].

Human beings act in some unpredictable way because they are driven by passions – above all, covetousness and ill-conceived ambition – are influenced by fallacious opinions, and, by their own simulations, mis-lead others into expecting different actions [Santoro 1978, pp. 366–7]. Yet, they are all motivated by self-interest,[64] and this is the only per-manent and constant feature of human nature on which Guicciardini's rationalism is based. The specific form that self-interest can take varies across individuals, and even in the same individual, and reflects the interplay between events and their impact on the mind of those who are called to decide. Thus, explanation is not grounded in self-interest alone but reflects the broader context, historically determined, in which a ruler, a group or a state finds himself/itself, defines his/its interests and acts accordingly. In other words, although individuals – and collective actors – are free to do what they do, the circumstances in which they find themselves at any given time provide them with the opportunities to fulfil their aspirations and, by predisposing them to act in a cer-tain way, affect their behaviour.[65] Now, at the individual level, and in domestic affairs, well-conceived self-interest is largely defined in terms of honour and profit. The former – a legitimate ambition of the best citizens – consists of the universal admiration elicited by the display of one's exceptional qualities at the service of the public good [Varotti

1998, pp. 395–418]; as for the latter, any honourable activity carries with it a licit reward that must offend nobody [Bianchi 1948, p. 45].[66] But among states, in international politics, honour and profit are always coupled with security – as the speeches will amply illustrate.

The Function and Structure of the Opposing Speeches

Both the relevance attributed to the external world and the conceptual and methodological framework that we have just sketched clearly emerge from Guicciardini's speeches. In a nutshell, the opposing orations disclose the pervasiveness of uncertainty, the importance of prudence and discretion, the awareness of the unpredictable, and the ineradicable presence of risk. At the same time, they are political debates all centred on the need to make a decision inspired by interest and expediency. Guicciardini's speeches have elicited widespread admiration throughout the modern age: Jean Bodin, Michel de Montaigne, Pierre Bayle and Charles Mills, to name but a few, entertained a flattering opinion of them [Luciani 1949, pp. 277–83]. Even Leopold von Ranke, who was quite critical of Guicciardini's historiography, called the speeches the 'main thing' (*Hauptsache*) of *The History of Italy* [Manselli 1985].

Out of the three historical works that Guicciardini wrote throughout his life – the *Florentine History*, *Le cose fiorentine* and *The History of Italy* – only the first one, the earliest, does not contain direct speeches. The other two do, in large numbers: *Le cose fiorentine* includes eighteen orations, *The History of Italy* as many as thirty-one. In addition, Guicciardini developed the habit of writing self-contained fictitious speeches in the early 1510s, and kept doing so for years: to the sixteen orations collected in the volume *Scritti politici e Ricordi*[67] one should add one more speech included in a previous edition of his miscellaneous writings,[68] four contained in the volume *Dialogo e discorsi del Reggimento di Firenze*,[69] and the three orations on his own personal situation after the sack of Rome and the collapse of the Medici regime in Florence, written in 1527.[70] Overall, there are more than seventy speeches, most of which are structured in pairs: that is, one in favour of a certain thesis, one against it. To come to this group, while their subjects vary widely – they range from fiscal reform to institutional procedures, from whether or not the 'Great Captain', Gonzalo de Córdoba, should accept the command of an expedition to Italy to Guicciardini's own examination of conscience – most of them deal with foreign policy decisions.[71]

It is evident that Guicciardini had a strong intellectual predisposition to examine the various issues under investigation by developing, in an antithetical manner, two sets of arguments of identical persuasive value. That he attributed great importance to the speeches is suggested, among other things, by the fact that when he definitively abandoned the writing of *Le cose fiorentine* he copied all the orations therein, as if they were the only thing that deserved to be saved [Ridolfi 1960/7, p. 235]; moreover, the speeches often incorporate some of his *Maxims and Reflections*, the work in progress to which he attended for almost twenty years, and the one he probably held dearest [Phillips 1977, p. 131]. Finally, according to the humanist standards of the time, debate was regarded as the best way to display one's best qualities as a leading citizen [Varotti 1998, pp. 414–15]. This veritable passion reflected, in part, his juridical training in so far as the pairs of speeches reproduced the trial procedure of orations in favour and against somebody or something:[72] in part, his own *forma mentis*, in so far as he apparently considered such a method the most appropriate way to shed light on complex situations and clarify the various alternatives and implications that each of them entailed;[73] in part, of course, humanist teachings.

Direct speeches are, in fact, a common feature of Roman historiography, imitated by the humanists.[74] But Guicciardini's opposing speeches – which continued the practice introduced a century earlier by Leonardo Bruni[75] – reflect in particular the rediscovery of Greek models, for in Latin historiography antithetical orations were not so common [Barucci 2004, pp. 106–7]. In addition, in the first half of the fifteenth century, Lorenzo Valla, the great humanist, had insisted that historians should adopt a rigorous methodology in their search for the truth. Such advice was less in line with the Ciceronian tradition than with Thucydides' teachings – and Valla himself rendered Thucydides into Latin. This meant that political historians were now called on not only to adopt the formal and rhetorical features of Roman writers, but also to deal with Thucydidean methodological principles, according to which history is less concerned with teaching by example than with finding out the truth, must be impartial, and must be based on a careful evaluation of the sources [Anselmi 1979, pp. 25–7].[76] The objective tone adopted by Guicciardini in his two later historical works, his systematic and critical use of archival material and secondary sources, and his steady effort to dig out the real causes of the events he wrote about seem to suggest that he had been exposed to these teachings. But there is more. It has been argued that some of the intellectual traits of Guicciardini's are, in fact, compatible with some typical features of sophistic thought: his relativism, his lack of faith in the 'good cause', his predisposition to engage in discussions and analyses in which a demonstration of reasonableness is always possible because even the slightest change in any minor detail can lead to opposite conclusions [Bianchi 1948]. Within this broader framework, the impact of the Thucydidean lesson perhaps becomes more visible. Apart from the search for the truth and the adoption of an adequate methodology for this purpose, some have suggested that Thucydides and Guicciardini also share a similar perspective on the historical process. The notion of the repetitiveness of things, common to both, is counterbalanced, in Guicciardini's thought, by the awareness of exceptions. This discloses a world made of diversity, the domain of chance – something not very different from Thucydides' notion of tyche: that is, the way things end up falling out. Thus, while the repetitiveness of things entails that human beings are predisposed to act in a certain way – a predisposition that should not be confused with determinism – once a choice has been made tyche sets in, and the consequences of that decision can no longer be controlled. In other words, choice triggers a mechanism that can easily lead to the irrational production of effects whose intensity and quality we can neither know in advance nor dominate [Marcucci 1985, pp. 429–30].[77] Reason should inspire choice for Thucydides too: it is the 'intelligence [. . .] which proceeds [. . .] by estimating what the facts are, and thus obtaining a clearer vision of what to expect'.[78] Yet, the final outcome is beyond reason's control: 'that imponderable element of the future is the thing which counts in the long run',[79] and even the most careful calculations can prove groundless, as illustrated by the rebellion of the Chians against Athens:

> One may think that this revolt was an example of overconfidence, but they never ventured upon it until they had many good allies ready to share the risk with them and until they saw that, after the disaster in Sicily, not even the Athenians themselves were any longer pretending that their affairs were not in a really desperate state. And if, *incalculable as is the life of man*, they made a mistake, there were many others who thought, like them, that Athens was on the point of collapse, and who came also to realise their error.[80]

Not to mention that, for Thucydides too, it is war, more than any other field of human action, that witnesses the power of fortune.[81]

The similarities between the great Greek historian and Guicciardini become even more visible, of course, when it comes to speeches, for the latter amount to more than one-fifth of Thucydides' work and constitute one of its most remarkable features. Although seemingly at odds with the need to write a truthful historical account of the events, speeches were considered useful and legitimate in Guicciardini's times too, in so far as, in line with the Thucydidean approach,[82] the verisimilitude of the words pronounced was to be combined with the truthfulness of the facts reported. This would contribute to enlighten any given situation further by identifying the various options at one's disposal. And Guicciardini, a keen student of exceptions and differences, could not but appreciate such a method, for this allowed him to point out the variety of the opinions, which in turn revealed the complexity of the matters under discussion [Palumbo 1991, pp. 17–22]. In this sense, the opposing speeches in Guicciardini's historical works go well beyond the humanist requirement of rhetorical embellishment but perform a clear analytical function.[83] Thesis and antithesis underline the many and often contradictory aspects of any situation, show how difficult it is to reduce reality to a single dimension, and lead to a more objective understanding of the forces at play [Cutinelli-Rèndina 2009, p. 213].

Although the central role played by individual psychology in Guicciardini's reconstruction of decisions should never be forgotten, in the opposing speeches the speakers express collective preferences and views. In fact, in many cases, the orators are figures of secondary importance who represent less their personality than the views of the group on behalf of which they speak. By and large, the speeches are deliberative exercises structured around three main features: they are about advising a political body, be that an assembly or a more restricted council; they look at the future – that is, at the likely consequences of each decision; and their benchmark is what is advantageous or disadvantageous for the ruler or the state as a whole.[84] Expediency is thus the criterion that is invoked all the time and *utile* (useful, convenient) is the term that comes up over and over again, always with reference to public, collective goals – an incipient doctrine, it has been noted, of *raison d'état* [Treves 1931, pp. 24–33].

The typical context in which the pairs of orations are placed is shaped by some impending threat that forces a collectivity to make a prompt decision. This sense of urgency and constraint is often conveyed by the frequent use of the term 'necessity'. Any alternative entails some risk. The speakers face each other in a rigorously interdependent manner, for each argument raised by one, in favour or against, is re-examined and rejected by the other. The strictly impartial way in which the orations are structured and the richness of the reasons of which the speakers avail themselves reveal that there is no predetermined solution, and leave the reader – and occasionally the speakers themselves – puzzled, at the end of the debate, in so far as it is almost impossible to say which thesis is more convincing.[85] Each argument can be contradicted and turned upside down as the speakers engage in a rhetorical struggle that fleshes out all the aspects and details of the circumstances in which those who are called upon to decide find themselves. In this sense, the debates are indeed a stringent interpretation of events. The net result is not only a very lucid analysis of the logical consequences of each argument once it is pushed to its extreme limits, but also a vivid illustration of the uncertainty with which any decision must inevitably coexist [Palumbo 1991, pp. 16–17 and 32–6].

As a general rule, the final deliberation is not based on some greater persuasive power of one speech vis-à-vis the other. At the end of the debate – in the historical works – Guicciardini explains why the decision was made, and the reasons he suggests are frequently different from the arguments on which the speakers insisted. He does not believe that rhetorical undertakings can affect politics in a significant way; on the contrary, in his search for causes he goes beyond words and appearance, and often comes to the conclusion that irrational forces tend to prevail: ill-founded fears, covetousness, hatred. Thus, the impartial attitude that characterises his presentation of different views does not keep him from expressing his own opinion at the end; nor does it prevent him from disclosing the gap between facts and the distorted assessment of the same under the influence of desires and passions: 'By means of speeches the historian fulfilled the function of a judge: Guicciardini indicated how policy was to be conducted if it were managed rationally, and how it was conducted in reality' [Gilbert 1965, p. 299].

In their effort to convince the audience, speakers engage in no abstract dissertation; nor do they aim at formulating universal laws. They explicitly put forward the principles that must inform policy; yet, while those principles are general, they only find an immediate – and controversial – practical definition in the specific context in which the debate takes place. As said, interest is the main criterion that guides policy, and interest, in turn, is articulated around three main components: honour (or reputation, glory, dignity), profit (or gain) and security. Here again, the parallelism with Thucydides is striking, for one cannot help noticing not only that the Greek historian availed himself of opposing speeches to a large extent, but that this similarity is not just structural and functional, but conceptual too. As a general rule, Thucydides' speakers invoke expediency, and expediency, in turn, is structured around the same three motives: security, profit and reputation.[86] These three themes run across virtually all Guicciardini's orations, as each speaker tries to show that the policy he recommends is consistent with the interest of the state in so far as it leads to an optimal combination of the three components; by the same token, each speaker tries to show that the policy suggested by his opponent is deficient, if not downright wrong, precisely because it does not satisfy those criteria.

Security, profit and reputation, in turn, are defined in specific ways. For example, security relates both to sheer survival and to the preservation of autonomy, independence and rank; profit is often associated with expansion or some form of indirect control over other states; reputation depends not only on the goals actually achieved but also on the legitimacy of the means employed. In addition, the three criteria are related to each other: reputation adds to security, gains consolidate reputation, and security brings about both gain and reputation. The three motives are usually arranged in some hierarchical order, security being, as a general rule, the most relevant. But the other two criteria play no minor role, as they contribute to make a point more solid and convincing. Finally, although the speakers invoke the same principles to frame their argument, they disagree on the actual content that must be assigned to them under the given circumstances. This is why, although they all express themselves in similar terms, their policy recommendations are at odds with each other. As such, not only do the opposing speeches disclose how variegated the notion of state interest can be, but they also illustrate the competition of different conceptions of the same interest that lies at the core of any foreign policy debate.

The Content of the Opposing Speeches: An Overview

War, peace and alliance are the great general themes of the disputations. Each of them is given a special twist according to the circumstances of the moment. How should we respond to somebody who has just tried to seize a part of our dominion by deception?[87] We must react by waging war against him, for our reputation and, above all, our security are at stake. If we do not, not only will our other enemies be encouraged to follow his example, but he himself, realising that we now know what he is up to, will openly attack us first. Preventive – or pre-emptive – war is thus requisite. Not at all: we are no longer under threat, and sheer revenge will be counterproductive. In fact, we would be making a war that we cannot possibly hope to win and suffer, in addition, a serious reputational loss.

Should we exploit this fair opportunity to expand our dominion?[88] Yes, for the enterprise is easy, just, honourable and profitable: our target is weak and isolated, nobody will assist him, and it will nicely add to our territory. We have been long waiting for this, and now that the moment has arrived, it would be shameful to waste such a great chance. Not really: we have no justification for attacking him, even if things were as easy as you say. If we do, everybody will believe that we are too ambitious and imprudent, not to mention that somebody will help him. As a result, we will become involved in a dishonourable, costly and dangerous war.

Should we accept a peace proposal that would finally normalise our relations with this ruler whom we do not trust much?[89] No, we should not. The current situation is just fine and there is no reason why we should alter it. Reason and experience suggest that he is not serious about peace; all he wants is to tie our hands and be left free to pursue his expansionist designs. Let us wait and see what he does, for if it turns out that he is genuinely interested in peace, we will always be able to sign an agreement with him later on. Yes, we should. If he is sincere, peace will bring a convenient arrangement structured around our respective spheres of influence and will allow us to consolidate our dominion. Should we flatly reject his offer, this would make him believe that we are hostile to him, and a spiral of uncertainty and insecurity would follow, to the detriment of all. In addition, our public opinion would suspect that some of us want war for their own personal advantage. If, on the other hand, he intends to cheat us, our display of good will will place us in a better position to convince other states to support us against him and we will be able to keep him at bay anyway.

Should we come to an agreement that would terminate a problematic war campaign, although such a deal might compromise our previous conquests?[90] No, for we still have the means to prevail; as such, it would be shameful to give up. In addition, the stakes are too high, for victory would bring about extraordinary results. Finally, our enemies, far from keeping their promises, would take advantage of the peace to seize all we have taken. Yes, for we are in no position to keep fighting. Although it is quite likely that they will violate the agreement, it remains to be seen if they will manage to inflict such a serious loss on us. And in any case, necessity forces us to settle: the agreement is the lesser evil.

What happens after a decisive victory? What are the options at the disposal of both the conqueror and the states that, although not openly at war against him, have tried to hamper his designs and now have reason to fear him? To begin with, how are we, the victorious power, to deal with the vanquished enemy?[91] A peace of reconciliation, based on self-restraint and even generosity, is the most promising policy. Not only would this elicit our enemy's gratitude, thereby predisposing him to observe the peace treaty, but also it would reassure all the other states that are now afraid of our power and that might therefore be tempted to join forces against us. Glory and security would thus follow, our leadership will be uncontested, and we will be able to address common issues with the support of all. No, all this is wrong. Generosity is dangerous and gratitude is rare. If we do not exploit our victory to the fullest, our reputation will be lost. The vanquished is inevitably resentful; as for the others, there is not much they can do against us. Hegemony that relies on superior power, and not leadership based on consensus, is what gets things done, and we should do all we can not to waste such a fair opportunity.

How shall we, the victorious power, establish the foundations of a new international order? Shall we come to an agreement with the great power that we have just defeated, or with the group of medium powers that stood aside in the hope that we would fail in our enterprise and that are now terrified of us?[92] With the latter, no doubt. The former is not reliable, for it has too much to lose: it is an enemy by position. If we settle with it, not only will it disregard its commitments, but also it will form an alliance against us with the others. Those medium powers, on the contrary, only want to be reassured. If we tranquilise them, they will be valuable partners and will not attempt anything against us. No, we should make an agreement with the defeated great power. The medium powers cannot be trusted: even if they acted out of fear at the beginning, by now they are nothing but enemies. In fact, one of them has already blatantly betrayed us, and it would be ignominious to forgive it. The deal with the great power is thus more honourable and more useful, provided it will keep its word – and it is likely to do so, in light of the pledges it is willing to give us.

Shall we, one of the medium powers, come to an agreement with the victorious great power?[93] It would not be a good idea at all: the great power is hostile to us, no matter what. If we sign a treaty with them, we will simply postpone war, and not avoid it – and time is not on our side. The simple fact that they are pressing us so much to settle reveals their designs: they simply intend to deactivate us, thereby discouraging all the others. If we do not bend, the others will not bend either, and this will keep the enemy at bay. Not really. If we do not come to an agreement, we will have war immediately, and this is the worst option for us at this time. And even if war should not break out now, we will be worse off without the agreement under all the possible scenarios that can materialise. By coming to terms, we will gain time; and the benefit of time can do wonders.

Finally, alliances. In this case too, the speeches display a rich variety of themes. Should we make an offensive alliance with a foreign great power for the sake of settling matters once and for all with a neighbour?[94] Yes, for this would allow us to avenge ourselves on him, expand our dominion and be more secure. Sharing the border with a great power, then, might be hazardous, granted; but precisely because it is a great power, all the other states will keep an eye on it and support us in case of need. No, this would be a foolish thing to do. The great power is much more dangerous than our neighbour. In addition, if we bring a foreign power in, our reputation will suffer, and no one will believe that we simply aimed at taking revenge on our neighbour or securing ourselves against him; they will all blame it on our ambition, will be afraid of us, and will not help us at all should the great power eventually turn against us.

We are allied with X but Y is asking us to shift sides. What should we do?[95] If we could only be sure that X and Y will not come to terms at our expense, honour and security would suggest that we should stick to the existing alliance. Yet, X is likely to fear that we abandon him for Y, is encouraged by all our neighbours to turn against us, and desires to seize part of our dominion. Y, for his part, is looking for any possible ally. In light of all this, we cannot be sure that the two will not come to an agreement, and the only way to prevent this is that we ally with Y. No, this would be a very bad decision. The alliance of X and Y is not likely at all, for Y would be a more dangerous neighbour for X than we are. If we shift sides and wage war with Y against X, not only will we be breaking faith, but also we will soon be in trouble: X is very powerful, all our neighbours will side with it against us, and Y will end up abandoning us, for we know how unreliable it is.

Several themes, in turn, cut across the debates – for example, the distinction between a real peace and a false one:

> Peace, I submit, is a sweet and holy thing when it brings security, when it does not increase the power of enemies, when it does not pave the way to a more dangerous war; but when it entails these effects, it is bitter and pernicious,[96]

and the belief that all princes are aggressive and never keep their promises:

> It is natural for princes [. . .] always to seek to increase their greatness, and the greater they are, the more they wish to reach the highest posts and [. . .] they take into little consideration and lay low all the other regards.[97]

A utilitarian notion of legitimacy comes up frequently:

> to take up arms against him cannot be done without incurring the reproach of violating our faith, to which this Senate ought to pay

the highest regard for the honour and service it does us in our daily transaction with other princes.[98]

And although the speakers are well aware that pretexts can always be found, especially if you are powerful,[99] they try to show that their advice is, in fact, consistent, at least with the letter, if not the spirit, of treaty obligations.[100]

The speeches are informed by a lucid sense of the interdependence of decisions – strategic interaction, in the language of political science. The relation of forces and the interpretation of the intentions that animate the other actors are the two main subjects about which the speakers debate. How do we stand vis-à-vis our enemies and allies, in terms of power? A survey of the military and financial means at each player's disposal, accordingly, is always there – and this is a first source of disagreement between the speakers. Second, what is our enemy up to? The answer is often based on 'reason and experience': that is, his past actions and what it is reasonable to expect from him in light of his identity and the situation in which he now finds himself. Not surprisingly, this is another issue on which opinions vary to a large extent. Finally, the speakers point out the concatenation of causes and effects that derives from those assumptions – how events will unfold, in an action–reaction sequence. Thus, by the end of the debate, the divergence between the opposing views – each of which, it is worth repeating, is plausible – reaches its maximum width.[101]

Within this broad context, it is not difficult to pinpoint other recurrent themes. As we have seen, Guicciardini has a deep appreciation for the notion of balance of power. Accordingly, speakers refer to it quite often, both directly and indirectly. By his aggressive policies, our enemy will bring about a countervailing coalition;[102] if we do not keep our expansionism under control, the other states will be afraid of us and join forces against us;[103] it is not in our interest that a state contiguous to ours be under the control of somebody who is stronger than we are;[104] we should have supported much more vigorously great power A in its struggle against great power B, for now B has grown too powerful and is threatening us;[105] 'if the King of France should get possession of the Duchy of Milan, affairs resting in a balance between two such princes [the King of France and the Emperor], whoever should have reason to fear the power of one would be spared and left alone on account of the power of the other.'[106] Balance aside, the speakers are also aware of other important repercussions that the policy they recommend can have on other states – enemy and potential allies as well. If we sign the treaty that our enemy is offering to us, we will no longer be feared and held in consideration by him, and instead of being entreated by others, we will have to entreat others when in danger, and experience how little are held in esteem those who find themselves in need.[107]

It may well be that great power A, a potential ally to us, and great power B, a threat to us and A, come to a union, but the terms of their deal will be affected by our own policy. If we do not settle with B, A will find itself in stronger bargaining position vis-à-vis B; conversely, if we come to an understanding with B, A will be forced to bend to B's demands and will be of little help to us:

> if we make an agreement with Caesar in order to escape the danger of this union, we head [. . .] towards our certain ruin, and we will find ourselves in such a situation that we can be assisted by nothing but unlikely accidents and events.[108]

Those who are familiar with the theory of international relations, in addition, will easily recognise a mechanism that is strongly reminiscent of the 'security dilemma': under the conditions of uncertainty that shape international politics, the measures one side takes for the sake of acquiring more security lead the other side to adopt similar measures. As a consequence of the spiral process thus triggered, even two parties that initially entertained no aggressive design but were simply aiming at security may end up caught in a situation in which they both are less safe, more fearful of each other, and therefore more predisposed to war. Guicciardini's speakers underline something very similar:

> And every little beginning, although not the result of hostile intentions, may take things further and lead them to a necessary war [. . .]. Thus, in order to be safe we will become suspicious, out of the will of defending ourselves we will begin to injure each other, and in order to escape war we will enter into war.[109]

This vicious circle can be broken only by some manifest sign of good will, a tangible pledge that usually the most powerful state alone can give: if your power is so great as to frighten all the other states, you can tranquilise them by showing moderation and self-restraint, and their security will be your security.[110] If, however, one side has reason to believe that the other entertains hostile intentions, then the dilemma is no longer a dilemma and the logic of security becomes implacable, for one can be safe only by undoing one's opponent:

he will know that his suspicion keeps you in suspicion by necessity, and your suspicion multiplies his suspicion. And such suspicions cannot be cured but by the one who will be in such a position that the other will not have the means to injure him.[111]

It is tempting to look at the situations crystallised in the debates as ideal-type cases whose essential traits nicely reflect both the state of affairs they address and the speakers' views. On the one hand, one should resist such an enticement: each case, if one looks closer, is characterised by specific features that relate to the historical circumstances in which the debate takes place and the identity of the actors, be those individual or collective. In addition, one should never lose sight of Guicciardini's diffidence towards 'examples' and 'rules', for the reasons noted above. On the other hand, each situation displays certain basic features that denote some regularities. As such, they cannot but elicit the attention of those who are interested in the theory of international politics. 'Examples' and 'rules' have a limited practical value, granted, but they perform an analytical function that must be emphasised. In general terms, the speeches address recurrent issues in international politics, and their conceptual framework can inform the analysis of similar situations, their differences notwithstanding. It is not difficult to imagine that a number of debates on war and peace must have taken into consideration at least some of the issues raised by Guicciardini's speakers: do we have the right to take up arms? Is our security at stake? What do we stand to gain from war? Similarly, the ambivalent nature of alliances and the uncertainties that afflict them are an only too familiar theme in international relations: will our ally stand by us, in case of need? Will it come to terms with our enemy behind our back? Will we end up entrapped in a war that is not ours? Should we shift sides? Even more generally, any international agreement carries a set of constraints on one's freedom of movement that must be carefully assessed and contrasted with the advantages it promises – and this, too, can be found in the speeches. None of this tells us what we should do, or what is likely to happen, under specific circumstances. Yet, these questions cast light on a set of predicaments and make them intelligible. Thus, leaving prediction and control aside, we are left with explanation – and in this Guicciardini excels. Although the reasons why a decision is finally made do not always follow from the motives invoked in the debates and are often the result of irrational forces, the speakers engage in a rational effort to examine the options at their disposal in terms of costs and benefits, and have a clear vision of what international politics is about. Security, honour and profit are not only the criteria that inspire the policy they support, but also the measure of the policies of the other states, the filter through which the behaviour of friends and foes alike is interpreted. What they all say is that superior power cannot be trusted, that weakness invites exploitation and that faith is often broken, provided some appearance of decency is saved. Their environment is imbued with risk, danger, fear, jealousy and suspicion; their compass is self-interest. The net result is a general conception of international politics whose main components, although not arranged in a systematic way, are highly consistent with each other.

Notes

1. For one of the few exceptions, see Berridge [2001].
2. The best biography is still Ridolfi [1960/7]. For two comprehensive works in English, see Bondanella [1976] and Phillips [1977]. More recent books in Italian that combine Guicciardini's biography and an analysis of his works include Cutinelli-Rèndina [2009] and Varotti [2009].
3. *The History of Florence*, Engl. transl. by M. Domandi, New York: Harper & Row, 1970.
4. Machiavelli was one of the closest aides to Gonfalonier Soderini, the head of the popular government that Guicciardini and the other oligarchs criticised.
5. Letter to Luigi Guicciardini, 29 November 1509. Engl. transl. in J. B. Atkinson and D. Sices (eds), *Machiavelli and His Friends: Their Personal Correspondence*, DeKalb: Northern Illinois University Press, 1996, p. 189.
6. *Maxims and Reflections (Ricordi)*, Engl. transl. by M. Domandi, Philadelphia: University of Pennsylvania Press, 1965.
7. *Discorso di Logrogno*, Engl. transl. by A. Moulakis in his *Republican Realism in Renaissance Florence: Francesco Guicciardini's Discorso di Logrogno*, Lanham, MD: Rowman & Littlefield, 1998, pp. 117–49. Logrogno was the name of the city in which Guicciardini found himself, at Ferdinand's court, in the summer of 1512.
8. *Dialogue on the Government of Florence*, Engl. transl. by A. Brown, Cambridge: Cambridge University Press, 1994.
9. *Consolatoria, Accusatoria, Defensoria*, in *Opere*, ed. by E. Lugnani Scarano, Turin: Utet, 1970, vol. I, pp. 485–604.
10. *Le cose fiorentine*, ed. by R. Ridolfi, Florence: Olschki, 1945.
11. *Considerations on the 'Discourses' of Machiavelli*, Eng. transl. by M. Grayson in Francesco Guicciardini, *Selected Writings*, ed. by C. Grayson, Oxford: Oxford University Press, 1965, pp. 57–124.
12. *The History of Italy*, Engl. transl. by A. Parker Goddard, 3rd edn, London: Stuart, 1763. This, as said, is the last English translation of the entire work. For a more recent, but abridged, edition, see the translation by S. Alexander, Princeton: Princeton University Press, 1969.

13. *Discorso di Logrogno*, op. cit., pp. 119–21. The same ideas are put forward in *Maxims and Reflections (Ricordi)*, op. cit., B 95 and C 48, and in the *Dialogue on the Government of Florence*, op. cit., pp. 158–9.
14. *Dialogue on the Government of Florence*, op. cit., p. 70.
15. See below p. 84.
16. See below p. 149.
17. *Dialogue on the Government of Florence*, op. cit., p. 59.
18. Ibid., p. 60.
19. Ibid., pp. 61–3.
20. Ibid., pp. 61–2.
21. Ibid., pp. 63–5.
22. Ibid., pp. 66–7.
23. *Discorso di Logrogno*, op. cit., pp. 135–42, and *Dialogue on the Government of Florence*, op. cit., pp. 111–14.
24. *The History of Florence*, op. cit., Ch. XXVI.
25. *Discorso di Logrogno*, op. cit., pp. 119–21.
26. *Dialogue on the Government of Florence*, op. cit., pp. 88–91 and 145–53.
27. Ibid., p. 150.
28. The same pragmatic attitude can be seen a few years later, as Clement VII, being rather at sea in the aftermath of the battle of Pavia, dispatched Machiavelli to Guicciardini – who was, at the time, Governor of Romagna – to see whether Niccolò's ideas about a citizen army could be put to any use in the papal dominions. To Guicciardini, the whole thing was not practical at all, for a series of reasons: the Pope had no friends in the region; the people were split into warring factions and arming them would be very dangerous; the militia would require financial resources that were not available, unless new taxes were introduced, which would make the papal government even less popular; and the enterprise would take a long time – in fact, longer than one could afford under those circumstances (Letter to Cesare Colombo, 23 June 1525, in Francesco Guicciardini, *Le lettere*, ed. by P. Jodogne, Rome: Istituto Storico Italiano per l'Età Moderna e Contemporanea, vol. X, 2008, pp.106–11).
29. *The History of Italy*, op. cit., I, i. My translation.
30. *Dialogue on the Government of Florence*, op. cit., p. 63.
31. *Maxims and Reflections (Ricordi)*, op. cit., B 28 and C 127; C 166; C 180; C 183.
32. *Dialogue on the Government of Florence*, op. cit., p. 63.
33. *The History of Florence*, op. cit., Ch. XI.
34. For example, see *Maxims and Reflections (Ricordi)*, op. cit., C 127, C 166, C 180, C 183; *Giustificazione della politica di Clemente VII*, in *Opere*, vol. VIII: *Scritti politici e Ricordi*, ed. by R. Palmarocchi, Bari: Laterza, 1933, p. 198, and below, p. 153.

35. *The History of Florence*, op. cit., Ch. XI.
36. Letter to Iacopo Salviati, 27 July 1513, in Francesco Guicciardini, *Le lettere*, ed. by P. Jodogne, op. cit., vol. I, 1986, p. 489.
37. *The History of Italy*, Engl. transl. by S. Alexander, op. cit., pp. 4–5.
38. 'Everyone [of the Italian potentates] who is ambitious, angry or fearful, unable to satisfy himself or protect himself by other means, will attempt to get the ultramontanes to come [. . .]. So not only do I see no guarantee that the French will not remain here or return to Italy, I am afraid that in addition the way is open to other nations. This will be our ultimate ruination. For while they are in agreement, they will eat up Italy; if they break up, they will lacerate it; and if by chance one of the ultramontanes chases out the others, Italy will remain in extreme servitude' (*Dialogue on the Government of Florence*, op. cit., pp. 69–70).
39. *The History of Italy*, op. cit., X, vi.
40. For example: 'It is a great error to speak of the things of this world absolutely and indiscriminately and to deal with them, as it were, by the book. In nearly all things one must make distinctions and exceptions because of differences in circumstances. These circumstances are not covered by one and the same rule. Nor can these distinctions and exceptions be found written in books. They must be taught by discretion.' And 'How wrong it is to cite the Romans at every turn. For any comparison to be valid, it would be necessary to have a city with conditions like theirs, and then to govern it according to their example' (*Maxims and Reflections (Ricordi)*, op. cit., C 6 and C 110, respectively. See also C 114 and C 117).
41. Letter to Niccolò Machiavelli, 18 May 1521. Engl. transl. in J. B. Atkinson and D. Sices (eds), *Machiavelli and His Friends*, op. cit., pp. 338–9; *Maxims and Reflections (Ricordi)*, op. cit., C 23 and C 76; below, p. 151.
42. *Maxims and Reflections (Ricordi)*, op. cit., C 78, C 79 and B 76, C 52 and C 31.
43. Ibid., C 136. See also C 1.
44. Ibid., C 23 and B 96.
45. Ibid., C 71 and B 140.
46. *The History of Italy*, Engl. transl. by S. Alexander, op. cit., p. 2.
47. *Maxims and Reflections (Ricordi)*, op. cit., C 79.
48. Ibid., C 126.
49. Ibid., C 96 and below, pp. 156–7.
50. Cf. *Maxims and Reflections*, op. cit., C 186.
51. Ibid., C 182. See also B 172.
52. Ibid., C 155 and B 171.
53. Ibid., C 194. See also C 96.
54. Cf. below, pp. 55, 76, 128.
55. Cf. below, p. 89.
56. Cf. below, pp. 156–7.

57. Below, pp. 123–4. Cf. also p. 42.
58. Santoro [1978], Phillips [1977], pp. 61–80, and Gilbert [1965], pp. 280–1.
59. *Dialogue on the Government of Florence*, op. cit., pp. 139–40.
60. *Consolatoria*, op. cit., pp. 499–500. In a similar vein, 'Giustificazione della politica di Clemente VII', op. cit.
61. On the role assigned to fortune by humanist historiography, see Wilcox's comments on Leonardo Bruni and Poggio Bracciolini (Wilcox [1969], pp. 64 and 147, respectively).
62. *The History of Italy*, op. cit., I, i.
63. There are, however, important exceptions. As Marchand [2002] has noted, in *The History of Italy* Charles V is always referred to as 'Caesar', which suggests that his role as emperor matters more than his personality. Similarly, the clash between Charles V and Francis I is presented less as a conflict between two sovereigns than a struggle between the two most powerful nations, as circumstances and events seem often to prevail over the natural inclinations of the two monarchs. In particular, several of Charles's decisions are interpreted as the result of a series of constraints rather than the reflection of his own political initiative.
64. 'There are more bad men than good, especially in matters regarding property or power' and 'In this world of ours, the men who do well are those who always have their own interests in mind and measure all their actions accordingly. But it is a great error not to know where true interest lies; that is, to think it always resides in some pecuniary advantage rather than in honour, in knowing how to keep a reputation, and in a good name' (*Maxims and Reflections (Ricordi)*, op. cit., C 201 and C 218, respectively).
65. This is the acute interpretation of Guicciardini's most famous concept – the *particulare* – suggested by Santoro [1978, pp. 365–6]. Often taken as sheer self-interest, the notion of *particulare* refers rather to the set of particular circumstances that encourage the individual to engage in a certain action or adopt a certain behaviour because this is conducive to the attainment of honour and profit.
66. In addition, 'life in this world being so corrupt as it is, anyone who wants a reputation is forced to seek wealth. For with wealth, those virtues shine and are esteemed which in a poor man are scarcely regarded and hardly known.' *Maxims and Reflections (Ricordi)*, op. cit., C 141.
67. *Opere*, vol. VIII: *Scritti politici e Ricordi*, ed. by R. Palmarocchi, op. cit., pp. 67–219.
68. *Opere inedite di Francesco Guicciardini*, ed. by G. Canestrini, Florence: Barbera, 1857, vol. I, 'Discorso decimoquinto', pp. 348–51.
69. *Opere*, vol. VII: *Dialogo e discorsi del Reggimento di Firenze*, ed. by R. Palmarocchi, Bari: Laterza, 1932, pp. 175–217.
70. *Consolatoria, Accusatoria, Defensoria*, op. cit.

71. More exactly, all the pairs of speeches related to foreign policy from *Le cose fiorentine* and *The History of Italy* have been included in the present volume. As for the four additional pairs coming from the collected writings (*Opere*, vol. VIII: *Scritti politici e Ricordi*, op. cit.), two (I–II and VIII–IX) were revised by Guicciardini himself and incorporated in *The History of Italy*; in this case, I opted for this last version. The other two (X–XI and XIII–XIV), on the contrary, were not integrated in *The History of Italy* and have been included in this volume.

72. Varotti [2009], p. 6. To Carta [2002], it is Guicciardini's legal training – and not some scepticism of his – that explains his attitude vis-à-vis 'rules' and 'exceptions'.

73. Sasso [1984], pp. 74 and 129; Palmarocchi [1947], p. 110; Ridolfi [1960/7], p. 186.

74. It was from Aristotle and Cicero that the humanists took inspiration for the writing of history, and this deeply affected their work. Latin historiography was considered superior to the Greek one, and the models most frequently invoked were Caesar, Sallust and especially Livy [Gilbert 1965, pp. 203–26].

75. Bruni's *Istoria fiorentina* (*Istoria fiorentina di Leonardo Aretino tradotta in volgare da Donato Acciajuoli*, 3 vols, Florence: Le Monnier, 1855–60) features several individual orations and seven pairs of opposing speeches. The latter can be found in vol. I. pp. 327–43; vol. II, pp. 69–77, 135–7, 241–51 and 519–39: vol. III, pp. 131–9 and 295–307. While Guicciardini's speakers belong to the same decision-making body and their speeches always have a deliberative connotation, Bruni's speakers represent different political actors (e.g. the Pope versus the Florentines, the Bolognese ambassadors versus the Florentine ambassadors), and are often simply engaged in mutual recriminations and accusations.

76. It should not be forgotten, however, that throughout the Renaissance the Greek model of political history is Polybius and not Thucydides [Momigliano 1990, pp. 35–58].

77. Bodrero [1940] offers a comprehensive comparison of Thucydides and Guicciardini, centred on their intellectual profiles and some significant parallels between their respective lives and times. See also Varotti [2012], especially pp. 330–2.

78. Thucydides, II, 62 (Engl. transl. by R. Warner, *History of the Peloponnesian War*, London: Penguin, 1972, p. 161).

79. Thucydides, IV, 62 (ibid., p. 301).

80. Thucydides, VIII, 24 (ibid., p. 551). Emphasis added.

81. Everybody knows it and everybody says so: the Athenians to the Spartans (ibid., I, 78), the Spartans to the Athenians (IV, 18), the Melians to the Athenians (V, 102), Archidamus to the Spartans (I, 80), Nicias to the Athenians (VI, 23; VII, 61) and Hermocrates to the Sicilians (IV, 62).

82. 'My method has been, while keeping as close as possible to the general sense of the words that were actually used, to make the speakers say what, in my opinion, was called for by each situation' (Thucydides, I, 22; Engl. transl., op. cit., p. 47).

83. The extent to which Guicciardini can be assimilated to humanist historiography is open to debate: see Wilcox [1984].

84. These are the three traits of Aristotle's deliberative genre of rhetoric, the one to be adopted before a political assembly: see Palumbo [1991], pp. 27–8.

85. Readers can easily convince themselves of this by skipping the last lines of the introduction to each debate, which is where I have revealed which resolution was adopted at the end.

86. In their reply to the Corinthians, in their very first speech, the Athenians put forward the reasons that have led them to create their empire: 'Fear of Persia was our chief motive, though afterwards we thought, too, of our own honour and our own interest' (Thucydides I, 75; Engl. transl., op. cit., p. 80). And the same criteria inform most of the other debates.

87. See Ch. 1, below.

88. See Ch. 3, below.

89. See Ch. 2, below.

90. See Ch. 4, below.

91. See Ch. 8, below.

92. See Ch. 11, below.

93. See Ch. 9, below.

94. See Ch. 5, below.

95. See Ch. 6, below.

96. Below, p. 50. Cf. pp. 96–7, and the general attitude that informs the first speech in Ch. 9 and the second speech in Ch. 10.

97. Below, pp. 147–8 and also pp. 51, 86, 97, 99, 143.

98. Below, p. 90. Cf. also p. 97. Vice versa: 'If we should, therefore, arm ourselves against one who has endeavoured to deceive us, none will cry out against us for breach of faith' (below, p. 87).

99. Cf. below, p. 116.

100. Cf. below, pp. 87, 99–100.

101. Although such features characterise many debates, the best illustration of all this can be found in Ch. 10.

102. Cf. below, pp. 54–5.

103. Cf. below, p. 79.

104. Cf. below, p. 97.

105. Cf. below, p. 147.

106. Below, p. 96.

107. Below, p. 52. Cf. also p. 117.

108. Below, p. 121.

109. Below, p. 54.

110. Cf. below, pp. 107, 145.
111. Below, p. 149.

References

Albertini, Rudolf von (1955/70), *Das florentinische Staatsbewußtsein im Übergang von der Republik zum Prinzipat*, Berne: Francke. (Italian transl., *Firenze dalla repubblica al principato: Storia e coscienza politica*, Turin: Einaudi.)
Anselmi, Gian Mario (1979), *Ricerche sul Machiavelli storico*, Bologna: Il Mulino.
Barucci, Guglielmo (2004), *I segni e la storia: Modelli tacitiani nella 'Storia d'Italia' del Guicciardini*, Milan: Led.
Berridge, G. R. (2001), 'Guicciardini', in G. R. Berridge, M. Keens-Soper and T. G. Otte (eds), *Diplomatic Theory from Machiavelli to Kissinger*, Basingstoke: Palgrave, pp. 33–49.
Bianchi, Dante (1948), 'Problematica e sofistica in Francesco Guicciardini', *Saggi di umanesimo cristiano*, 3, 37–62.
Bodrero, Emilio (1940), 'Francesco Guicciardini', in *Francesco Guicciardini nel IV centenario della morte (1540–1940)*, Florence: Centro Nazionale di Studi sul Rinascimento, pp. 29–48.
Bonadeo, Alfredo (1981), 'Guicciardini on War and Conquest', *Il pensiero politico*, 14:2, 214–42.
Bondanella, Peter (1976), *Francesco Guicciardini*, Boston: G. K. Hall.
Carta, Paolo (2002), 'Guicciardini scettico?', in E. Pasquini and P. Prodi (eds), *Bologna nell'età di Carlo V e Guicciardini*, Atti del convegno internazionale di Bologna, 19–21 October 2000, Bologna: Il Mulino, pp. 265–81.
Chabod, Federico (1933), 'Francesco Guicciardini', in *Enciclopedia italiana di scienze, lettere ed arti*, Rome: Istituto della Enciclopedia Italiana, vol. 18, pp. 244–8.
Cutinelli-Rèndina, Emanuele (2009), *Guicciardini*, Rome: Salerno.
Fournel, Jean-Louis and Jean-Claude Zancarini (2009), *La Grammaire de la république: Langage de la politique chez Francesco Guicciardini (1483–1540)*, Geneva: Droz.
Fueter, Eduard (1911/63), *Geschichte der neueren Historiographie*, Munich–Berlin: Oldenbourg. (Italian transl. *Storia della storiografia moderna*, Naples: Ricciardi, vol. I.)
Gagneux, Marcel (1970), 'Nature et condition humaines selon François Guichardin', *Revue des études italiennes*, 16:3, 231–63.
Gilbert, Felix (1965), *Machiavelli and Guicciardini: Politics and History in Sixteenth-Century Florence*, Princeton: Princeton University Press.
Jodogne, Pierre (2002), 'La "potenza" di Carlo V: Il commento del Guicciardini nel carteggio del 1525', in E. Pasquini and P. Prodi (eds), *Bologna nell'età di Carlo V e Guicciardini*, Atti del convegno internazionale di Bologna, 19–21 October 2000, Bologna: Il Mulino, pp. 19–39.

Luciani, Vincenzo (1949), *Francesco Guicciardini e la fortuna dell'opera sua*, Italian edn ed. by P. Guicciardini, Florence: Olschki (an expanded edition of the author's *Francesco Guicciardini and His European Reputation*, New York: Otto, 1936).

Manselli, Raoul (1985), 'Il Guicciardini nel giudizio storico di Ranke', in *Francesco Guicciardini*, Giornata lincea indetta in occasione del V centenario della nascita (Rome, 12 December 1983), Rome: Accademia Nazionale dei Lincei, pp. 47–56.

Marchand, Jean-Jacques (2002), 'Carlo V e l'Impero in Machiavelli e in Guicciardini prima della battaglia di Pavia', in E. Pasquini and P. Prodi (eds), *Bologna nell'età di Carlo V e Guicciardini*, Atti del convegno internazionale di Bologna, 19–21 October 2000, Bologna: Il Mulino, pp. 251–64.

Marcucci, Marcello (1985), 'Storia e salvezza: Tucidide, Guicciardini e la ragione laica', *Critica storica*, 22, 421–38.

Martelli, Mario and Francesco Bausi (1996), 'Politica, storia e letteratura: Machiavelli e Guicciardini', in E. Malato (ed.), *Storia della letteratura italiana*, Rome: Salerno, vol. 4, pp. 251–351.

Momigliano, Arnaldo (1990), *The Classical Foundations of Modern Historiography*, Berkeley: University of California Press.

Palmarocchi, Roberto (1947), *Studi guicciardiniani*, Florence: Macrì.

Palumbo, Matteo (1991), 'I discorsi contrapposti nella *Storia d'Italia* di Francesco Guicciardini', *Modern Language Notes*, 106:1, 15–37.

Phillips, Mark (1977), *Francesco Guicciardini: The Historian's Craft*, Toronto: University of Toronto Press.

Pocock, J. G. A. (1975), *The Machiavellian Moment: Florentine Political Thought and the Atlantic Republican Tradition*, Princeton: Princeton University Press.

Ridolfi, Roberto (1960/7), *Vita di Francesco Guicciardini*, Rome: Belardetti. (English transl. *The Life of Francesco Guicciardini*, London: Routledge & Kegan Paul.)

Santoro, Mario (1978), *Fortuna, ragione e prudenza nella civiltà letteraria del Cinquecento*, Naples: Liguori, 2nd edn.

Sasso, Gennaro (1984), *Per Francesco Guicciardini: Quattro studi*, Rome: Istituto Storico Italiano per il Medio Evo.

Scarano, Emanuella (1981), 'Introduzione alla *Storia d'Italia*', in F. Guicciardini, *Opere*, ed. by E. Scarano, Turin: Utet, vol. 2, pp. 9–68.

Treves, Paolo (1931), *Il realismo politico di Francesco Guicciardini*, Florence: La Nuova Italia.

Varotti, Carlo (1998), *Gloria e ambizione politica nel Rinascimento: Da Petrarca a Machiavelli*, Milan: Bruno Mondadori.

Varotti, Carlo (2009), *Francesco Guicciardini*, Naples: Liguori.

Varotti, Carlo (2012), 'Lo sguardo "autoptico" di messer Francesco', in C. Berra and A. M. Cabrini (eds), *La Storia d'Italia di Guicciardini e la sua fortuna*, Milan: Cisalpino, pp. 329–58.

Wilcox, Donald J. (1969), *The Development of Florentine Humanist Historiography in the Fifteenth Century*, Cambridge: Harvard University Press.

Wilcox, Donald J. (1984), 'Guicciardini and the Humanist Historians', *Annali d'Italianistica*, 2, 19–33.

Chapter 1

On Whether or Not the Florentines Should Wage War against the Church*

From 1309 to 1377, the popes resided in Avignon, and many of their dominions in Central Italy fell into the hands of local lords. In 1353, Pope Innocent VI sent Gil Álvarez Carrillo de Albornoz, Cardinal of St Clement, into Italy, for the sake of restoring the papal temporal authority. The energetic policies of the Cardinal led to the rapid establishment of a strong and cohesive state that surrounded Florence on all sides and that included cities and territories to which the Florentine republic, in turn, aspired. The full restoration of papal jurisdiction over Perugia (1371), in particular, elicited palpable concern across all Tuscany. In addition, many in Florence feared that the faction connected to the Church (the Guelph party and the Albizzi family) might now be tempted to rely on the Pope's external support to rid itself of its political enemies. Finally, the arrogant style of government of the papal legates who were dispatched from Avignon to the dominions of the State of the Church soon alienated the various peoples who were subject to their rule and created additional tensions with their neighbours: above all, Florence. Despite all this, Florence joined a general anti-Milanese coalition with the Pope in 1372 (and renewed it in 1374), for the sake of checking the expansionist policies of Bernabò and Galeazzo Visconti, lords of Milan, in Northern Italy.

It is against this backdrop that, in the winter of 1374–5, the Legate of Bologna denied Florence permission to buy grain in Romagna, a region under his jurisdiction. In the following summer, a truce being signed with the Visconti (4 June 1375), he dismissed Sir John Hawkwood and his mercenary company, who immediately headed for Tuscany, looking for plunder and ransom. In Florence, many suspected that Hawkwood had passed into Tuscany upon the Legate's encouragement, for it was believed that the latter intended to take revenge on the Tuscan cities that had refused to contribute funding for his war against the Visconti,

* From: *Le cose fiorentine*, ed. by R. Ridolfi, Florence: Olschki, 1983, pp. 39–45.

thus forcing him to suspend it. A plot designed to make Prato – a town under Florentine dominion – fall into Hawkwood's hands was foiled and Florence was forced to pay a huge sum of money to convince the English mercenary to evacuate her territory. As a result of all this, the outrage in Florence was immense. This is the context of the debate below.

The Florentines resolved to make an alliance with the Visconti (26 July), and found themselves involved in a war against the Church the following year. Although Guicciardini is critical of such a decision – to him, considerations relating to the 'just indignation' prevailed over those relating to 'expediency' – and although Florence did suffer many of the difficulties that the second speaker had predicted, the repercussions of the wave of rebellions across the papal dominions, soon coupled with the Western Schism (1378–1417), destroyed Albornoz's achievements and removed any significant threat to Florence from the State of the Church for longer than a century.

The Priors,[1] having summoned the main magistrates and a great multitude of citizens, asked for advice on what one should do. At this point, [. . .] spoke like this:

— The injury that the Legate of Bologna[2] has done to our city has been so perfidious and so grievous that even if we were not under the necessity of taking measures to secure ourselves against the dangers we are facing, the concern alone of preserving the glory of our republic would oblige us to resent it vigorously. For, what behaviour can be more treacherous than his? While he and we are in the same confederacy, which we have thoroughly observed, he, having forgot about both his faith and the articles of our treaty, having uttered no protest, not even the slightest complaint, has not been ashamed to attack us. What design could be more vicious than trying to starve into submission a city that has always been devoted to the Apostolic Seat and that both in the remote past and in more recent times has taken up arms so many times against the enemies of the Church? In addition, what infamy could be greater for us than, by remaining passive in the face of such malice, proving so different from our great-hearted ancestors, who being often provoked by slight injuries, underwent any danger to preserve the dignity of this city? The injuries done by the Pisan ambassadors to the Florentine ambassadors at the court of Rome were of so little importance that one can still hardly believe that so great consequences followed from such weak causes;[3] and yet, those affronts induced our ancestors to fight very long and very cruel wars against the Pisans. Rightly so, for the deliberations of republics require no mean and private considerations, or which tend only to expediency, but magnificent and high goals by which they may increase their glory and keep their reputation among their neighbours; and nothing is more detrimental to reputation than giving occasion to think that you want courage or strength to resent affronts, or you are not prone to take revenge, not so much for the pleasure attending vengeance but rather because the punishing of the offender may serve as an example to deter all the others, so that they will not have the boldness to provoke you.[4] In such a way glory and expediency are combined and noble and great-hearted resolutions produce security and profit. In such a way, by dealing with one difficulty, many are prevented, and one short exertion often frees you from many, and prolonged, efforts.

But it looks as if necessity, to a much greater extent than great-heartedness, pushes us to make war, for no one can deny that, if we do not, we will find ourselves in the most evident danger, and that those legates, who one cannot believe would have dared such evil deeds without the consent of the Pope,[5] realising that their wicked intentions have become manifest to us, will no longer have any scruple in harming us. Remember how great the danger has been this time, how vast the opportunity they have to injure us, surrounded as we are by the dominions of the Church on many sides and rounded about by several others who are unfriendly to us. Surely, if I mistake not, even if our undertaking appeared hard and most hazardous, we would be necessitated to attempt it, for no difficulty has reason to extinguish in our breasts the desire to preserve the dignity and the magnificence of this republic, and no danger can be so great that running it and tempting fortune is more perilous than choosing to perish shamefully out of cowardice. What infamy is greater than waiting for a certain death out of an immoderate fear of dying?

But such difficulties and dangers are not there, for, although our enemies are very powerful as long as we wait to be attacked or betrayed by them, if we attack them first they will prove very weak, because due to the long absence of the pontiffs, the unjust and insolent ways of governing of their officials, and the many iniquities and brutalities inflicted upon their subjects, all the peoples of the Church are reduced to the utmost despair, and as soon as they see our arms, as soon as they are given the hope of liberty, they will all turn against those wicked tyrants, who, for want of revenues – since they will be fighting a war on their own territory – and finding themselves oppressed by infinite difficulties, it is not to be doubted that will soon no longer be able to resist; and all the more, since we will be able to join with Bernabò [Visconti], who is a most bitter enemy of the Pope and has been recently injured by him.[6] Thus victory will be easy, and its fruits will be very great, that is the security and the eternal glory of our city. Nor will we save ourselves only, but we will also be the liberators of many peoples, who, thanks to us, will get out of the throat of these wolves.

No one should be withheld by the name of the pontiffs, the authority of the Apostolic Seat, the fear of offending God, for those names have reason to inspire awe and pious feelings to those who intend to injure them out of malice or ambition. God is the severe avenger of the affronts to his Church, but he is no enemy to the arms that one takes up only for the sake of one's safety; and all laws, both divine and human, condemn those who try to oppress others, not those who aim at defending themselves. Our intention has not to be to occupy the dominions of the Church or to crush the authority of our religion, but to rid Italy of so much tyranny, to make bad shepherds remember that they are pontiffs before they are emperors, to restore the Apostolic Seat to the ancient majesty that used to induce people to obey more out of reverence than fear, more out of devotion than force.

Therefore, most excellent Lords, my advice is that, in order to preserve the dignity of our city, which we inherited from our ancestors in all its greatness, to maintain our liberty, for which they spared themselves neither dangers nor expenses, and out of compassion for so many people who are oppressed by such a cruel and iniquitous tyranny, we make this just, necessary and holy war, not against the Church of God or the vicars of Christ, but against the bad shepherds, against the wicked governors, with the firm decision, so that our undertaking is more justified and without any suspicion of ambition, not to take possession for ourselves of any place that currently belongs to the Church, but only to procure the freedom of those peoples and leave them to their own will. And once we have decided to make war, I advise that a less numerous council should be in charge of all the matters pertaining to the ways and the timing of its beginning and continuation, for in a free and popular government wars have to be decided upon by many but, if they are to be successful, have to be managed by few.[7] —

This speech was heard with the very great approval of most [. . .]; but as soon at the crowd noise had settled a bit, Carlo Strozzi,[8] a man then of great authority, spoke like this:

— The greater and juster our indignation against the governors of the State of the Church, and the more offensive the injuries they have inflicted upon us, the more it is necessary to be prudent, so that our passions do not lead us to decisions that might prove useless to our republic. For resisting the forces or desires of others is not always difficult;

the difficulty consists in being able to moderate yourself and overcome the desire of a just revenge, with reason and with considerations related to the interests of the state. The injury that the Legate of Bologna has done to us could be neither more unfair nor more cruel, on account of the conjunction and the alliance that subsist between the Pontiff and us, and even more on account of the ultimate end of his designs and the inhuman way by which he has tried to satisfy such a wicked desire. But this is no reason for us to concentrate so much on what we could justly do to him that we lose sight of the great infamy, loss and danger that are to result to our city from an unnecessary war against the Roman pontiffs for the purpose of making the State of the Church rebel.

I take it for granted that the Legate is extremely ill disposed towards us and that should he have any chance to injure us seriously he would have fewer scruples now than he has had in the past. I do not know how the Pope is inclined, for if we do not want to deceive ourselves, we have not hitherto seen any sign that can make us conclude that these infamous undertakings proceed with his consent. Be that as it may, it seems to me that the harm they could have done to us has passed, and that we have discovered and escaped danger at one and same time. For this Legate, although full of ambition and arrogance, was normally of the opinion that he could not be a match for us, but he suddenly hoped to be able to oppress us when, on account of the war he had fought against Bernabò, he found himself armed with a most powerful army, when we were utterly lacking provisions, when we did not expect any threat from him on account of the security provided for by the alliance and our ancient devotion to the Church, when we were extremely short of supplies, and it was the appropriate time to spoil the harvest: not only do all these conditions cease to exist now, but they will also never occur again at the same time – and if they do not, they do not possess force enough to injure us. Thus, if we want to form a sound opinion, this war is not forced upon us by danger; and, to be sure, if it were more honourable, more easy, more safe, although not necessary, the considerations related to the injury we suffered would perhaps be more important, to me too, than those pertaining to expediency. But the burden we are debating about is just too heavy to shoulder, for many reasons.

To begin with, the war will not be fought against the Legate who has injured us, since the dominions of the Church are not his, but against the Roman Pontiff, who may have consented to his undertaking. But how can we justify this? With what face shall we reply to the King of France[9] and the other Christian princes to whom the Pope will complain of us? Or how will we be able to invoke a reason that, should he deny it, we cannot possibly prove? And how will we excuse ourselves by alleging a cause which, even if it were proved, would not justify us? For if the Pope has injured us, the Church has not, and it is not appropriate that we, out of revenge against one pontiff, attempt to violate God's bride, to seize the patrimony of the Church, the donations made by the Roman emperors to the apostles.

Our city has no greater reason for praise, no more precious treasure – although this is not the thing in which our ancestors and we take pride most often – than having always assisted the Apostolic Seat, having always been Catholic, always defenders of the Church. Of what else are all our memories, all our archives, fuller? What else is the meaning of the name of the Guelphs, which is so revered in this city, and of the glorious flags, victorious in so many wars, that the Roman pontiffs donated to us? Yet, we are now debating about depriving ourselves of such a glory, acquired with the endless blood of our ancestors; and whereas previously, both in the court of Rome and throughout all Christendom, we praised with much confidence the deeds we had carried out in the defence of the Church, while in all our troubles we used to resort to the pontiffs, as their beloved and special sons, we want now to deprive ourselves of this patronage, to thoughtlessly throw so glorious a treasure away, with our own hands. To what end? With what hopes?

The initial phase of the war will perhaps be easy, now that the State of the Church lacks arms and the people are hostile to them. But consider how things will go then. This is not a temporal prince whose authority and state one can take away from him with the rebellion of his subjects, but a Roman pontiff, whose power does not consist in the dominion over the cities he possesses in Italy but in the reverence that princes, in the obedience that Christendom, pay to him, both of which grow as much as he is troubled and harassed. Thus, when we believe we have defeated him, he will resurge with more power than before, with more facility to injure us. He will not be wanting the assistance of the princes, or ways to incite all the peoples against us as against enemies of the Christian name – all weapons which, in different occasions and with less justification, have been resorted to by the Church, which fights less with foot and horse than with censures and edicts. It is folly to hope to defeat in battle him who can wage a very great war against you from his apartments while at rest, to believe you can defend yourself with shields and spears against him who can mortally wound you with bells and papers. He will soon interdict our city; if we comply, the suspension of the Mass and other Christian offices and sacraments will look very serious and will give rise to great scandal in the mind of an infinite number of people; if we do not, this will amount to nothing else but curing the lesser disorder with a greater one. Declaring us heretics and infidels, he will deprive us of our possessions everywhere, and the goods and the persons of our merchants will be given as prey by him. Do you believe that, before princes and peoples, our justifications would be of greater moment than the authority of the Church? Or that the respect for justice, provided we could demonstrate the justness of our cause, would prevail over the cupidity to steal so many riches from us? Thus, we will make war at an immense expense; to help sustain it, we will be robbed of so many goods; and having been deprived of the opportunity to trade with other countries, we will be left with no hope to earn. And the facility that may now look great will become more difficult by the day, because on account of so many expenses, so many losses, so much damage, the mind of our citizens will change, and the city will be filled with ill disposition, so with endless troubles we will sustain a war which, even if it went well, would be of no use to us, for we cannot aim to take possession of any territory. And the peoples who will rebel against the Church will hurt us more than those who will stay with it, for we will have to support them with our purse, on account of the fact that they are not used to spend money in the defence of their liberty, nor will they be as stubborn as we are in preserving it. In fact, as soon as they are free they will split into factions, and perhaps most of them, due to the losses and troubles of war, will be inclined to return to their ancient allegiance.

Nor should you be induced to take such a great risk by any consideration of great-heartedness. He who, with a just cause, enters troubles and dangers with a plausible hope to succeed is great-hearted; he who, for the sake of taking revenge for the injuries he has suffered, harms himself no less than his enemy, is unwise; he who harms himself without comparison more than the others is most imprudent beyond any measure. The ways of the pontiffs are unfair, I admit, and the tyranny with which they rule their peoples is wicked and inhuman. But it is not our duty to protect all our neighbours, and thinking to reform the world is beyond our rank. And whereas the great princes adore the iniquities of the clergy, we are at least to tolerate them.

To conclude, I do not think that danger forces us to undertake this enterprise, nor do I believe that considerations of honour induce us to be imprudent, to harm ourselves, and to initiate a war which cannot be waged without shame, enormous expenses, and intolerable damages, and which it would be most dangerous to lose and useless to win. Thus, my advice is that, in order to provide for our safety with no danger and no loss, we send ambassadors to the Pope to complain of the Legate's insult to us and ask for reassurances of our security, and do the same with the King of France. In the mean time, let us not fail to be well alert, to be provided with some troops, to come to a sound agreement with our neighbours and allies, to try and make an alliance with Bernabò in the defence of our states. His reputation, as long as we are at peace, will be useful for us to put a bridle on those who might intend to injure us; but, should we enter into war, I do not know how advantageous his company would be to us, on account of the natural hatred he feels for us, and because, as you all know, he is man of much cunning and little faith. Thus, in my view, we will enjoy a safe peace and, if in the end we have to, we will be ready to make war, to which no reason must push us, except extreme necessity. —

Notes

1. At the time, the six Priors – the representatives of the most important guilds – were the heads of the city.
2. Guillaume de Noellet (c. 1340–94), Cardinal of St Angel.
3. According to the thirteenth-century chronicle by Ricordano and Giacotto Malispini (*Storia fiorentina*, Milan: Sonzogno, 1927, Ch. CVIII, pp. 107–8), upon the crowning of Frederick II as emperor in Rome (November 1220), the Florentine and Pisan ambassadors came to a violent brawl over who should be entitled to a little dog, which his owner, a Roman cardinal, had promised as a gift first to a Florentine ambassador and the following day, having forgotten about his previous commitment, to one of the Pisan ambassadors. The actual fighting that ensued between the members of the two delegations led Florence and Pisa to take various retaliatory measures against each other, until war broke out two years later. The same episode is also described by Giovanni Villani in his fourteenth-century chronicle (*Cronica*, VII, 2, Florence: Coen, vol. I, 1844, pp. 225–6).
4. Cf. *Maxims and Reflections (Ricordi)*, Engl. transl. by M. Domandi, Philadelphia: University of Pennsylvania Press, 1965, C 74.
5. Pierre Roger de Beaufort, pope as Gregory XI from 1370 to 1378.
6. Bernabò Visconti, Lord of Milan (together with his brother Galeazzo) from 1354 to 1385. Gregory XI was the inspirer and an active member of an anti-Viscontean coalition that launched a very serious attack against the state of Milan in 1372. After the failure of the allied offensive, the Pope still opposed a general peace of compromise, determined as he was to abase, if not destroy, the Visconti lordship.
7. The ad hoc institution here invoked was, in fact, established soon afterwards, in August. Composed of eight men, it went under the name of the Eight of War. As its members were excommunicated, the Florentines ironically began to call them the Eight Saints, and the conflict was from then on referred to as the War of the Eight Saints (1376–8).
8. A leading figure of the Guelph party, Carlo Strozzi was ambassador and Prior on several occasions. He died in 1383.
9. Charles V of Valois, King of France from 1364 to 1380.

Chapter 2

On Whether or Not the Florentines Should Accept the Peace Agreement that the Duke of Milan is Offering[*]

Throughout the fourteenth century, Florence was a tenacious opponent of the expansionist policies of the Visconti, the lords and then dukes of Milan who aimed at establishing a solid and large state in Northern Italy. Between the late 1390s and the early 1400s, Gian Galeazzo Visconti extended his dominions and influence to Bologna, Perugia and Tuscany itself, thereby posing a serious challenge to the very position held by Florence in Central Italy. His sudden death, in 1402, and the almost immediate disintegration of his powerful duchy – which was soon reduced to a conglomerate of cities and territories ruled by local lords – seemed to liberate Florence and other Italian states from such a threat. In 1412, however, his younger son, Filippo Maria, became duke. Filippo engaged in a gradual and skilful restoration of the dominions that had been lost in the previous decade. First, he neutralised the hostility of the local lords around Milan; then, after consolidating his power, he ridded himself of them in various ways and began to regain the other dominions. While doing this, the young Duke needed to make sure that the other Italian powers, above all Venice and Florence, would not interfere with his designs. He kept Venice quiet by giving up his claims on Verona and Vicenza, seized by the Venetians after his father's death; as for the Florentines, whose attitude was instrumental to the recovery of Genoa, he offered them a treaty of peace and non-interference in their respective spheres of influence – a reciprocal guarantee that his ambassadors presented as a manifestation of his good faith and desire to break with his family's expansionist tradition.

The debate that follows is about this offer, which was indeed accepted by the Florentines (the treaty was signed on 8 February 1420). To Guicciardini, the decision reflected in particular the desire not to antagonise the popular party, whose members suspected that those who spoke against Filippo's peace plan stood to gain some personal advan-

[*] From: *Le cose fiorentine*, ed. by R. Ridolfi, Florence: Olschki, 1983, pp. 149–56.

tage from war. Thus, the supporters of the peace became more vocal, those who held a different view turned more reserved, and those in between embraced the prevailing opinion, 'whose good was evident and whose evil was so hidden that only a perspicacious eye could see it'. The same interpretation can be found in the Dialogue on the Government of Florence, *Book I. Niccolò Machiavelli, in his* Florentine Histories *(IV, iii), expresses a different view on the decision:*

> *Many others thought it best to make such a treaty and by virtue of it to impose conditions upon Filippo, the transgression of which would make his evil intentions manifest to anybody; and that then, in case he broke the peace, they might with greater justice make war against him.*

This, incidentally, is also one of the reasons invoked in the second speech. As the first speaker had predicted, far from being content with what he possessed, the Duke seized Genoa in 1421 and intervened in Romagna in 1423, which eventually induced Florence to wage war against him.

The issue became the subject of a huge debate and, opinions being asked for, Niccolò da Uzzano,[1] most prudent citizen, who was then a man of immense authority in the republic, spoke like this:

— In my view, our city has never had to make any decision to which she has been less induced by necessity than this. Since we have been at peace, albeit a tacit one, with the Duke of Milan[2] for many years, there is no reason at all which now forces us to explicitly accept or refuse to sign a peace agreement with him. And yet, either some presentiment that comes from my heart, or the knowledge I have, out of a long experience, of your ways of proceeding, makes me greatly fear that our aspirations will lead us to where neither ambition nor necessity guides us. For I know how much peace is appreciated in a city whose nourishments are based upon peace, how hateful is the fear of having to spend money to those who know that war must be financed more from their own purses than by public revenues, how little is believed the man who suggests something that almost all dislike, and how much more that which one sees at present, rather than that which one fears in the future, naturally sets men in motion. The more such things are true and potent, the more they encourage me to advise against the general inclination, because the more rare those who advocate the public good regardless of the impu- tations this might entail for themselves, the more those who do so are to be commended. And he who, in his advice, takes into account what is expedient to the city more than what pleases the people, may perhaps be judged to act out of imprudence, but not out of adulation or malice.

The peace the Duke is asking for, provided it is asked for sincerely and is aimed at the goal his words indicate, is most useful to this city, for it brings us reputation and security; in addition, being asked for by him and being negotiated in Florence, it comes with very great dignity for our republic. Yet, even if the Duke were after peace with honest intentions, the damage we would suffer in rejecting his offer would not be so great as the danger we would incur in accepting it in case he were not sincere. For if we reject it, our situation will not worsen, nor will we have more reason to fear war from any side; but if we accept it, and he intends to carry out evil designs, we place him in a better position, for, being sure of us, he will be able to boldly attempt those enterprises for which he now shows little enthusiasm out of the fear of us, and many who, relying on our assistance, would either resist him or not bend to his will, once they despair of our help will either yield to him or look for his friendship.

Peace, I submit, is a sweet and holy thing, when it brings security, when it does not increase the power of enemies, when it does not pave the way to a more dangerous war; but when it entails these effects, it is bitter and pernicious. Nor have we to look for examples of this from others, for we have very many ourselves. The first peace that, contrary to the opinion of many wise citizens, we made with King Ladislaus was the means by which he freed himself from enormous dangers, and the cause that he defended his kingdom, then occupied Rome and almost all the State of the Church, and that at last placed us under the necessity of either entering a most dangerous war against him or making with him another peace, more pernicious than war, which led us to such a situation that, if God (who is often more of a patron of good, rather than wise, men) had not come to our assistance with the unexpected death of the King, that peace would have caused us the loss of our liberty.[3] We are to be aware of the same things now, for reason and experience teach us that the Duke is not asking for peace in order to have peace with us, but to consolidate his own state, rid himself of his troubles, and be able, in the end, to strike us with greater force.

I am not saying that sons are always like their fathers, but those who suspect as much are not without reason, and it would be less surprising that the Duke should imitate his ancestors than that he should be different from them. His forefathers never had any goal more important than extinguishing our city, destroying our republic. Azzo[4] had such a desire, Galeazzo[5] too; the archbishop[6] attempted to do so, as did Bernabò.[7] As for the Duke's father,[8] his memory is still so fresh that any reference to it would be superfluous. And with what manners, with what cunning? They all proceeded with sweet words, with insidious promises, with showing a most burning desire for peace under the promise of the treaty, of the alliance, under a thousand oaths. Thus, in this uncertainty, we have to fear that he has the same cunning and not a different purpose, especially because the same reasons are there, and perhaps some others. He is a prince as powerful as they were; as such, he has the same ambition to expand his state as they had and as all great princes have; he is a Ghibelline, as they were; as such, he has the same desire to subjugate this city, the head of all the Guelphs of Italy; his father passed down to him a heritage of hatred against our republic that was more intense and profound than the one he had received; ambition pushed his ancestors to that which shame seems to induce him to do, for he has so fresh a memory of the enterprises undertaken by his father, who was lord of Bologna, Siena, Pisa and Perugia. How can we believe that he remains content with his ancient borders, that he desires our friendship, that he has turned his mind to peace? Do we not see his deeds? Have we not seen with how much cunning, how many simulated peaces, how many breaches of faith he has recovered his father's state? Pandolfo Malatesta is witness to it; so is Gabrino Fondulo;[9] so are many others, first assured and then deceived by him. Should anybody doubt the allegiance of these princes, the ambition of the Visconti, I would think it appropriate that he should call on us to bear witness; are we so imprudent as to have learnt nothing from so many losses? The very name Ghibelline is frightening in this city, and every little increment of that camp generally has us in suspense and fills us with distrust. Are we now to provide a large space for the growth of a head of the Ghibelline camp, a most powerful prince who has many causes for enmity with us?

I am not advising that we seek war with the Duke, nor that we do anything which, if he is truly well inclined, may give him cause to change his mind, nor that we reject peace in such a way as to seem eager for war. But I am not recommending either that, by assuring him, we remove the bridle that can keep him moderate, nor that we give him the opportunity to grow bolder towards us. We are now in such a position that, by simply remaining in suspense, we keep alive and on their feet many who will give up as soon as they see us bound; we are now in such a position that, should it be necessary, we can prevent him, with very little expense, from undertaking any enterprise which we do not find convenient to us; we are now in such a position that we are feared and entreated by him and all those who fear him call on, and entreat, us. If we commit to this peace, his power will grow in such a way that we will not then be able to defend ourselves without incurring enormous expenses and dangers, we will no longer be feared and held in consideration by him, and instead of being entreated by others, we will have to entreat others when in danger, and experience how little are held in esteem those who find themselves in need – of which the immoderate demands that the Venetians made on us when the old Duke seized Bologna[10] serve as an example. We should be thinking of containing and extinguishing his ambition; instead, we are trying to set it alight. Where is our prudence? What about the proverb that says that the Florentines see things in advance? I wish to God that we will not resurrect that other old adage – that we are blind!

I therefore recommend that we respond to the ambassadors with grateful words, showing the same desire for peace; that we take our time in concluding the negotiations under the pretext that we intend to consult with our allies or any other excuse that will sound better; and that we say we entrust the decision to those ambassadors we intend to send to him for this purpose. We shall then send them, with careful reflection and some delay, always keeping negotiations open, so that he understands that we hesitate out of a lack of trust in having a safe peace, and not out of a desire to make war against him. His behaviour and ways of proceeding will enlighten us step by step. If we see that he is content with what he has, that he does not upset his neighbours, that he relinquishes his ambitious thoughts, we will always be able to make peace with him; if we realise that he is following the steps of his ancestors, we will be able to make new decisions to our advantage at any time. Thus we will maintain ourselves with more security and more reputation, and keep our friends more reassured and braver. Otherwise, I am afraid that, sooner rather than later, and with enormous expenses and dangers, we will know for ourselves (and will also serve as an example to the others), how pernicious it is, on account of an excessive desire for peace, to bind ourselves by an unsafe peace ahead of time, how foolish it is not to act with foresight on dangers from the beginning, and how very imprudent it is to deprive our friends of hope while temporising with the enemies. —

The truthful arguments of Niccolò, and the immense esteem in which his reputation was held, made everyone listen very carefully and struck the minds of most. But after him, . . . stood up and spoke like this:

— I admit that although peace is a most desired and most holy thing, it is the duty of all those who govern a state not to let its sweetness dazzle them to such an extent that out of fear of losing it they enter into greater wars and dangers than would those who do not love it too much. Nevertheless, I advise that one has no reason to enter into war on account of any fear of war, for those who do so often enter without any need into danger in order to escape danger, and since no peace is ever so safe and so firm as to be wanting of some fear of war, this would be the way not to ever have peace but, out of the desire of it, to become involved in war after war. Therefore those deserve to be commended who, in seeing a manifest danger of war, are not kept by the sweetness of peace from recommending to procure all the appropriate provisions; and those deserve to be blamed who increase the occasions of war only because they fear war more than is needed.

The peace the Duke of Milan is offering to us, provided it is not a fraudulent one, cannot be more convenient to this republic because it diverts him from the affairs of Tuscany, and we are not concerned about his successes in Lombardy, provided he has no cause to get involved on this side of the Apennines. Nor does such a peace stabilise our condition of tranquillity with him only, but also with all the other states, for the situation of Italy is such that if we do not have war with him, we are not to fear war from anybody else for many years to come. And how useful peace is to us – a peace that is cloudless and is established in such a way that the minds of all are safe from any fear of war – how much it is in fact the safety and the life of our city, can easily be judged by those who remember the heavy damages that the previous wars inflicted upon us, and by those who consider how much our city has grown in goods, in riches, and in reputation in the few years of peace that we have had, and how much it is to grow every day, if the peace holds, for it is the natural tendency for things to rise from the bottom to the middle with more difficulty and slowness than they do from the middle to the top. We therefore have to ardently desire peace, nor should we hold it less dear because it is offered to us and we are entreated to accept it, for peace is good and useful when it is not made out of necessity and when we are induced to it not by the difficulties in which we find ourselves but by the sort of terms proposed. Nor do I believe that the foundation that Niccolò da Uzzano – a prudent man – has laid is very safe, that even if we do not accept the peace not for this we will become involved in a war, and that it will always be in our power, according to the behaviour of the Duke, to embrace it or get away from it, because the nature of these things is such that they do not have a middle ground and it is hardly ever the case that he of whom you do not want to declare yourself friend will not consider you as an enemy. The Duke may well attempt a number of undertakings of no concern to us within the borders of Lombardy, neither against us nor with the intention of injuring us; so we may, with the same attitude, in Tuscany. If we make peace and establish our respective borders, such deeds will be of no concern to one, and held in no consideration by the other; but if we do not make peace, the same deeds will give umbrage and may be the cause of new turbulences. And every little beginning, although not the result of hostile intention, may take things further and lead them to a necessary war; in addition, it is to be apprehended that our rejection of peace might make the Duke suspect that we intend to harm him at some point. Suspicion cannot be moderated, nor are good reasons enough to make it safe. Thus, if he attempts something that displeases us, if he tries to gain adherents in Tuscany, friends in Bologna or in Romagna, not with a desire to injure us but in order to be better able to defend himself against us, will we not have been the cause of these motions? Our suspicion will then be the cause of his suspicion, and his will increase ours, and in the multiplication of suspicions on both sides, one will be under the necessity of thinking to prevent the other. Thus, in order to be safe we will become suspicious, out of the will of defending ourselves we will begin to injure each other, in order to escape war we will enter into war. If nothing else, the doubt that peace is ill-founded and can break down any day will interrupt the flow of our goods and profits, which stop out of any insignificant opinion, of any uncertainty, men may have.

I do not know what might be the intentions of the Duke, and it is difficult to judge the human heart which God, as he shaped men, placed in a covered place in order for it to be occult. But it would not be surprising if he desired that quiet which his ambassadors have mentioned, for those princes who in their youth have known nothing other than felicity are warm and dangerous, but those who have experienced the adversity of fortune are colder, nor are those who have been heated too much by the fire likely to willingly approach it. The Duke has never experienced what felicity is, what peace is, what rest is; in fact, there is no greater example in the world of the variations of fortune than when we consider the felicity of the father and the calamities of the sons. Everybody was already taking it for granted that the Duke's father would be king of Italy when, in the blink of an eye, one of his sons was killed[11] and the other not only lost the state that his father had passed down to him, but was almost reduced to begging. If we concede this peace to him, he will grant us all the rights he can claim over Pisa, which is not something to be held in low esteem, for it is always good to combine force with all the titles and justifications that one can.[12] Should he attempt anything at all against the articles of the peace agreement, his ambition will be manifest, so will our righteousness and we will be able to take up arms against him with more praise and more authority, and it will be easier for us to induce the other princes and states of Italy to oppose his enterprises. On the other hand, we are giving him nothing more than that which we are willing to grant him anyway, for we have deliberated many times not to interfere in the affairs of Lombardy, and even if the wisest citizens were of a different opinion, the people would not be induced to it without the most evident reason.

Thus I am not sure if it is wise advice, remaining in the situation in which we find ourselves, to abandon a good that is already here and is certain out of the fear of an evil that is far away and dubious, to lose the most precious fruits of peace out of a perhaps vain fear of war. The affairs of the world depend on many accidents, and are therefore so uncertain that our opinions about them are often most misleading, and experience shows that almost always the opposite happens to what men, no matter how wise, expected. The difficulties that the Duke is facing in Lombardy are not of such a sort that he can disengage from them in one day. How many unforeseen events, how many unhoped-for things may occur which, should he think of violating peace, would free us from such a danger! In addition, we are not so weak, nor are our forces held in such a low esteem, that – should he be wicked – either the easiness of the enterprise has to tempt him, or, even in case he attempts it, we are to lack the means to defend ourselves. We resisted his father, a most powerful prince and no doubt the greatest that Italy had had in a very long time, for twelve years; we filled Lombardy with armies and he, being put in the utmost danger of losing his state, saw our flags not far from the walls of Milan.[13] Will now the courage to face him fail us, the lord of a duchy that is plagued and devastated by so many plunders, so many fires, so much ruin? [His father] Duke Gian Galeazzo had nobody to fear in Italy, for all of Lombardy was obedient to him, the Venetians were oriented towards nothing but sea affairs, and the popes were extremely weak on account of the schism.[14] Now the Venetians address themselves to land affairs and, since they possess in Lombardy many of the cities which his father held, are understandably afraid of his power; the Pope,[15] having solved the schism and being restored to so many dominions of the Church, is powerful and has cause to have the same fear on account of Bologna and Perugia;[16] the name of the Empire has more authority now than it has had in many years. Thus, he has many obstacles to overcome and we will be able to expect many favours in resisting him.

I remind you, finally, that our people desire peace, and if in the past, when we fought against the old duke and King Ladislaus wars that were so necessary, they often believed that those conflicts were incited by our chiefs, what will they say now if they see us reject such an honourable, advantageous and safe peace? And how pernicious it is to the republic to pave the way with pretexts for slanderers and make the people suspicious of those who govern is so well known that any reference to it would be superfluous. Not to mention that it is not imprudent but rather necessary to sometimes govern free cities more by the opinion of the people than reason; but it is more often a greater imprudence, and it leads to worse consequences, to want to oppose the general inclination of the citizens and give birth to sinister conceptions of those whose continuing trustworthiness in the eyes of the people is useful to the city. Liberty produces such evils, but since it entails many and greater goods, it is better to adjust to, than recalcitrate against, the nature of things.

For all these reasons, I recommend that we conclude the negotiations and accept the peace, since we can have it under the terms that have been proposed; nor will I ever commend that, out of an uncertain fear of having war, we lose the benefits that the establishment of peace brings to us and give cause for war with our own hands. —

Notes

1. Niccolò da Uzzano (1359–1431) held important political offices from the 1390s onwards, and was ambassador several times. He was a leading exponent of oligarchic politics.
2. Filippo Maria Visconti, Duke of Milan from 1412 to 1447.
3. Ladislaus of Anjou, King of Naples from 1386 to 1414. He entertained the ambitious design to unify most of Italy under his rule. The 'first peace' mentioned by Niccolò da Uzzano was signed in 1411, and the second one shortly before Ladislaus's death, in 1414.
4. Azzone Visconti, Lord of Milan from 1329 to 1339.
5. Galeazzo Visconti, Lord of Milan from 1322 to 1328.
6. Giovanni Visconti, Archbishop and Lord of Milan from 1333 to 1354.
7. Bernabò Visconti, Lord of Milan from 1354 to 1385.
8. Gian Galeazzo Visconti, Lord and then Duke of Milan from 1385 to 1402.
9. Pandolfo Malatesta and Gabrino Fondulo were two *condottieri* who took advantage of the collapse of the Duchy of Milan after Gian Galeazzo's death in 1402 and became lords of Brescia and Cremona, respectively. It took Filippo Maria years, endless negotiations, cunning and force to recover both cities.
10. In 1402. The Venetians were not inclined to fight the Duke at this time, and in return for their alliance with Florence asked her, among other things, for the right to conclude a separate peace with him, should they find it advantageous.
11. Giovanni Maria Visconti, killed in 1512.

12. Florence had bought Pisa from Gabriele Maria Visconti, the natural son of Gian Galeazzo, in 1405. Thus, the risk was there that his stepbrother would not acknowledge the transaction and claim rights to the city.
13. In the campaign of 1391.
14. The Western Schism (1378–1417).
15. Oddone Colonna, pope as Martin V from 1417 to 1431.
16. Gian Galeazzo Visconti seized Perugia in 1400 and Bologna in 1402. Following his death, his wife gave both cities back to Pope Boniface IX in 1403, in an attempt to alleviate the external pressure upon the Duchy.

Chapter 3

On Whether or Not the Florentines Should Launch a War of Aggression against Lucca[*]

At the end of the war that had followed the 1420 agreement with the Duke of Milan (see the previous debate), Florence remained empty-handed and embittered by the territorial gains achieved by her ally, Venice. Now that the threat posed by the Duke seemed under control, however, the Florentines resumed their century-long design to take Lucca, the conduct of whose lord, during the last war, provided a pretext. The debate below is introduced by the words of Niccolò Machiavelli, who, in his Florentine Histories *(IV, 18), offers an account of the events that is fully consistent with Guicciardini's:*

> *Niccolò Fortebraccio [. . .] had been for a considerable time in the service of the city of Florence during the wars with the Duke of Milan Filippo Maria Visconti. Upon the declaration of peace he was discharged by the Florentines [. . .]. Rinaldo degli Albizzi persuaded Niccolò to attack Lucca under some pretext, pointing out to Niccolò that if he did so, he, Rinaldo, would make the Florentines openly declare war against Lucca, and that then Niccolò would be made commander of their forces [. . .]. [Thus Niccolò] with 300 mounted men and 300 infantry, seized, in November 1429, the Lucchese castles of Ruoti and Compito, and then descended into the plain, where he took a large amount of booty. When this became known in Florence people of all sorts gathered in groups throughout the city, the greater part of which wanted war to be waged against Lucca. Of the principal citizens who were in favour of this were the adherents of the Medici with whom Rinaldo had sided, being influenced either by the belief that it would be advantageous for the republic, or perhaps by the ambitious hope that he would have the merit of victory. Those who were opposed to it were Niccolò da Uzzano and his party. It would almost seem incredible that in the same city*

---

[*] From: *Le cose fiorentine*, ed. by R. Ridolfi, Florence: Olschki, 1983, pp. 204–10.

there should be such a diversity of opinion as to the undertaking of this war; for those very citizens and the same people who, after ten years of peace, had blamed the war undertaken against Duke Filippo in defence of the independence of the republic, now, after the heavy expenditures and affliction in which that war involved the city, eagerly demanded that a war should be undertaken against Lucca to suffocate somebody else's independence. And, on the other hand, those who had been in favour of the former war now strenuously opposed this one. So wildly do opinions change with time, and so readier are the multitude to seize upon the goods of others than to defend their own, and so greatly are men more influenced by the hope of gain than by the fear of loss; for the latter, unless very near, is not felt; and the former, being still remote, is believed in. And thus the people of Florence were filled with hopes by the conquests already made and yet expected to be made by Fortebraccio, and by the letters written by their rectors from near Lucca. For the governors of Pescia and Vico were writing that, if permission were given them to receive those castles that were willing to surrender to them, the whole Lucchese territory would very quickly be acquired [. . .]. The Signoria assemble[d] the Council, at which 498 citizens came together, before whom the question was discussed by the principal men of Florence.

Of those, after a secret vote, only 98 were against war. Guicciardini comments that the desire to take Lucca was so irresistible that it prevented the Florentines from seeing the difficulties and the dangers that the enterprise entailed and, in such a large assembly, 'where votes were not weighed but counted, the prudent men turned out much less numerous than the imprudent men, with whom the partisans [i.e. the supporters of the Medici] had joined'. The same view is put forward in the Dialogue on the Government of Florence, *Book I. War was decided upon on 15 December 1429, and Rinaldo was appointed as one of the two commissioners of the Florentine army. Thanks to the support of Siena, and above all the Duke of Milan, however, Lucca managed to defend her independence.*

The Council having been summoned, Rinaldo degli Albizzi,[1] who had very warmly supported this enterprise in restricted meetings, spoke thus:

— I know very well, most excellent citizens, how much our republic has desired and needed peace and how little convenient it is for her to enter into new expenses and dangers at this time. But I also know how great is the opportunity now at hand to take Lucca with little trouble and very little expense, and how this enterprise is just, honourable and full of invaluable advantage. Nor is there anybody to whom it is not known that opportunities are by their own nature very short-lived, and that those who cannot take them when they occur are always visited by regret but most rarely by remedy.

It is plain to all of Italy what the behaviour of the Lord of Lucca[2] has been towards our republic, and that, although this city has never injured him, he has always, in all our troubles, sided less with us than with our enemies: Giovan Galeazzo,[3] Ladislaus,[4] lately Filippo.[5] And given that he has been doing so ever since he became the tyrant of Lucca, we can be most certain that these are his natural inclinations and that he will always have the same tendency. In fact, he will have much more of it in the future, for, besides having multiplied his injuries, he has been able to understand some signs of our ill disposition towards him, considering that we rightly put forward the request that he not be included in this last peace.[6] Therefore, those who recommend that we undertake the enterprise of Lucca suggest not only that we seek an acquisition that is useful and appropriate in itself, but – and this makes such acquisition even more important – that we attempt to remove a lord who is a most bitter enemy to us, and who can easily put us often in the most serious dangers on account of Pisa[7] being close to his city and Lucca being oriented towards Lombardy, whence our storms almost always come.

Thus, the acquisition is very great; but consider, most excellent citizens, that it is no less easy. He already has war at home and has lost a number of castles in the countryside; he utterly lacks provisions and is so weak that he barely resists a poor *condottiero*. He is a tyrant; as such, the people are hostile to him, so that not only will he have to fight the enemies outside but also guard against those inside. He has neither friends nor subjects outside of Lucca, since everybody left him out of this last peace; nor is the situation of Italy such that he can hope for any assistance. All in Tuscany are either our subjects or our allies; nor is there anybody so powerful as to be able to venture upon such an enterprise. The Venetians would not move against us, and the Duke [of Milan] cannot succour him, according to the peace treaty; nor is it credible that he intends to violate it after having wished for it so much. In addition, the memory of what he went through in war is too fresh, and he has no interest in Lucca. The Pope[8] may dislike any prosperity of ours, but if we consider his natural inclinations and ways of proceeding, there is no danger that he will interrupt our undertaking. The power and reputation of Pisa were much greater, and yet we seized her, because we had, I believe, a just cause, but no less because Italy was disposed in such a way that nobody had the courage or the means to assist her. Italian affairs are now in the same disposition, so that we can expect the same outcome, and all the more easily as Lucca is weaker.

If we lose this opportunity, we will not perhaps see it ever again, of which Lucca herself can serve us as an excellent example. Our ancestors could have safely taken her by paying eighty thousand ducats to the Germans who were in Lucca. As they were reluctant to spend that sum of money, as they were hoping to acquire her with greater ease, she slipped out of their hands. They ran after her, bought her for almost three hundred thousand ducats, fought various wars over her, but all to no avail. Not only did they not take her, but also they fell into so many dangers that they ended up losing their own liberty.[9] Let us take care that we and Lucca herself will not serve as an example to our posterity. What an infamy, what an ignominy if we do not accept this opportunity! To what purpose did we strive with so much insistence that Paolo Guinigi should not be mentioned in the peace treaty, if our timidity was to give him back that which justice and the will of all of Italy had taken away from him? It would have been a lesser fault for us had he been mentioned, for if we were not allowed to injure him our cowardice would not be noticed. I am certain that, if we do not undertake this enterprise, we will acknowledge our sloth at our expense in any trouble Italy may have, if not sooner. We will deplore that we have not been able to assure ourselves, but our complaints will sooner serve to increase our grief than rid us of dangers. The room for exhorting you is immense, for reasons are legion, but I do not wish to add anything else, for I do not know what can make you decide to act if such a manifest ease of being able to acquire enormous honour, advantage and security by a short-lived expense and action cannot. —

At the end of the speech all the Council remained utterly silent, for it was known that Niccolò da Uzzano[10] had expressed completely different views in restricted meetings, and everybody was waiting for him to speak. And he, being waited for and almost called on by all, stood up and spoke like this:

— I have very often wondered, most excellent citizens, why the hope of acquisition induces peoples to enter into war more easily than the fear of being attacked does, and finding the cause has not been as easy for me as realising that this thing is out of reason, for the desire to preserve what one has should be a more powerful motive for men than the desire to take possession of what belongs to others. In the latter case, war is voluntary, in the former, necessary. Defence is always just and honourable; attacking others is often unjust and comes with imputations of ambition. Examples are many in all states, especially yours. As this city has often been slow to give credence to those who have showed the need to fight dangers, so that she has run into most serious difficulties, so she has almost never been offered any hope of gain which she has not willingly hastened to take. Thus, since I now fear that we follow this almost natural inclination of ours, I urge and entreat your excellencies as much as I can to examine, with careful and thorough reflection and evaluation, the resolution under consideration, not by the first motions of the soul, but by the reasons which, if I mistake not, do not entail at all that we should go into this venture at this time. I do not know if I would be prepared to recommend this enterprise even if it were as easy as Rinaldo has presupposed, for we lack justice, which is to be considered as the main foundation for all the actions of men.

The Lord of Lucca has been discordant with us on many subjects and has had with our enemies more harmony than we would have desired. Yet, those who examine his conduct over time in a reasoned way shall notice that he has temporised with our enemies more out of his own security than to injure us; nor has he ever waged war on us, nor has he ever assisted those who did. Thus I do not know what reason we have to want to deprive him of his lordship. But even if it were just with regard to him, it cannot be just with regard to the people of Lucca, our ancient friend and ally, in whose company our fathers made and sustained many wars; nor did they have a more secure foundation than this in attacking, and defending against, the Pisans. Therefore, if the people of Lucca are now oppressed and subjugated by tyranny, it would be our duty to attempt to free them, not to put them in an even more odious slavery. More odious, I say, because a free city, when the time of its calamities comes, has reason to consider being oppressed by the tyranny of one of its citizens to be a lesser evil than being enslaved by a stranger, because it can hope to free itself from the former more than the latter, because the former is less shameful and it does not damage the ways of life of the city in so far as it retains many of the customs, some parts of its traditional institutions, and some shadow and semblance of liberty. Thus, besides the injustice of the cause, we will be making war not only against the tyrant but also against the people of Lucca; nor will they be less stubborn in defending themselves than he will; nor will they attempt anything against him only to be enslaved by the Florentines. Let me remind you that when we attacked Genoa with Tommaso Fregoso and the Catalan fleet, at the beginning of the war, [11] no reason preserved the lordship of the Duke – who was greatly hated in that city – more than the fact that hatred of the Catalans was a more powerful motive for the

Genoese than hatred of the Duke. Likewise, hatred of the Florentines will be a more powerful motive for the Lucchese than hatred of Paolo Guinigi. Their defence will thus be stubborn, and therefore, even if they are unaided, the war will be long, because armies do not take big cities by force these days, but by treason or siege. Treasons are not safe; as for the siege, it will be extremely long, because when one meets with obstinacy one has to reduce men to necessity by wearing them down utterly. And campaigns and sieges that are to be won by attrition are like bodies sick with slow fever, whose life always stretches much longer than expected by all because the illness does not suffocate the vital energy but steadily consumes it.

Throughout such a lengthy time, what hope do we have that at least the Duke, if nobody else, will not succour him? He is restless by nature, he is our enemy out of both his longstanding inclination and the current situation; this acquisition of ours would be dangerous to him on account of its proximity to Genoa. He usually seeks war with immense expenses and difficulties; and now that he will be offered an easy opportunity, and cheap too, on account of the great treasure of the Lord of Lucca, should we believe that he will let it pass? He made peace only to be able to start war again on more advantageous terms. Neither our state of exhaustion from long and enormous expenses nor the memory of so many dangers holds us back – in fact, as soon as we have ended one war, we want to enter into a new one. Do we want to believe that those reasons, which are impotent in our case and which proceed from nothing but our being led less by wisdom than by passion, will hold him back?

This case is similar to that of Pisa neither in terms of justice nor of ease, for we bought Pisa legitimately from her Lord,[12] and the Italian situation was such that we were certain that nobody could succour her. The state of the Visconti was dismembered, the Roman Church was suffocated by the schism,[13] the Kingdom of Naples was rent by the disobedience of the barons, and the Venetians were very far from us and busy with the acquisition of Padua. We then found an agreement with the Genoese and, through their governor and upon the authorisation of the King of France,[14] who was then the Lord of Genoa, we bought Pisa. Now the Duke of Milan, in Lombardy, is very powerful and an enemy to us; Genoa obeys him and, by both her own disposition and the will of the Duke, will be inclined to assist Lucca; the Pope is no great friend to us; the Sienese will perhaps do now in company that which they could not do then alone. Shall we count on the friendship of the Venetians, who are by natural inclination no great friends to us? If they did not let the Duke oppress us out of their own interest, perhaps they will not be displeased if he prevents us from acquiring Lucca. They will not take up arms to make us more powerful; they will not spend money for our greatness, accustomed as they are to grow with our money and become great with our assistance; and should we call on them in our troubles, you know what loss of dignity, what harsh conditions, what disadvantage this would entail. The greatest convenience we enjoyed in the last war was that the Duke had no easy access to Tuscany, no way to wound us in our very bowels. The Sienese sided with us, the Lord of Lucca did not oppose us. And now we are doing anything we can in order that these two cities, both gates to our city, are opened to him, receive him, call on him. We do not remember how pernicious to us the disputes with the Sienese were in the war against the old Duke,[15] for it was thanks to the quarters granted by them that he always kept his armies on our territory, and the beginning of the war was born out of the encouragement and hope they gave him.

Nobody in Italy wished for this last peace more than we did, nobody had better grounds for wishing it more than we had, because we were exhausted by intolerable expenses to such an extent that it seemed impossible to us to keep sustaining them. Now that we have barely come out of that war, have not re-established ourselves yet, and have scarcely resumed breathing, we start a new war with vain hopes, with frivolous designs, and put ourselves back, with our own hands, into those very expenses and dangers from which we prayed with such insistence that God should free us. What will all of Italy say, except that we are ambitious and restless, that we can neither make war nor preserve peace? What will the Venetians say, whom we induced to peace almost by force by exclaiming and complaining of our exhaustion, our impotence? For many years we have had a long and dangerous war, in which, if do not want to deceive ourselves, we put not a little part of the dignity of this city, spent an immeasurable sum of money and wore out our forces. Do reason and the memory of so many and so fresh troubles not prevent us from going back to a war that will be not just, not short, and replete with expense and dangers, a war that can occasion all of Italy to take up arms again? Should we run into adversity, scorn will be greater than damage, for everyone will be of the opinion that we have got into troubles by our own hand, and will blame our ambition and imprudence.

I am speaking so freely because the importance of the thing requires it; and since I urge peace, one cannot doubt that my advice is loyal, for the people always suspect that the citizens of some authority wish for peace less than war out of their own private interests. I know well that, if I took my own honour into consideration, I should wish not to be listened to, for good counsels are more recognised and commended at the end when they have not been followed at the beginning. I advised against the first peace with this Duke;[16] although my opinion was beneficial to the city, it was not approved. The troubles that followed gave me reputation with you, and many often recalled my counsel in the subsequent difficulties. I pray God that I am proved a false prophet and that your decision to make war at a time when you have the supreme necessity to preserve peace will not increase the esteem – perhaps a groundless one – in which my wisdom is held at the cost of loss and dishonour to the city. —

Notes

1. Rinaldo degli Albizzi (1370–1442). Diplomat and politician, he was extremely influential, especially in the 1420s.
2. Paolo Guinigi, Lord of Lucca from 1400 to 1430.
3. Gian Galeazzo Visconti, Lord and then Duke of Milan from 1385 to 1402.
4. Ladislaus of Anjou, King of Naples from 1386 to 1414.
5. Filippo Maria Visconti, Duke of Milan from 1412 to 1447.
6. This peace between Florence and Venice, on the one hand, and Milan, on the other, had been signed in April 1428.
7. Pisa had been part of the Florentine dominion since 1406.
8. Ottone Colonna, Pope as Martin V from 1417 to 1431.
9. Under the Ghibelline lordship of Castruccio Castracani (1316–28), Lucca was a bitter enemy to Florence. After Castruccio's death, the Florentines were determined to seize her. At that time (1329) the city was occupied by German troops, who, out of lack of money, decided to sell her to Florence; as the Florentines hesitated, Lucca was sold instead to a Genoese. In the following years, despite Florence's military efforts, the city fell under several different lordships, until she ended up in the hands of Mastino della Scala, Lord of Verona, who agreed to give her to Florence in return for a large amount of money. As the Pisans heard of the deal, however, they lay siege to Lucca, and the city eventually surrendered to them in 1342. The Lucca affair, which entailed a number of humiliations and cost Florence a fortune, coincided with a period of military setbacks, deep domestic divisions and severe financial crisis, all of which contributed to a momentary eclipse of republican institutions and the ephemeral lordship of Walter VI of Brienne, the Duke of Athens (1342–3).
10. Niccolò da Uzzano: see the previous debate, fn. 1.
11. In 1425, Tommaso Fregoso, Doge of Genoa, was supported by Florence in his attempt to retake the city that had been seized by the Duke of Milan in 1421. Alfonso V, King of Aragon, contributed to the effort with a Catalan fleet in retaliation for the Duke's involvement in the struggle over the Kingdom of Naples.

12. Gabriele Maria Visconti, Lord of Pisa from 1402 to 1405.
13. The Western Schism (1378–1417).
14. Charles VI of Valois, King of France from 1380 to 1422.
15. From 1390 to 1402.
16. In 1426.

Chapter 4

On Whether or Not the King of France Should Make Peace with the Duke of Milan*

Claiming dynastic rights to the Kingdom of Naples, Charles VIII, King of France, passed into Italy in September 1494. The inability of the Italian states to coordinate their moves on account of old and new rivalries, coupled with what looked like the frightening military superiority of the French, paved the way to an effortless campaign: after marching unmolested along the peninsula, the King entered Naples in February 1495. The very ease with which the enterprise had been accomplished, however, finally induced the Italian states to take action. A large coalition was thus created (March 1495), which included Milan, Venice, the Pope, the King of Spain and the Emperor, for the sake of expelling the French from Italy.

As Charles heard of this, his control over the Kingdom of Naples was far from consolidated. He then decided to leave part of his troops in his new dominion and withdraw with the rest of his army (May 1495). While the King was on his way back, the French contingent left in Asti (about 50 km south-east of Turin) the year before seized Novara, a city of the Milanese, thereby prompting the Duke of Milan to lay siege to it and the Venetians to come to his assistance. After forcing his way in the only serious battle of the entire campaign, on the north-western side of the Apennines (Fornovo, 6 July 1495), Charles engaged in negotiations with the enemy coalition, especially the Duke of Milan. A truce was signed, which allowed for the evacuation of the French from Novara except for the citadel (September 1495); although both parties managed to increase the size of their armies during that time, neither was inclined to come to battle again. In fact, the Duke submitted a proposal for what amounted to a separate peace with the King of France, which is the subject of the debate below.

Much to the disappointment of the Venetians (who will eventually make the Duke pay for this and the Pisan affair – see the next debate), the

---

* From: *The History of Italy*, II, xii.

peace was signed on 10 October 1495. This decision, to Guicciardini, was occasioned by the prevailing mood among the French:

> *the inclinations of most of the council, and of almost the whole army, were for accepting peace, the desire of returning into France being so strong in all, and in the King as much as the rest, as to suppress all sense of the danger of the Kingdom of Naples and of the disgrace they would incur by suffering Novara to be lost before their eyes, and by departing out of Italy on terms which, for the uncertainty of their performance, were highly iniquitous.*

The French army left Italy at the end of the same month, and Charles, in Guicciardini's words, 'after so many victories, returned over the mountains, more like a vanquished than victorious prince'; in the Kingdom of Naples, Ferdinand II was soon restored to his throne with the help of the Venetians and the Spanish.

As soon as the King's[1] deputies informed him about the terms of peace, he summoned a council, in which many were of different opinions. The Lord of la Tremoille[2] thus gave this speech:

— If in this present debate we were only to discuss, noble King, how to bring additional glory to the French crown through valiant deeds, I would perhaps with more caution recommend a decision that might expose the person of Your Majesty to further perils, though your own example should suggest you to do the opposite. For inflamed by love of glory, you determined against the advice and entreaties of almost the whole kingdom to pass last year into Italy, in order to conquer the Kingdom of Naples. And since the expedition succeeded with so much honour and renown, it is most manifest that the question now is not only whether one is to refuse an opportunity of acquiring further honour and glory, but rather whether one is to scorn and lose the glory you have acquired with so much danger and expense, convert the honour into the greatest ignominy, and make you reprove and condemn your own deliberations.

Your Majesty might, without any reproach, have remained in France; nor could what now will be attributed by all to the utmost timidity and cowardice have been imputed to any other motive than carelessness and the pleasures of youth. Your Majesty, on your late arrival at Asti, might have kept going all the way back to France with much less shame, demonstrating to all that what was going on around Novara was not of your concern. But now that you have fixed here with your army and declared that you have done so to free Novara from the siege, and for this purpose sent for so many of your nobility out of France, and enlisted so great a body of Swiss at an immense expense, who can doubt that your own, and the kingdom's, glory will be converted into eternal shame if the siege is not raised?

But there are still stronger or at least more necessary reasons, provided that in a king's magnanimous breast there can be any more powerful and urgent inducement than the desire of glory and renown. For our return into France, after giving up Novara by agreement, is in reality giving up the whole Kingdom of Naples, abandoning to destruction so many commanders and French nobles left there on your promise of a speedy assistance, of which they will have reason to despair when they hear that on the frontiers of Italy, at the head of such a powerful army, of so many forces, you have given in to the enemies. Everyone knows that reputation has no small share in the success of a war; and as reputation declines, so does the valour of the soldiers, the loyalty of the people, and also the revenues necessary to support the war, while on the contrary the courage of the enemies increases, the undecided walk away from you, and all the difficulties grow larger and larger. Therefore, our army deprived of its vigour by the unhappy news of our retreat and the reputation and the strength of the enemy increased, who can doubt we shall soon hear that all the Kingdom of Naples has rebelled, that our army is destroyed, and that our enterprise, undertaken and prosecuted with so much glory, has produced no other effect than disasters and incalculable infamy? For whoever asserts that this peace is made in good faith betrays a poor understanding of the present posture of affairs and the temper of those we are treating with. It is obvious to everyone that as soon as we have left Italy, not one of the terms of the agreement will be observed, and instead of our receiving the stipulated support, succours will be sent to Ferdinando[3] against us. In addition, those very people who will boast they have shamefully chased us out of Italy will enrich themselves with our spoils at Naples.

This ignominy might be better borne if there could be any plausible doubt of our coming off victorious. But how can that be possible, considering the number of our forces and the opportunity we have to avail ourselves of the country around us? Call but to mind how lately, though tired by a long march, lacking provisions, very few in numbers and in an enemy country, we valiantly fought a very large army at the Taro.[4] That day, the river ran with great momentum, fuller of the enemy's blood than of its own waters. With the sword we opened our way, and for eight days we marched victorious through the Duchy of Milan, despite the difficulties we were facing from all sides. Now we have double the number of

cavalry and many more French infantrymen than before, and instead of
three thousand, we have twenty-two thousand Swiss. As for the enemies,
though their number has grown thanks to German foot, such an increase
is modest if compared to ours, for their cavalry is almost the same, and
the same the commanders who, after being seriously defeated by us once,
if forced to engage, have reason to fight with terror.

Besides, are the fruits of victory at this juncture so inconsiderable as
to be contemned? Or rather are they not such as to encourage us to run
any risk to get them? Our fighting at present is not only for the preservation of so much glory acquired and the Kingdom of Naples and for the
safety of so many commanders and nobles left behind; what is at stake
is the domination over all of Italy. The whole country, if we win here,
will thoroughly be the prey of our victory. For what other forces will
be left to our enemies? Their camp contains in a manner all the arms
and commanders they have been able to assemble. We need pass but a
ditch, or force a barrier, to achieve so great results as the control over,
and all the riches of, Italy, and the ability to avenge all our injuries. If
these two motives, sufficient to animate mean and ignoble souls, have
no effect on our warlike, brave people, we need not hesitate to affirm
that our quality, rather than our fortune, has deserted us. For the latter
has provided us with the opportunity to gain, in a few hours, in so
undemanding an enterprise, prizes so ample and so noble as to exceed
our own expectations. —

But, in the opposite vein, the Prince of Orange[5] spoke as follows:

— If our affairs, Most Christian King, were not reduced into such a
narrow compass of time, but were in a condition to give us leisure to
accompany our strength with prudence and operosity, and did not put
us under the necessity, if we continue the war, to proceed rashly and
against all the rules of the military art, I too should be one of those who
advise to reject the proposals of peace. For truly there are many reasons
against them, and the continuation of the war would be both very honourable and very appropriate for our affairs in Naples. But the condition
to which Novara and its citadel are reduced, where there is not a day's
provision left, forces us, if we intend to relieve it, to attack the enemies
immediately. And if we should give it up with a design of transferring
the war to some other part of the Duchy of Milan, the winter that is
approaching (a time very unseasonable for armies in those low countries
full of water); the state of our army, which, in light of the temper and
number of Swiss, if it is not immediately put on action, will prove more
pernicious to us than to our enemies; the severe scarcity of money, on

which account we cannot long subsist here: all these reasons compel us to put a very speedy end to the war. This, if we reject the agreement, can only be accomplished by engaging the enemies straight in battle, which, due to their and the country's present conditions, is so dangerous that it would be called extreme rashness and imprudence to attempt it.

For the enemy's camp is so strong, by both nature and art, they having had so long a time to consolidate it and fortify it, the places about so well provided for, guarded, and suitable for their defence, the country, on account of many ditches and waters, so inconvenient for the horse, that whoever undertook to assault them frontally at once, as opposed to getting closer to them slowly and securing the ground inch by inch, would be doing nothing but taking a risk that entails a most severe and almost certain danger. For by what reasoning, by what rule of war, by what example provided by excellent commanders is so vast an army to be impetuously attacked in its strong entrenchments, so well lined with artillery? It would be necessary, unless we leave all to chance, first to dislodge them from their fort by acquiring some positions from which we might command their camp, or by hindering them from procuring their provisions. But nothing of this, so far as I can judge, is possible unless we proceed cautiously and rely on the work of time – a luxury we all know we cannot afford.

Not to mention that our cavalry is neither so strong nor so numerous as some imagine, for it is well known that many of our men are sick, many others with and without permission are returned into France, and most of the remainder fatigued and more disposed to repass the Alps than to fight. The great number of Swiss, the principal strength of our army, is perhaps as dangerous to us as a small number would be useless. For everyone who knows the nature and customs of those people has also to know how difficult it is to keep so large a body of them in order. And who will ensure us that they will not be mutinous, especially if things proceed slowly? Due to their pay, of which they are so greedy, and which might not be regular, and to other accidents, a thousand occasions may arise that would lead them to unrest. So we remain in a state of uncertainty, whether their presence would do us good or harm. In this situation, how can we consolidate our decisions? How can we undertake any great and brave action? No one doubts that a victory would be better than a peace, for both the preservation of Naples and our honour. But in all human affairs, and especially in wars, decisions must often be accommodated to necessity, and one must not, in order to attain something that is too difficult and almost impossible, expose the whole thing to the most manifest danger. Nor is wisdom less the part of a great commander than courage.

You have not taken the initiative in the affair of Novara, Sire, which is only indirectly your concern, for you claim no right to the Duchy of Milan; nor did you come from Naples with a design to stop and wage war in Piedmont; but to return into France in order to procure money and men to succour more effectually that kingdom, which being in the mean time assisted by your fleet from Nice, the soldiers of the Vitelli,[6] the help and the money of the Florentines, will sustain itself to such an extent that it will easily be able to wait for the powerful provisions that you will make once you are back in France.

I do not claim that the Duke of Milan[7] will observe the treaty; but as he and the Genoese are to give hostages and deliver the citadel [of Genoa] according to the terms of the agreement, you will at least have some guarantee and pledge. I would not be very surprised if he desired to live in peace, since his dominions lie in the way to be always the first attacked by you. In addition, as the nature of leagues where many are concerned is not so firm and solid, one may entertain hopes of making someone lukewarm or separating someone from the rest:[8] each small opening we could make, every little crack that might appear would deliver into our hands a sure and easy victory.

In conclusion, Most Christian King, my counsel is for peace, not because it is in itself advantageous and laudable, but because it becomes wise princes, when they deliberate upon intricate and disagreeable cases, to make themselves easy with the decision that is necessary or is attended with least difficulties and displeasure.[9] —

Notes

1. Charles VIII of Valois, King of France from 1483 to 1498.
2. Louis de la Tremoille (1460–1525), Chamberlain of Charles VIII.
3. Ferdinand II, King of Naples (1495–6).
4. Battle of Fornovo, 6 July 1495.
5. Jean de Chalon-Arvay (1443–1502).
6. The Vitelli brothers – Paolo, Camillo and Vitellozzo – were three Italian *condottieri* then at the service of the King of France.
7. Lodovico Sforza, Regent and then Duke of Milan from 1480 to 1499.
8. The same view is also expressed in the second speech of the next debate (and shared by Niccolò Machiavelli: see *Discourses on Livy*, III, 1 and *Florentine Histories*, VIII, 26).
9. Cf. *Maxims and Reflections (Ricordi)*, Engl. transl. by M. Domandi, Philadelphia: University of Pennsylvania Press, 1965, C 213.

Chapter 5

On Whether or Not the Venetians Should Sign an Offensive Alliance with the King of France[*]

On his way to Naples (see the introduction to the previous debate), Charles VIII, King of France, entered Pisa in November 1494. The city immediately rebelled against the Florentines – who had taken her in 1406 – and came de facto *under French rule. Despite his repeated assurances, the King never restored the city to Florence. As the French left Italy the following year, Lodovico Sforza, Duke of Milan, along with the Venetians, managed to prevent the Florentines from taking Pisa back. Under the pretext of defending her independence by financial and military means, both Milan and Venice were in fact attempting to bring her under their control. The Venetians went as far as sending an army into Tuscany at the end of 1498. From the beginning of the Pisa affairs, as the Venetians seemed better placed to succeed, the Duke did his best to thwart their design, first indirectly, then in an ever more manifest manner, thereby provoking a bitter resentment in Venice on account of the huge amount of money they had been spending on the enterprise.*

In April 1498 Charles VIII died and was succeeded by Louis XII, who, as an Orléans, claimed rights to the Duchy of Milan. In order to second his ambitions, the new French king needed the support of Venice, in exchange for which he was ready to cede a part of the Duchy to her. Thus, Venice had a fair opportunity to expand her dominion significantly, at the cost, though, of finding herself with a far more powerful prince than the Duke as a neighbour. The two speeches below summarise the various views that were expressed in the Venetian Senate on this issue, in an impassioned debate that lasted for days, in November 1498. The alliance was eventually signed on 9 February 1499. In August the two allies launched a simultaneous attack, and in a few weeks they managed to partition the Duchy, as stipulated in the treaty.

To Guicciardini, the reasons against the alliance were 'cogent' and seconded by 'the gravest and most prudent senators'. Yet, 'hatred and

* From: *The History of Italy*, IV, vi.

covetousness to dominate, vehement instigators of any dangerous deci-sion', prevailed. In other words, the desire to take revenge on Sforza was coupled with no less a desire to include in the Venetian dominion a rich city, Cremona, and a fertile land, the Ghiaradadda (that is, the ter-ritory between the Adda and Serio rivers) – the prizes promised by the French. Not only was such an acquisition important in itself, but also it looked very promising for further reasons. As the first speaker argues, the Venetians expected that the French would not be able to sustain themselves in Milan, just as they had failed to consolidate their acquisi-tion of Naples in 1495, in which case the whole Duchy would fall into their hands. The Venetian decision contributed to the second French invasion of Italy in five years, which brought about the end of the inde-pendence of the Duchy of Milan (and the Kingdom of Naples, shortly afterwards). Although Venice did acquire her desired new dominions, less than a decade later she would be facing a formidable coalition made up of all those who resented her expansion – and led by the same French king.

As the members of the Council of the Pregadi[1] were summoned one day for coming to a final resolution, [Antonio Grimani],[2] a man of great authority, spoke as follows:

– When I consider, illustrious senators, the immense favours Lodovico Sforza[3] has received from our Republic, which in these latter years has often preserved his dominions, and on the other hand his ingratitude and the most serious injuries he has done us in order to oblige us to abandon the defence of Pisa, to which he himself had encouraged and incited us, I do not in the least doubt that we all agree we must do any-thing we can to take revenge on him. For no infamy could be greater than, by remaining passive under so many affronts, proving so different from our great-hearted ancestors, who when provoked but by slight injuries, never refused to undergo any danger to preserve the dignity of the Venetian name. Rightly so, for the deliberations of republics require no mean and private considerations, or which tend only to expediency, but noble and high goals by which they may increase their glory and keep their reputation; and nothing is more detrimental to reputation than giving occasion to think that you want courage or strength to resent affronts, or you are not prone to take revenge, which is supremely necessary, not so much for the pleasure attending vengeance as rather because the punishing of the offender may serve as an example to deter others from giving the like provocation.[4] In such a way glory and expe-diency are combined, and noble and great-hearted resolutions produce convenience and profit; in such a way, by dealing with one difficulty, many are prevented, and one short exertion often frees you from many and prolonged efforts.[5]

But if we consider the situation of affairs in Italy, the disposition of several princes against us, and the continuous snares of Lodovico Sforza, we cannot but conclude that necessity, to a no lesser extent than any other consideration, leads us to such a decision. For the Duke of Milan, incited by his natural ambition and his hatred of this most excellent Senate, makes it his perpetual study to set all Italy, the King of the Romans,[6] and the whole Germanic body, against us; in fact, he has begun to negotiate with the Turk for the same purpose. You are all sensible that it is through his means that we meet with such difficulties, as almost to lose any hope, in supporting Pisa and waging war in Casentino,[7] which if continued will become extremely dangerous, and if abandoned without otherwise securing our interests, will result in such a loss of reputation that would elate the spirits of those who seek our ruin. And you all know how much easier it is to overwhelm those who are on the decline than those who still are at the height of their reputation.[8]

Of all this, illustrious senators, you would infallibly see the effects, and our state would soon be replete with the noise of war and tumults, were not Lodovico kept in suspense by his apprehension of our joining with the King of France[9] – an apprehension that cannot keep him in suspense for long, though. If the King loses the hope of making an alliance with us, either he will get involved in some enterprise beyond the Alps or he will come to a composition with Lodovico, drawn by his artifices, corruption and other most powerful means of which the Duke can avail himself in the French court. Thus, both the necessity of preserving our ancient dignity and glory and, to an even larger extent, an imminent and most severe danger that cannot otherwise be escaped, force us to join with the King of France. And I think we ought to congratulate ourselves on our good fortune, which has inclined a mighty king voluntarily to entreat from us what we should entreat from him; and all this on such advantageous and honourable offers as may make this senate entertain hopes, greater by the day, and imagine the noblest designs, above all because all those expectations could become real very easily. For who can doubt that Lodovico Sforza will not be able to resist two so mighty and contiguous powers?

We should not be kept from this decision by the fear that the nearness of the King of France, once he has acquired the Duchy of Milan, will become dreadful and dangerous to us. In fact, if you look carefully you will see that in this case many circumstances will appear in our favour that are now against us. For it is not to be doubted but such an increase of power in the French will alarm all of Italy and provoke the resentment of the King of the Romans and the Germanic body due to their rivalry and the bitterness that must derive from seeing so noble a member of the Empire[10] taken over by the King of France. Thus, those very states that now fill us with apprehensions of their confederating with Lodovico against us, will then, for their own interest, desire to preserve us and join with us. And such is the universal reputation of our power, so current the fame of our riches, and still greater the opinion of our own union and constancy in the preservation of our state, which is confirmed by so many and illustrious examples, that the King of France will not venture to attack us but in conjunction with many, or at least the King of the Romans – a confederacy for several reasons attended with so many difficulties that it would be vain for him to expect it or for us to fear it. Nor will the peace he is now endeavouring to settle with his neighbours beyond the Alps be permanent; in fact, envy, rivalry, and fear of his increase of power will awake all those who had before found matter for hatred or emulation.

It is well known that the French are more resolute in acquiring than prudent in preserving and how soon they become hateful to their subjects by their rash and insolent behaviour. For which reason, once they have conquered Milan they will be rather under the necessity of attending to its preservation than find leisure to enter on other projects. For a new conquest, neither well settled nor prudently governed, rather diminishes than increases the power of the conqueror. And have we not a recent and convincing proof of this in the management of the late King?[11] The unbelievable love and fondness with which he had been received in the Kingdom of Naples were soon converted into extremity of hatred and aversion.

The danger therefore to be apprehended from a French victory in time to come is neither so certain nor so great that to avoid it we should choose to remain in present and immense danger. To refuse, for the sake of future and uncertain losses, so rich and commodious part of the Duchy of Milan, could be imputed only to pusillanimity and want of resolution, despicable in private life, but much more so in a republic that, except for the Roman, is the most glorious and powerful that ever existed on earth. Opportunities like this are rare and transient, and it is the part of prudence and a generous resolution to lay hold of them, as on the contrary it would be highly reproachable to reject them. Wisdom that is over scrupulous and ponders future events too nicely is often blameable; for human affairs are subject to so many and so different vicissitudes that only rarely do future events conform to the expectations of men, no matter how wise. And that person who does not embrace a present good for fear of a future danger – unless that danger is very certain and close – often ends up losing, much to his regret and shame, the opportunity of acquiring glory and advantage out of fear of some danger which he finds afterwards vanished.[12]

These are the reasons that induce me to give my opinion for entering into an alliance against the Duke of Milan. Such a confederacy is conducive to our present security, has us held in great esteem among the other powers, and is attended with such an acquisition as at any other time we should spare neither trouble nor expense to obtain; not only for the importance of the thing itself, but as it opens a door to an extraordinary augmentation of the glory and power of this most potent republic. —

This speech was heard with great attention and very favourably received. Many applauded the speaker's greatness of mind and his love for his country. But [Melchiorre Trevisan][13] thus replied:

— It cannot be denied, most prudent senators, that the injuries inflicted on our republic by Lodovico Sforza are exceedingly great, and very offensive to our dignity. Yet, the greater they are, and the more they excite our indignation, so much it becomes prudence to moderate our just resentment with maturity of judgement and with considerations related to the interests of, and to what is expedient for, our republic. To be able to exert self-control and overcome one's passions is all the more commendable the more rarely one knows how to do it and the juster the reasons that excite one's anger and passions.

It is therefore the business of this Senate, so renowned for its wisdom, and which has lately professed to be the liberator of Italy from the French, to consider of what infamy it will be charged if the French by its means should return, and even more to reflect on the danger to which we should lie constantly exposed whenever the King of France becomes master of the Duchy of Milan. Those who do not appreciate such a danger should recall the terror we were in when King Charles [VIII of France] made the conquest of Naples. We never thought ourselves secure until we formed a confederacy of almost all the Christian princes against him.[14] But what a disparity between one danger and the other! That king, in a manner destitute of nearly all the royal virtues, was an almost ridiculous prince; and the Kingdom of Naples, so far distant from France, kept his forces so divided as to rather weaken than increase his power; and that acquisition, on account of the fear for their dominions that were so near, made the Pope[15] and the Kings of Spain[16] his bitter enemies. But now the former proceeds on other views, and the latter, tired with the affairs of Italy, are determined not to get involved, if not under the most pressing necessity. The present King is endowed with such natural parts that he is rather to be dreaded than despised, and the state of Milan is so nigh the Kingdom of France that, due to the ease with which it can be succoured, we cannot hope to expel him without putting all the other powers in motion. Hence it appears that as we are near to so formidable a power we will be at a vast expense and in great apprehension in time of peace and in time of war so exposed to his attack that defending ourselves will be most difficult.

I must own my astonishment at what was advanced by the person who spoke last. He seemed to be under no fear of a King of France master of the Duchy of Milan and, on the other hand, professed so great a dread of Lodovico Sforza, a prince much inferior to us in strength and who through his timidity and avarice has always jeopardised his undertakings. He sounded scared by the assistance the Duke might get from others, as if it were easy to make an alliance in such a diversity of inclinations and desires and in such a variety of conditions, or as if one great power, collected within itself, were not to be feared much more than a confederacy made up of many who, having different motives, must of consequence disagree in their operations. He expected that those who, out of hatred or for some other reason, wish our destruction would be so wise as to keep their resentment and passions under control while not even we are wise enough as to curb our own ambitions. Nor do I quite understand why we should expect that the rivalry with, and the old and new resentment against, the King of France, should he take Milan, will be a more powerful incentive for the King of the Romans and the Germanic body than the inveterate hatred they hold against us, who took and keep so many territories wrested from the House of Austria and the Empire. Nor do I see why the King of the Romans should sooner join with us against France than with France against us. In fact, it is more likely that those barbarians, eternal enemies to the Italian name, should unite with a view to have an easier prey. For the King of the Romans has more reason to expect to defeat us with the help of France than to defeat France with our help. Moreover, I see no reason why we should at all covet an alliance with the King of the Romans when we consider his conduct in our late alliance with him and his operations in Italy.[17] Lodovico has injured us grievously, I admit it, but it can never be prudence to expose our own affairs to such a severe danger merely out of revenge; nor will it be shameful to wait for proper opportunities and favourable circumstances, as a republic can do,[18] in order to avenge ourselves. In fact, being carried away by resentment before the time has come is highly blameable; and in state matters imprudence followed by losses is the supreme shame.

It will not be thought that we have undertaken such a rash enterprise just to take revenge, but everyone will judge that we have been dragged by the desire of acquiring Cremona. Thus, everyone will lament the ancient wisdom and prudence of this senate, everyone will be surprised at us for being ourselves guilty of the very same imprudence we were so surprised to see in Lodovico Sforza, I mean, inviting the King of France into Italy.[19] The acquisitions promised are very considerable and in many respects commodious, but then we ought to consider whether putting the King of France in possession of the Duchy of Milan does not vastly overbalance this convenience. When are our power and reputation greater? When we are the chief in Italy, or when we have in Italy a prince so vastly superior, and so near, to us? We have been in times past sometimes in amity, at other times at enmity with Lodovico Sforza, and this is no more than what may happen continually. The difficulties concerning Pisa are not so perplexing but that some way of accommodation may be found; nor are they of that consequence as to make us adopt dangerous measures. But we shall never want occasions to quarrel with the French when they become our neighbours, for the same reasons for friction will persist forever: the diversity of minds between the barbarians and the Italians, the pride of the French, the hatred with which princes, by nature, always persecute republics, the ambition that is constantly moving the more powerful to oppress the weaker. For these reasons, I am not at all allured with the acquisition of Cremona. On the contrary, I rather dread the issue, as it will give the King of France more opportunity and incitement to attack us, for which purpose he will be constantly solicited by the Milanese, who can never be easy at the alienation of Cremona from their duchy. The German body and the King of the Romans will be highly offended for the same reason, for both Cremona and the Ghiaradadda are members of the Empire. [If we decide not to join with the French], if nothing else, our ambition will not be blamed so much, nor will we create every day new enemies with new conquests, nor will we grow more fearsome to everybody. Conversely, we must either reduce all under our dominion or be beaten by all; and which of the two is more likely to happen let anyone judge who is not resolved to deceive himself.

The wisdom and caution of this senate have often been admired and exalted in every corner of Italy and all the world over. I trust it will suffer no disgrace at this time from any rash and dangerous resolution. To be carried away by resentment against one's own interest is fickleness; to be under a greater concern for small than for great dangers is imprudence; both which, being directly opposite to the wisdom and gravity of this senate, I cannot but persuade myself that your resolution on this head will be moderate and circumspect, as it usually is on the like occasions. —

Notes

1. A body composed of 120 citizens elected by the *Maggior Consiglio*. To Guicciardini, it 'supplies the place of the Senate'.
2. Antonio Grimani (1434–1523) held important public offices and became doge in 1521.
3. Lodovico Sforza, Regent and then Duke of Milan from 1480 to 1499.
4. Cf. *Maxims and Reflections (Ricordi)*, Engl. transl. by M. Domandi, Philadelphia: University of Pennsylvania Press, 1965, C 74.
5. The reader may have noticed that these are almost exactly the same words that Guicciardini put in the mouth of the first speaker, in the first debate above. By the same token, the opening of Melchiorre Trevisan's speech, below, is strongly reminiscent of Carlo Strozzi's reply in the same first pair of speeches. The first debate comes from *Le cose fiorentine*, a Florentine history on which Guicciardini worked between 1527 and 1531, only to leave it incomplete. A few years later, as he was writing his masterpiece, he must have found it convenient to avail himself of this material.
6. Maximilian I of Habsburg. 'King of the Romans' was the title of the heir apparent to the imperial throne. Maximilian was made King of the Romans in 1486; when his father died, in 1493, he was elected emperor of the Holy Roman Empire, but never managed to be crowned by the Pope, as the centuries-old custom required. This is why he is here referred to as 'King of the Romans'. In 1508, with the permission of the Pope, he took the title of 'Elected Roman Emperor', thereby putting an end to the tradition of papal crowning.
7. Region of the Florentine dominion.
8. Cf. *Maxims and Reflections*, op. cit., C 72 and C 144.
9. Louis XII of Orléans, King of France from 1498 to 1515.
10. That is, the Duchy of Milan.
11. Charles VIII of Valois, King of France from 1483 to 1498, in 1495.
12. Cf. *Maxims and Reflections*, op. cit., C 23.
13. Melchiorre Trevisan (c. 1440–1500), *provveditore* of the Senate and military commander.
14. The alliance of March 1495 (see the introduction to the previous debate).
15. Rodrigo Borgia, pope as Alexander VI from 1492 to 1503.
16. Ferdinand II, King of Aragon from 1479 to 1516, and Isabella I, Queen of Castile from 1474 to 1504.
17. Although a member of the 1495 anti-French coalition, Maximilian did not intervene militarily in the campaign against Charles VIII.

18. Unlike a princedom, whose enterprises depend on a single ruler who may die at any moment, a republic can afford the luxury of waiting for the right time to come. Cf. *The History of Italy*, XVI, x: the same Venetians 'might have hopes to trust their affairs to length of time and to opportunities that republics, which, in comparison to princes, are immortal, have reason to expect'.

19. It was almost unanimously believed at the time that Lodovico Sforza had played a decisive role in convincing Charles VIII to pass into Italy in 1494.

Chapter 6

On Whether the Venetians Should Ally with the King of the Romans or Stick to the Alliance with the King of France*

In the spring of 1507, Maximilian I, King of the Romans, was getting ready to pass into Italy for the sake of being finally crowned emperor by the Pope and, in particular, of settling matters with Louis XII, King of France, over the Duchy of Milan, to which both monarchs claimed rights and which the French had seized in 1499. To that purpose, he asked the Venetians for leave to pass through their dominion and invited them to make an alliance with him against the French. Should they refuse his offer, he threatened to find an agreement with Louis at their expense. The French King, in turn, invoked the existing alliance with the Venetians, urged them to oppose the coming of Maximilian, and offered a new alliance and the assistance of all his forces. The Venetians thus found themselves in a very delicate position, as reflected in the debate below. On the one hand, they were afraid to deny Maximilian a passage because this entailed the risk of being the first to be attacked by him; on the other hand, they were reluctant to grant it because this would offend the French king. In which case, it would be dangerous not to declare themselves openly for the Emperor, for Louis would then be their bitter enemy and Maximilian, having obtained nothing more than free passage, would not be much obliged to them. The Venetian predicament can be better understood by looking at the broad picture.

Since the first French invasion of 1494, Venice had managed gradually to expand her dominions in Italy. In exchange for her support for the restoration of the King of Naples, overthrown by the French in 1495, Venice occupied a number of ports in Apulia, which were now claimed back by the Spanish, the new lords of Naples. In 1499, in cooperation with the French, the Venetians seized a portion of the Duchy of Milan – the city of Cremona and the Ghiaradadda (see the previous debate), only to realise how dangerous it was to have the French king as a neighbour. In 1503, in keeping with an expansionist policy in Romagna that

---

* From: *The History of Italy*, VII, x.

dated back to the mid-fifteenth century, Venice took advantage of the
death of Pope Alexander VI to extend her dominion further in a region
that was part of the State of the Church, thereby outraging the new
pope, Julius II. Finally, relations with the Empire in general, and the
House of Habsburg in particular, were traditionally tense, on account
of several cities and territories taken by the Venetians in the past. In
short, the Republic was surrounded by powerful enemies (not to men-
tion the minor Italian powers, especially Ferrara and Mantua, that had
reason to fear and resent Venetian policies). As early as 1504, Julius II
had managed to reconcile Maximilian and Louis in a broad scheme that
contemplated, among other things, an offensive alliance against Venice.
Although nothing came of it, the two monarchs discussed the same
matter on other occasions, as the Venetians knew only too well.

The debate produced a cautious response: invoking their obligations
with the French alliance, the Venetians told Maximilian's ambassadors
that they would grant him passage if he came without an army for the
sake of being crowned, but would oppose him if he passed into Italy
with an armed force; they also resolved not to sign any new treaty with
the King of France, 'being desirous to intermeddle as little as possible
in the war between them, in hopes perhaps that Maximilian, to avoid
plunging himself in new difficulties, would let their frontiers remain in
peace'. The nightmare of a general anti-Venetian coalition would even-
tually materialise in December 1508 (League of Cambrai) and lead to
the disastrous battle of Agnadello (15 April 1509), which resulted in the
– albeit temporary – loss of virtually all the Venetian dominions in Italy.

After they [the Venetians] had delayed coming to a resolution for as long
as they could, they were no longer able to resist the pressing instances
that each of the parties made them. The Council of the Pregadi[1] con-
vened to come to a decision, and [Niccolò Foscarini[2]] made the following speech:

— If it lay in our power, most excellent senators, to pass a resolution by
which the peace of our republic, in the midst of these movements and
troubles that are coming up, might be preserved, I am very certain that
there would be no difference of opinion among us, and that no proposal
would be sufficient to incline us to a war attended with so much cost and
danger as the present appears to carry with it. But since, for the reasons
so often of late mentioned in our debates, there is no hope of preserving
our peace, I persuade myself that the principal reason on which we are
to found our resolution is to consider closely with ourselves whether it
be probable that the King of the Romans,[3] despairing of our friendship,

will join with the King of France,[4] or that the enmity between these two princes is so powerful and deep as to prevent any such union. For if we could be secure from that danger, without a doubt I would recommend not to break the alliance with the King of France, because when our forces are heartily united with his for the common defence, we would easily protect our state; it would be more honourable to continue our confederacy with him than to renounce it without any apparent reason; and it would be more laudable and carry a better aspect in the sight of all to enter into a war with a professed intention of preserving the peace of Italy than to join our arms with those that one cannot but know are taken up with a design to raise the greatest disturbances. But presupposing the danger of this union,[5] I believe that no one will deny that we must prevent it. And it would be much more useful to us to join with the King of the Romans against the King of France rather than to wait until they unite together against us.

But as to whether such a conjunction will take place it is difficult to form any certain judgement because it depends not only on the will of others but on such a multitude of accidents and causes as hardly leave the decision in the power of those whom it concerns. Yet, from what we can understand from conjecture and what past experience teaches us about the future,[6] it appears to me a very hazardous affair and to be greatly dreaded by us. For it is more than probable that the King of the Romans will overcome all difficulties, considering his ardent desire to pass into Italy, which it would not be easy for him to accomplish unless he joins with the King of France or with us. And although he should rather choose to join with us, yet who can doubt that, if he were refused by us, he would not of necessity agree with the King of France, having no other way to attain the completion of his desires?

On the side of the King of France, there seem to be greater difficulties, but they are not such as, in my view, can promise us any security. For he may be induced to take such a resolution from fear and ambition, two powerful incentives, and each of them often sufficient of itself to execute much greater movements. He is well aware that the King of the Romans solicits our union, and measuring, although falsely, our intentions and desires merely by his own, he may fear that the suspicion we entertain of being prevented by him may induce us to prevent him; especially since he knows that we are well informed of what he and the King of the Romans have so long a time been treating together against us. He may also be apprehensive that we are incited by ambition, since he cannot doubt that we are offered very large shares; and what means are sufficient to secure him from such fear? Nothing is, by nature, more apprehensive than states.[7] Next to fear, he might be moved by ambition, through the desire that we know he has for the city of Cremona,[8] which is excited in him by the incitements of the Milanese and to a no lesser extent by his own desire to seize on what formerly belonged to the Visconti – to which, as well as to the rest of the Duchy of Milan, he claims an hereditary title, and which he can have no hope of obtaining but by joining with the kings of the Romans; for our republic is powerful in itself, and if we are attacked by the King of France alone we shall always have in our power to join with Maximilian. And that this may possibly be in his thoughts, or rather was never out of his mind, is demonstrated by the fact that he never attempted to oppress us without this union, which being the only way that can conduct him to his desired end, ought we not believe that at last he will attempt to effect it? Nor can our fears be removed by considering that it would be an impolitic resolution, for the sake of two or three cities, to introduce into Italy the King of the Romans, his natural enemy, and from whom he can never meet with anything else but troubles and wars, and no friendship but what is uncertain, and even that uncertain friendship must be procured and kept up by immense sums of money. For if he should entertain a suspicion that we shall unite with the King of the Romans, he will imagine that, by preventing us, he shall put himself in a state not of danger, but of security. And even if he should not be apprehensive of this union, he will perhaps judge it necessary to confederate with Maximilian in order to secure himself from the troubles and dangers that may arise from him, assisted by the Germans or other adherents and by favourable circumstances. Although he might be facing more serious dangers should the King of the Romans begin to set foot in Italy, it is the common nature of men to be more afraid of dangers that are nearer and to set a greater estimate on things present than is due to them and to pay too little regard to things future and at a distance, to which one can hope that time and opportunity may offer several remedies.[9]

Moreover, even if this union were not for the benefit of the King of France, we cannot be sure that he will not engage himself in it. Do we not know how men are blinded, sometimes by dread, sometimes by covetousness? Do we not know the nature of the French? That they are quick and ready for new enterprises, and that their hopes of success are never less than their desires? Are we not apprised of the encouragements and offers, sufficient to rouse the quietest disposition, by which the French King is stimulated against us by the Milanese, the Pope,[10] the Florentines, the Duke of Ferrara[11] and the Marquis of Mantua?[12] All men are not wise; in fact, very few are so. And he who takes upon himself to foretell the resolution of another must, if he has not a mind to be deceived, consider not so much what a wise man would probably do as the intellectual qualities and the natural inclinations of the person who is to take those resolutions.

Therefore, he who would judge what the King of France will do, must not so much take into consideration the duties that prudence would require as the natural temper of the French, who are remarkable for their restlessness, levity, and proceeding with more heat than judgement. He must take into account the natural inclinations of great princes, which are not like our own, nor so easily resist their appetites as those of private men. For, accustomed to be adored in their own kingdoms, where their looks are understood and obeyed, they not only are haughty and insolent, but cannot bear to be disappointed of obtaining what they imagine to be their just due (and whatever they desire appears to them as such), as they persuade themselves that they can level all impediments with a word, and surmount the nature of things. In fact, they reckon it a shame not to indulge their inclinations on account of difficulties, commonly measuring affairs of greater moment with the same rule by which they are used to proceed in matters of less concern, conducting themselves not by prudence and reason but by will and caprice.

These defects being so common among princes in general, none will say that the French are exempt from them. Have we not fresh before our eyes the example of the Kingdom of Naples? Half of which the King of France, induced by ambition and thoughtlessness, consented should go to the King of Spain so that he himself might enjoy the other half, not considering how much he weakened his power, which was the sole among all the Italians, by introducing into Italy another king, of equal power and authority with himself.[13] But what need have we to go by conjectures in things where we have certainty? Is it not known to all that the Cardinal of Rouen[14] negotiated with this same Maximilian at Trent about dividing our state? And what more certain than that the same negotiation was afterwards concluded at Blois?[15] And that the same cardinal went to Germany on the same business and brought back with him the ratification of Caesar,[16] confirmed with his oath? These treaties had no effect, I admit, on account of some intervening difficulties; but who shall secure us that, since the principal intention continues the same, some solution may not be found for removing the obstacles that have thwarted their common desire?

It is your part now, most worthy senators, diligently to consider the imminent dangers, together with the imputations and the shame that, in the face of all the world, will be cast upon our Senate, so renowned for prudence, if, making a wrong estimate of the present condition of affairs, we should suffer others to make themselves formidable, in order to attack us, with those arms that are offered us for our security and advantage. Consider, I beseech you, for your country's sake, what difference there is between attacking our enemies and waiting until we are attacked by them, between treating about dividing the states of others and waiting until your own be divided, between joining in company against one alone and remaining alone against many in company. For if these two kings join together against us, they will be followed by the Pope, on account of the towns of Romagna, the King of Aragon,[17] on account of the ports of the Kingdom of Naples, and all Italy, some to recover what they have lost, others to secure what they possess. Everyone knows what has been treating so many years between the King of France and Caesar against us. If we should, therefore, arm ourselves against one who has endeavoured to deceive us, none will cry out against us for breach of faith, none will wonder at us, but all will account us wise; and, to our great commendation, one shall see that distress fall upon him, which everyone knows he was deceitfully contriving to bring upon us. —

To this speech [Andrea Gritti[18]] made the following reply:

— If it were proper, on the same issue,[19] to keep dropping a dubious ball,[20] I must confess, most illustrious senators, that this would be my inclination, because there are so many arguments on both sides of the question in debate that for my part I am often confounded. Nevertheless, it being necessary to come to a decision, which cannot be based upon certain foundations or suppositions, our business is to weigh those reasons that contradict one another, and to follow those that are most probable and rely on the strongest arguments.

When I examine these reasons, I can by no means understand why the King of France, either out of apprehension of being prevented by us, or out of an ambitious desire of those towns that formerly belonged to the Duchy of Milan, should enter into an agreement with the King of the Romans to induce him to pass into Italy against us. For the dangers and losses he must sustain by such a step are, without doubt, greater and more manifest than the danger of our joining with Caesar, or the advantages he can hope for from such a resolution. In addition, besides the enmity and the vast injuries they have suffered from one another, there is also the competition of dignity and states, which is wont to breed hatred between the greatest friends. To imagine, therefore, that the King of France will call into Italy the King of the Romans is the same as to say that instead of a quiet republic, which has always been in peace, and has no controversy with him, he would choose to have as his neighbour a king of the most restless spirit, whom he has injured, and who has a thousand causes for contending with him about dignity, dominion and revenge. Let it not be said that, because the King of the Romans is poor, irregular and unlucky, the King of France has no reason to fear his vicinity; for due to the memory of the ancient factions and inclinations of the Italians that are still alight in many places, [21] and especially in the Duchy of Milan, a Roman emperor can never set the least foot in Italy but with great danger to the others; especially Maximilian, because his hereditary dominions are contiguous to Italy, because of his reputation as a prince of great courage and of much skill and experience in war-like affairs, and because he keeps with him the children of Lodovico Sforza,[22] a powerful motive with multitudes to raise disturbances. Not to mention that in all the wars he may have with the King of France, he may expect to have the Catholic King[23] for his ally, if for no other reason, because they share a successor.[24] In addition, the King of France knows very well how powerful Germany is, and how much easier it will be to unite that entire nation, or part of it, once an entrance is opened into Italy and the hopes of plunder shall present. Have we not seen how much he has always stood in fear of the motions of the Germans and of this king, how poor and irregular so ever he may be represented?

And if Maximilian came into Italy, the King of France would be assured he would have with him nothing but a dangerous war or an extremely precarious and immensely expensive peace. Louis may possibly have a desire to recover Cremona and perhaps some other towns; but it is not likely that, for the sake of a small acquisition, he should subject himself to the hazard of a much greater loss, and it is more credible that he will proceed in this case with prudence than with temerity. All the more, if we take into consideration those errors which that king is said to have committed, for we shall find them to proceed from nothing but a too eager desire of ensuring his undertakings. For, what else induced him to divide the Kingdom of Naples, to make a cession of Cremona to us, but that his desire to facilitate the victory in those wars? It is more credible then that he will also now follow the wiser advice and his own custom rather than rash counsels. And the more readily, since this method will not leave him deprived of all manner of hope of obtaining his ends at another time, with greater security, and a more favourable opportunity – which men are wont to promise themselves with great facility, because he who promises himself nothing but changes in the affairs of this world is less mistaken than he who convinces himself of their firmness and stability.

Nor am I terrified at what is said to have been negotiated at other times between these two kings. For it is the custom of princes in our age artfully to entertain one another with vain hopes and dissembled talks, which after a course of many years together having taken no effect, must be construed either to have been fictitious or to involve in them some difficulty that cannot be resolved; for the nature of the things is repugnant to the removal of the diffidence between the parties, and without such a foundation they cannot come to conjunction. I do not fear, therefore, that the King of France will precipitate himself into such imprudent resolutions out of an ambitious desire of acquiring our towns. Nor will he do it, in my view, on account of any apprehension he may entertain of us; for, besides the long experience he has had of your disposition, as there have not been wanting many incitements and many opportunities to break off our confederacy with him, the same reasons that render us secure of him render him in like manner secure of us. For nothing in the world would be more pernicious to us than for the King of the Romans to have states in Italy, because of the authority of the Empire, the increase of which must always give us umbrages, as also on account of the House of Austria, which claims a right to many of our towns, and the vicinity of Germany, whose invasions are too dangerous to our dominions. In addition, we are universally reputed to be very deliberate in our resolutions, and are accused rather of slowness than speed.

I do not deny that these affairs might take a turn different from the opinions of men, and therefore that it would be a right measure to secure ourselves if we could do so easily. But since this is not to be done without exposing ourselves to extreme dangers and difficulties, we are to consider that vain fears are oftentimes as prejudicial as too much confidence. For if we enter into a confederacy with the King of the Romans against the King of France, the war must be commenced and prosecuted with our money, which must also supply all his prodigality and extravagances; otherwise, he would either come to an agreement with our enemies or retire into Germany, leaving us encumbered with all the burdens and dangers. We are then to manage a war against the most potent King of France, Duke of Milan and Lord of Genoa, abounding in valiant men-at-arms and furnished more than any other prince with artillery, and whose money attracts a concourse of soldiers from every nation. How then can it be expected that such an undertaking should be easily attended with a happy success? For there is reason also to suspect that all the potentates of Italy, who either pretend we are in possession of what belongs to them or stand in fear of our power, will join together against us, and the Pope above all others, who, besides the grievances he has against us, would be very sorry to see the Emperor become powerful in Italy, on account of the natural enmity between the

Church and the Empire, by which the popes stand in as much dread of the emperors in temporals as of the Turks in spirituals. And this conjunction would perhaps be more dangerous to us than one between the King of France and the King of the Romans, of which we stand so much in fear. For when princes who claim to be equal unite, apprehensions and contentions will easily arise between one another, by which means it often happens that those enterprises that were commenced with vast expectations and hopes of success become attended with a multitude of difficulties and at last prove abortive.

Nor ought we to postpone to all other considerations that although the King of France has indeed held negotiations contrary to our confederacy, yet it appears not from the effects that he can be said to have failed us; therefore, to take up arms against him cannot be done without incurring the reproach of violating our faith, to which this senate ought to pay the highest regard for the honour and service it does us in our daily transactions with other princes. Nor is it our interest continually to increase an opinion that we seek to oppress all our neighbours and that we aspire to the monarchy of Italy. And I wish to God that we had hitherto proceeded with more caution, because most of the apprehensions we have today arise from our having injured too many in times past. It will never be believed that our fears excite us to a new war against the King of France our ally, but an ambitious desire of gaining from him, by means of our conjunction with the King of the Romans, some part of the Duchy of Milan, as we had before, in conjunction with the King of France, gained a part from Lodovico Sforza. If, back then, we had conducted ourselves with more moderation, and not stood too much in fear of groundless concerns, the affairs of Italy would not be in the present agitations, and we, having sustained ourselves with a reputation of more modesty and gravity, should not now find ourselves under the necessity of entering into a war with one or the other of these princes, either of whom is more powerful than we are. But since we are reduced to such a necessity, I believe that it would be more prudent not to relinquish our confederacy with the King of France than from a motive of vain fear or hope of uncertain and dangerous gains to enter into a war that we would be unable to sustain alone and in which the allies proposed would in the end be rather a burden than a help to us. —

Notes

1. Cf. Ch. 5, fn. 1 above: the equivalent of a Senate.
2. Niccolò Foscarini (1442–1506) held a number of important political and administrative posts. His name was not mentioned by Guicciardini, but

was added to the manuscript by some unknown hand. In fact, Foscarini died in December 1506: that is, a few months prior to this debate. It is true, however, that he favoured Maximilian over the French.

3. Maximilian I of Habsburg, Emperor of the Holy Roman Empire from 1493 to 1519. On the title of 'King of the Romans', cf. Ch. 5, fn. 6 above.

4. Louis XII of Orléans, King of France from 1498 to 1515.

5. That is, an alliance between Maximilian I and Louis XII.

6. Cf. *Maxims and Reflections (Ricordi)*, Engl. transl. by M. Domandi, Philadelphia: University of Pennsylvania Press, 1965, C 76.

7. Cf. p. 149, below, in the second speech: 'jealousy is only too natural for states'.

8. Venice took Cremona in 1499, as a result of the partition of the Duchy of Milan with the French (see the previous debate).

9. Cf. *Maxims and Reflections*, op. cit., C 23.

10. Giuliano della Rovere, pope as Julius II from 1503 to 1513.

11. Alfonso I d'Este, Duke of Ferrara, Modena and Reggio from 1505 to 1534.

12. Francesco II Gonzaga, Marquis of Mantua from 1484 to 1519.

13. With the Treaty of Granada, at the end of 1500, Louis XII and Ferdinand II agreed to attack and partition the Kingdom of Naples between themselves. Such cooperation, however, was short-lived: three years later, the French were expelled from Southern Italy by the Spanish and left the Kingdom of Naples in Ferdinand's hands.

14. Georges Amboise (1460–1510), Cardinal of Rouen, close adviser to Louis XII and one of the most influential figures at the French court.

15. Treaty of Blois, 22 September 1504.

16. That is, Maximilian.

17. That is, Ferdinand II of Aragon, King of Aragon from 1479 to 1516 and Regent of Castile from 1506 to 1516. The titles of King of Spain and King of Aragon are used interchangeably.

18. Andrea Gritti (1455–1538), a highly successful tradesman, was then taking the first steps in a military and political career that would lead him to become doge in 1523.

19. It is likely, then, that the Council had already come to a vote on the same issue.

20. The members of the Council of the Pregadi voted by casting little balls of linen into three different boxes – one for the affirmative votes, one for the negative votes, and one for those who would abstain: that is, the 'dubious'.

21. The traditional rivalry between Guelphs and Ghibellines.

22. The Duke of Milan, who was bereaved of his state by Louis XII (and Venice) in 1499. While Lodovico was taken prisoner in 1500 and brought to France, his children were hosted by Maximilian.

23. That is, Spain's Ferdinand II.

24. Charles of Habsburg, who will become king of Spain in 1516 and emperor in 1519, was the nephew of both Maximilian and Ferdinand II.

Chapter 7

On Whether the Venetians Should Ally with the Emperor or Stick to the Alliance with the King of France*

In the previous debate, which took place in 1507, the Venetian senate was called upon to choose between remaining loyal to the existing alliance with the King of France or accepting the Emperor's offers. In the debate below, which takes place in 1523, the issue looks the same, yet many things had changed in the mean time. To begin with, the King of France was now Francis I. Within a few months of his crowning, in 1515, Francis took the Duchy of Milan, from which his predecessor, Louis XII, had been expelled in 1513 at the hands of the Swiss. The Venetians, who had joined the French in yet another alliance, contributed to his success, and recovered part of what they had lost in 1509. In 1516, Charles of Habsburg became king of Spain, and three years later Holy Roman Emperor, thereby concentrating under his rule an enormous mass of dominions, stretching from the Netherlands to the Kingdom of Naples. Despite this vast territorial extension, many still considered France as the more formidable power of the two: her central position, wealth, population, military capabilities and centralised government were contrasted with the dispersion of Charles V's dominions, the economic backwardness of some of them (Spain), the large autonomies of others (the Netherlands and the Holy Roman Empire) and the Lutheran movement, all of which suggested that the Emperor could have but a precarious hold on all his territories, except for the lands of the House of Habsburg. The most evident bones of contention between Francis I and Charles V, in territorial terms, included Burgundy, Navarre, Naples and Milan.

In Italy, a papal–imperial alliance was made (May 1521) for the sake of driving the French out of Milan once more and restoring the Sforza dynasty. Guicciardini, incidentally, was dispatched as a commissioner to the papal army, and witnessed the military operations that led to the liberation of Milan (except for the citadel) in November and the

---

* From: *The History of Italy*, XV, ii.

almost complete withdrawal of the French from Lombardy the follow-
ing spring. Although Francesco Sforza was now the ruler of Milan, it
was clear that his position depended on the benevolence of Charles,
who, at this point, was the master of most of Italy. His eyes were now
set on Venice.

Although they had not come to a clear rupture with the Emperor, the
Venetians had dutifully performed their role in the war on the French
side, and were now rather at sea as to what they should do next. As
in the previous debate, they found themselves under steady pressure
from both sides. On the one hand, Francis incited them to hold on,
for he would soon send another army into Italy; on the other hand,
Charles was trying to detach them from the French alliance with various
reassurances and offers. The matter went on for months, from 1522
to 1523. While some senators were not inclined to leave the French –
Venice being territorially surrounded by dominions that either belonged
to Charles or were friendly to him, others, who cited the letters of the
Venetian ambassador to France, no longer believed that Francis would
pass into Italy soon; still others were intimidated by Charles's strong
position. In Italy, the Emperor could now rely on the cooperation
of Milan, Genoa, Florence, and possibly the new Pope, Adrian VI;
abroad, he was in close alliance with the King of England. The attitude
of Charles's brother, Archduke Ferdinand, a neighbour to the Venetian
state, contributed to keeping the Republic in suspense, for it was feared
that he would take advantage of the situation to press his territorial
claims against Venice. All this is captured in the debate below.

The election of Andrea Gritti (the first speaker) as doge, on 20 May
1523, deprived the French party of its most authoritative representative.
Although Gritti was an energetic supporter of the alliance with France,
once he became doge he adopted a line of utter impartiality, leaving the
resolution entirely to the Senate. The Venetians repeatedly warned the
King that, unless he took more resolute action, they would be forced to
come to terms with the Emperor. Francis's prolonged procrastination,
the fall of the citadel of Milan (15 April 1523) and Charles's moderate
terms – to which his brother eventually adhered – eventually pushed
Venice to sign not only a peace treaty but also a defensive alliance with
the Emperor (Treaty of Brussels, 29 July 1523).

The Council of the Pregadi[1] was at last convoked in order to come to
a final decision. Here Andrea Gritti[2], a person of the highest authority
in that republic for the most important positions he had held and his
remarkable exploits, and whose name was very famous over all Italy
and in the courts of foreign princes, made a speech, as it is said, like this:

— Though I am sensible, most excellent senators, that there is cause to fear that, if I should give my advice not to separate ourselves from our confederacy with the King France, some may understand by it that I am more influenced with respect to the long familiarity I have had with the French than by a regard to what is expedient for our republic, I shall not forbear on that account to express my mind freely, as it is the duty of a good citizen. In fact, that citizen and senator is of no service who, for any reason whatsoever, refrains from persuading others of what he thinks in his own mind to be for the benefit of the republic. I am convinced, however, that this interpretation will not take place with men of prudence, because they will consider not only what have been my manners and actions at all times, but also that I have never treated with the King of France,[3] or with his men, but as your official, and by your commission and orders. And besides this, I shall be justified, if I deceive not myself, by the reliability of the reasons that induce me to embrace this opinion.

We are debating whether we ought to make a new confederacy with Caesar,[4] contrary to the faith we have given and the obligations, of the alliance in which we are engaged with the King of France – a point that, in my view, means nothing but to establish the power of Caesar, already frightening to everyone, in such a manner as that, it being impossible ever to find any remedy for moderating or repressing it, we shall see it continually increasing, to our manifest prejudice. We have no reason that can justify this resolution, for the King has always observed our confederacy; and if the effects have not answered in being so ready to renew the war in Italy, it is well known that, since he was stimulated to do it by his own interest, there can be no other cause for his backwardness than the impediments which he has met with, and still finds, in the Kingdom of France, which indeed have been sufficient to make him defer his designs but will not be able to crush them. For so ardent is his desire to recover the state of Milan, so great is his power, that as soon as he has repelled the first attacks of his enemies – which he will easily resist – nothing will retard him from sending afresh a very great force on this side of the Alps. We have before our eyes in both these respects the repeated example of King Louis [XII],[5] who, when France was attacked by armies much more potent than those which at present molest it, almost all the other states having joined together against him, by the greatness of his force, the strength of the places on his frontiers, and the loyalty of his people, easily defended himself. And when all men were of opinion that the fatigues of the war must have laid him under a necessity of taking some time for rest, on a sudden sent powerful armies into Italy.[6] Did not the present King do the same in the beginning of his reign, when everyone believed that because he was newly come to the crown and found the royal treasury exhausted by the infinite expenses of his predecessor, he must have been under the necessity of deferring the war to another year?[7] We ought not, therefore, to be intimidated by this slowness, nor would it be a sufficient excuse for shifting sides, since our confederate is not retarded by his will but by the impediments that have intervened; as such, he gives us neither a just cause to complain nor a decent pretext to break the alliance.

A regard to decency, a regard to the dignity of the Venetian senate, demand of us this resolution; but a regard to our interest, better still, to our security demands no less. For who is not aware of what great benefit it may be to us, and from how many dangers it may free us, if the King of France recovers the state of Milan, and what a peaceful situation for many years it may produce in our affairs? This we may learn from the example of what happened but a few years ago, when the recovery of Milan by that king was the cause that we, who before at a vast expense and hazard attended to the defence of Padua and Treviso, recovered Brescia and Verona;[8] was the cause that, while he kept quiet possession of that Duchy, we enjoyed absolute peace and security in all our dominions. These are examples that ought to have much greater weight with us than the ancient memory of the League of Cambrai,[9] for the kings of France comprehended by experience what they had not comprehended by reason: that is, the great damage they would receive by being separated from our alliance[10] – a point of which they will without comparison be more sensible at the present juncture, in which that king has for a rival an emperor, so great a sovereign of so many dominions, whose power necessitates him to desire and to set the highest value upon our confederacy. On the contrary, who is he that sees not, and knows not, in what dangerous situation our affairs will remain should the King of France be totally excluded from Italy? For, who can hinder Caesar from appropriating to himself or to his brother[11] the Duchy of Milan, of which he has not to this day ever granted the investiture to Francesco Sforza?[12] As if, as it is very plain, he will have the power to do it, what security can be given of his will? Who can promise that, since the Duchy of Milan serves as stairs for ascending to the control of all Italy, Caesar will be more influenced by a regard to justice and honour than by ambition and a covetousness proper and natural to all great princes? Shall we perhaps be secured by the moderation and temperance of his officials in Italy, who are almost all Spanish, a nation deceitful, most rapacious, and insatiable above all others? If Caesar then, or Ferdinand his brother, should seize Milan, what will be the condition of our state, when surrounded by them on the side of Italy and of Germany? What remedy can we expect for our dangers, the Kingdom of Naples being in his hands, the Pope[13] and the other states of Italy his dependants and everyone so worn out and exhausted of money and troops that no assistance can be hoped from them?

But if the King of France should get possession of the Duchy of Milan, affairs resting in a balance between two such princes, whoever should have reason to fear the power of one would be spared and left alone on account of the power of the other. In fact, the fear alone of his coming secures all others, since it constrains the Imperials to lie still and not to get involved in any enterprise. Therefore, it seems to me that we are rather to laugh than to be terrified at the vanity of their threat that if we do not confederate with Caesar they will turn their arms against us – as if to engage in a war with the Venetian senate were an easy undertaking and there was reason to hope for a speedy victory, and as if this were means for preventing the passage of the King of France and not rather the cause of the contrary: for who doubts that, when they have provoked us, we shall be under the necessity of proposing such conditions to the King as would induce him to pass even if he were averse to it? Was not this the very case in the time of King Louis, when their injuries and treacherous dealings[14] induced us to stimulate that king in such a way (when I from his prisoner became your ambassador[15]) that at a juncture when he was the most apprehensive of being very powerfully attacked in France, he sent his army, although with ill fortune, into Italy?[16] Do not believe that if the Imperials had thought that the way to procure them our friendship or to be secure from the passing of the King of France into Italy was to fall upon us, they would have hitherto delayed to begin hostilities. Do not their generals have any covetous desire to enrich themselves with plunder and the gains of war? Have they not been under the necessity of easing the country of their friends of the burden of quartering troops, of getting money for disburdening it, and to maintain the army upon free quarters in the territories of others? But they know that our power renders it too difficult to coerce us, that it is not in their interest, being every day apprehensive of a war with the King of France, to involve themselves in another war, and to give occasion to a state powerful in forces and money to stimulate a French intervention with vast offers. While they remain in these apprehensions and doubts they will not seize the Duchy of Milan for themselves; nor will they act against us but with vain threats. If we secure them from this fear, it will lie in their power to accomplish both things; and if they should put their scheme in execution, as probably they will, of whom can we chiefly complain but of ourselves and of our excessive timidity and immoderate desire of peace? Peace indeed is desirable and a blessing when it secures one from one's apprehensions, when it increases not the danger, and when it induces men to think themselves at liberty to enjoy rest and free themselves from expenses. But when it produces contrary effects, it is, under the insidious name of peace, a pernicious war, and under the name of wholesome medicine, a destructive poison.

Therefore, if our joining in confederacy with Caesar excludes the King of France from Italian affairs, gives Caesar the liberty of seizing at his pleasure the Duchy of Milan, and once he has done this, of studying our destruction, it follows that, with the greatest reproach to our name and with the violation of the faith of this republic, we purchase the aggrandisement of a prince whose ambition is no less vast than his power, and who claims, along with his brother, that all we possess on land in Italy belongs to them; and that we exclude from Italy a prince who by his power would secure the liberty of all the others and who would be necessitated to be most strictly united with us.

Now, a person who proposes such evident and palpable reasons cannot be charged as under the influence of affection rather than of truth, of private interest rather than love to the republic, of whose safety we have no reason to doubt if it shall please God to grant so much success to your resolutions as he has bestowed wisdom on this most excellent Senate. —

But Giorgio Cornaro,[17] a citizen of equal authority, and of as high a reputation for wisdom as nobody else in that Senate, made the following speech in opposition to this advice:

— The present decision, most illustrious senators, is certainly of great importance and very difficult. And yet, when I consider the ambition and faithlessness of the princes of our times and the difference between their nature and the nature of republics, which being governed not by the will of a single person but by the consent of many, proceed with more moderation and caution, nor ever impudently depart, as is frequent with princes, from what has some appearance of justice and honour, I cannot but conclude that it must be very pernicious to us that the Duchy of Milan should be under a prince more powerful than ourselves. For such vicinity will of necessity keep us under continual fear and uneasiness and always preoccupied with war, although we may be at peace and despite any confederacy or convention that may subsist between us. Of this we find infinite examples in ancient historians, and some in our own writers; but what greater and more illustrious example can there be than that whose bitter memory is engraved in all our hearts? This senate introduced Louis King of France into the Duchy of

Milan, at which unfortunate resolution many of us were present.[18] We faithfully observed the articles of our confederacy with him, although we were invited by the Spanish and Germans, with great rewards and on different occasions, to detach ourselves from him, and were assured that he was often plotting against us.[19] Not the benefit received, nor the faith given, nor the perpetual train of our good offices was capable of mollifying his spirit, which was so replete with the desire to injure us that, to this purpose, he eventually reconciled with his ancient and bitterest enemies and joined with them against us in the most pernicious League of Cambrai. To avoid therefore the dangers that will be continually hanging over our heads from the insidious and deceitful neighbourhood of great princes, we are under the necessity, if I mistake not, of directing all our resolutions with a view that the Duchy of Milan might not fall into the hands of the King of France nor of the Emperor, but may come into the possession of Francesco Sforza, or some other who is not formidable for his kingdoms or great dominions. On this depends our present security, and, if the condition of the times should alter, on this may depend the future augmentation and distinction of our state.

We are debating whether we ought to continue in friendship with the King of France or join in confederacy with Caesar. The former resolution totally excludes Francesco Sforza from the Duchy of Milan and gives admittance to the King of France, a prince so much more potent than ourselves; the latter intends to confirm and secure Francesco Sforza in the possession of that Duchy, whom Caesar proposes to include in our confederacy as one of the principals, and whose safety he has promised the King of England.[20] Therefore, if Caesar should attempt to deprive Sforza of that state, he would not only offend us and the other Italian states, to whom he would give occasion to have recourse once more to the French, but disoblige the King of England, for whom, as everyone knows, he must have the greatest respect, and would besides provoke the Duchy's people, who are perfectly devoted to Sforza. By such a step he would involve himself into a multitude of difficulties and dangers and, highly to his dishonour, be guilty of a breach of faith, which he has hitherto, for ought that appears, preserved inviolable, which cannot be said of the French. As a matter of fact, his restoring to Francesco Sforza, after the death of Pope Leo [X],[21] the state of Milan, resigning into his hands the fortresses successively as he acquired them, and at last, contrary to what many expected, putting him in possession of the castle of Milan, must be taken as manifest signs that he intends to fulfil his engagement.

Why then should we hesitate in preferring a resolution that gives us great hopes of answering our intentions before one that manifestly tends to an end repugnant to our needs? In opposition to this we are told that it would be more dangerous to this republic for the Duchy of Milan to be under the dominion of Caesar than of the King of France. For that king, by the power of Caesar and the emulation between them, would be in a manner necessitated to persevere in alliance with us, but from Caesar we may expect quite the opposite, both on account of his power and of the claims that he and his brother pretend to have on our dominions. I believe that those who have such an opinion of Caesar are not deceived, considering the nature and manners of such great princes. I heartily wish he may not deceive himself who has not the same opinion of the King of France! Many of the same reasons were in force under his predecessor, who was however more swayed by covetousness and ambition than by a sense of honour or his own interest. Besides, the reasons that might oblige him to continue united with us are not perpetual, but vary from time to time, according to the nature of human affairs. Caesar too is subject to the common lot of mortals, and, like other princes greater than himself, liable to infinite accidents of fortune. How long ago is it that, when all Spain was in an insurrection against him, he appeared more worthy of commiseration than envy?[22] And at least there is not so much difference between one danger and the other as there is between a resolution that certainly excludes us from obtaining our end and one that probably will lead us to its accomplishment.

Moreover, the reasons alleged [by the previous speaker] concern a future and distant time; yet, if we consider the present state of affairs, it is not to be doubted that if we refuse an alliance with Caesar we shall immediately expose ourselves to greater distresses and dangers. For if we break off our confederacy with the King of France, it is probable that Caesar will defer war until a more convenient time and opportunity; but if we are in conjunction with him, Caesar may perhaps think fit immediately to enter upon action, which will of necessity create us trouble and expense. But in what case is war likely to be attended with the greatest danger to us? If we join with Caesar, we may almost conclude for certain that victory will fall on our side – an event that we cannot so well promise ourselves by an union with the King of France. And by confederating with Caesar, even the victory of the King would not prove so dangerous to us as would be the victory of Caesar while we are united to the King: in this latter case, the whole force of the victorious arms would be turned against us, and Caesar would find himself not only under less restraint, and fewer impediments, but prompted in a manner by necessity to seize the Duchy of Milan.

To what is urged concerning our tie of confederacy, the answer is easy; for we promised the King of France to defend the states that he possessed in Italy, not to recover them after he had lost them. This is not what the instrument of our treaty requires of us; nor can the same reasons be invoked to that purpose. We fulfilled our obligations when at the loss of Milan,[23] occasioned by their want of provisions for its defence, our troops suffered more than the French; we fulfilled them when we sent out our forces to the assistance of Lautrec[24] on his return with the Swiss; and we have gone beyond our obligations now that, being fed by them with vain hopes and promises, we have been waiting so many months for the coming of their army. If will detains the King, why should we seek to bear the punishment of his own fault? If necessity, is not that a reason sufficient to justify us, even if we were under any obligations? I know not for what we should be any longer bound to the King of France, since we have first been abandoned by him. I know not what farther is required of one confederate for another, or how our dangers can do him any service. I am not saying that the imperial generals have at present any thoughts of going to war with us; at the same time, I will not presume to assert the contrary, considering the necessity they lie under of subsisting the army on somebody's territory, and the hopes they may have of drawing us by that means into an alliance with them, especially if the King of France should not pass, of which if anyone doubts, he has, in my opinion, sufficient reason for his doubting from the negligence of the French, their want of money, and the war in which they are engaged beyond the Alps with two such princes.[25] Nor can he be blamed who believes all this to be true on the credit of your ambassador, for ambassadors are the eyes and ears of states.

In short, I repeat it again that we ought to use our utmost endeavour, and be most solicitous, that the Duchy of Milan may be settled on Francesco Sforza, whence it follows that a resolution that may conduct us to this end is more expedient to us than one that totally excludes us from it. —

Notes

1. Cf. Ch. 5, fn. 1, above: the Venetian Senate.
2. Andrea Gritti is the second speaker of the previous debate (see Ch. 6, fn. 17). As stated in the introduction, he was about to be elected doge.
3. Francis I of Valois, King of France from 1515 to 1547.
4. Charles V of Habsburg, King of Spain from 1516 to 1556 and Holy Roman Emperor from 1519 to 1556.
5. Louis XII of Orléans, King of France from 1498 to 1515.

6. In 1513, after being forced to leave the Duchy of Milan the previous year.
7. Francis I became king of France on 1 January 1515 and passed into Italy in the summer of the same year.
8. As Francis was seizing Milan, in 1515, his Venetian allies were retaking Brescia and Verona. This is contrasted with the desperate situation the Venetians were facing after being defeated by the same French at Agnadello in 1509, as they laboured hard to defend Padua and Treviso against the imperial army.
9. The general anti-Venetian coalition of 1508, in which the French played a leading role.
10. After the crushing of Venice, Pope Julius II became concerned about Louis XII's preponderance in Northern Italy and inspired the creation of the Holy League in 1511 for the sake of driving the French out.
11. Ferdinand of Habsburg (1503–64).
12. Francesco II Sforza (1495–1535), son of Lodovico Sforza, the Duke of Milan overthrown by Louis XII in 1499, returned to his home town in 1521, as the papal and imperial forces expelled the French from the city, and became the lord of it. Many feared, however, that Charles V would now seize the Duchy of Milan – which he indeed did when Francesco died in 1535.
13. Adriaan Florenszoon Boeyens d'Edel, pope as Adrian VI from 1522 to 1523, had a long familiarity with Charles: when the future Emperor was a child, he was his tutor, and later performed important functions in preparing Charles's succession to the Spanish throne. In addition, Charles made him regent of Spain in 1520, as he left for the Netherlands.
14. The alliance of Pope Julius II and Emperor Maximilian I (November 1512), at the expense of Venice.
15. Captured by the French at the siege of Brescia in February 1512 and taken to Lyon, Gritti was held in great esteem by Louis XII and played a key role in the negotiations that resulted in a new Franco-Venetian alliance, signed in March 1513.
16. The joint Franco-Venetian campaign of 1513 witnessed the defeat of both allies.
17. Giorgio Cornaro (1452–1527), Procurator of San Marco (that is, the second most important life appointment in Venice next to the doge).
18. In 1498. See the debate on this, Chapter 5.
19. On the ambiguous French attitude towards their Venetian allies, see the previous debate.
20. Henry VIII Tudor, King of England from 1509 to 1547.
21. Giovanni de' Medici, pope as Leo X from 1513 to 1521. He died shortly after the expulsion of the French from Milan, on 1 December.
22. Cornero is probably referring to two almost simultaneous uprisings, the so-called Revolt of the Comuneros (1520–21), in Castile, and the Revolt of the Brotherhoods (1519–23), in Aragon.
23. As has been said, in 1521, at the hands of the Pope and the Emperor.

24. Odet de Foix, Viscount of Lautrec, Governor of Milan from 1516 to 1521. Forced to leave Milan in the autumn of 1521, he quartered his army in Venetian territory for a few months and was finally defeated at the Battle of Bicocca (27 April 1522), after which the French troops abandoned Lombardy (except for the castles of Milan, Novara and Cremona).
25. That is, the Emperor and the King of England.

Chapter 8

On Whether the Emperor Should Be Magnanimous towards the King of France, Whom He Holds Prisoner, or Impose Severe Terms on Him*

Despite the scepticism of the Venetian Senate (see the previous debate), the French did pass into Italy in 1523 – to no avail – and once more in the autumn of 1524. This time, Francis I himself was at the head of a powerful army. The Imperials did not have enough forces to defend Milan, devastated as it was by the plague; accordingly, they locked themselves up in several fortified places. Francis then began to lay siege to the most important of them: that is, Pavia. Despite the coalition that Charles V had managed to make in August 1523 with Henry VIII and all the most important Italian states, not to mention the alliance with the Venetians signed the month before, the Imperials received no assistance. In addition, their poor financial resources made their position even more precarious. Being concerned about their ability to sustain themselves further, upon the arrival of a contingent of Landsknechts the imperial generals decided to launch a surprise attack upon the French camp, in coordination with the troops under siege. In the early morning of 24 February 1525, Francis's army was annihilated in a two-hour battle that would change the course of history, and the King himself was wounded and captured, while a number of French noblemen who were fighting next to him were killed. Not only did this sensational result leave Italy at the mercy of Charles V, but also it pointed at a clear French inferiority vis-à-vis Spain on a European scale – an inferiority that the French kings will be able to attenuate, but not cancel, in decades of war to come.

The news of this astonishing victory reached Charles on 10 March. According to Guicciardini, his public reaction was extremely sober:

> He did not consent, as was customary with others, that there should be any demonstrations of rejoicing by bells or bonfires, or in any other manner, saying that it was proper to make rejoicings for

---

* From: *The History of Italy*, XVI, v.

victories obtained over Infidels, and not for such as are got over Christians.

Nor *did he show 'either in his words or gestures, any sign of immoderate gladness, or of being puffed up in mind'. The debate below took place a few days later.*

The opinion of the Duke of Alba was enthusiastically supported by the entire council, 'every one having already proposed in his mind the empire of almost all Christendom'. Charles himself endorsed it, 'though rather to show that he was not willing to reject the counsel of his men than by declaring what his own inclination was'. Accordingly, Francis was notified of the harsh conditions upon which he would be set free: among other things, he was to give up all his claims to Italy, Flanders and Artois, and restore to Charles Burgundy and all the dominions that had been annexed by the French crown in 1477. Not surprisingly, the French King found all this unacceptable. Francis was kept prisoner in Italy until June, and then taken to Spain upon his request, for he intended to talk to Charles in person. The Emperor, however, refused to see him, except for once, as he fell ill and seemed about to die. Charles's negotiations with Francis and the Regentess of France (his mother) went on for almost one year, until the French King capitulated on Charles's terms, which entailed the dismemberment of France and other humiliating conditions (Peace of Madrid, 14 January 1526). As the Bishop of Osma had predicted, however, as soon as the King was back in France, he made no secret of the fact that he did not intend to observe the agreement that had been extorted from him.

[Caesar[1]] called a council and signified to them that he desired their advice on how to regulate his conduct with regard to the King of France, and what ends he ought to serve by this victory, commanding everyone to express his views with freedom in his presence. In consequence of this command, the Bishop of Osma,[2] who held the office of confessor to Caesar, made the following speech:

— Though we are assured, most glorious Prince, that whatever happens in this lower world proceeds from the providence of the Supreme Being, which daily gives motion to things, on some occasions its operations can be noticed more clearly. Yet never did it give more evident tokens than in the present victory – a victory which on account of its greatness, the ease with which it was obtained, and the great power of the enemies, who abounded with all the necessary provisions of war to a far greater degree than ourselves, everyone must own to have been by the express will of God, and almost miraculous. The greater therefore and more manifest the favour of Heaven, the more strictly is Your Majesty obliged to acknowledge it and to show a just gratitude.

This behaviour consists principally in directing the victory in such a manner as may best promote the service of God and answer those ends for which we may believe it has been granted. And indeed when I consider to what a low ebb the state of Christendom is reduced, I cannot see that anything can be more holy, more necessary and more pleasing to God than a universal peace between Christian princes, without which we must be sensible that religion, the credit of religion itself, and a good life must fall under most manifest decay and disrepute. On one side we have the Turks, who, taking advantage of our divisions, have made such a progress that they now threaten Hungary, the kingdom of your brother-in-law.[3] And if they should get possession of Hungary – as no doubt they will if the Christian princes do not join forces – they will have an open road into Germany and Italy. On the other side, this Lutheran heresy, so hateful to God, so reproachable to him who has power to suppress it, and so dangerous to all princes, has now gained such a footing that without due care it will fill the world with heretics, and no provision can be made against it but by your power and authority, which, while Your Majesty is involved in other wars, cannot exert themselves for the extirpation of this most pernicious poison.[4]

But besides all this, had we nothing to fear either from the Turks or heretics, what can be more unseemly, more wicked and more pestiferous than that so much Christian blood, which might be gloriously spent for propagating the Christian faith, or at least reserved for more necessary occasions, should be idly shed for the gratification of our passions, attended with so many rapes, sacrileges and horrible outrages? Evils of which whoever is the author by his own will can never hope for pardon from God, and which whoever commits out of necessity deserves no excuse if he has not at least a full intention to redress them as soon as it shall lie in his power. The end, therefore, that you are to have in view ought to be universal peace among Christians, a work above all others honourable, holy and necessary, and which we are now to consider by what means it may be accomplished.

There are three resolutions that lie at Your Majesty's choice concerning the King of France. One of keeping him a perpetual prisoner; another of setting him at liberty with marks of affection and in a brotherly manner, without any other conditions than such as may serve to establish a perpetual peace and friendship between the two of you and to heal the sores of Christendom; the third way is to give him his liberty but with care to take the greatest possible advantage from it.

Of these resolutions, the first and last, if I mistake not, prolong and increase the wars, while the loving and brotherly liberation is the only one that extirpates them forever. For who can doubt that, if treated with such generosity and liberality, the King of France, from the sense of so extraordinary a benefit, will be more bound in mind and more in your power than he is at present in body? And if a sincere union and harmony should be effected between the two of you, all the rest of Christendom will betake themselves to follow the road that shall be marked out for them by two such princes. But a resolution to keep him in perpetual custody, besides entailing an unbearable reputation for cruelty, and discovering a mind ignorant of the power of fortune, is the ready way to propagate wars without end, since it presupposes an intention to conquer all, or part, of France, which is impossible to accomplish without new and very destructive wars. If we choose the middle way – that is, to set him free, but on such conditions as to yield us all the gains that can possibly be made of it, it is, in my view, the most complicated and dangerous resolution of all the others. For whatever affinity he may contract, whatever articles, obligations he may consent to, he will always remain your enemy and he will never want for the assistance of all those who fear your power, whence may be expected new wars, and those more bloody and more dangerous than the past.

I am sensible how much this opinion differs from the general sentiment, that it is quite new and unprecedented; but these singular and extraordinary resolutions well become Caesar. Nor is it surprising that his soul is very capable of such notions as are above the comprehension of all other men, whom he ought to excel in magnanimity as much as he is advanced above them in dignity; and therefore he ought to know, above all others, how full of true glory an act of such great generosity would be, and how much it is the duty of Caesar to pardon and show kindness rather than to make conquests; that God has not in vain almost miraculously put into his hands the power of giving peace to the world; that it is incumbent on him, after so many victories, after so many favours bestowed upon him by God, after seeing all prostrate at his feet, to proceed no longer as an enemy to anybody, but to provide, as a common father, for the welfare of all. The names of Alexander the Great and Julius Caesar were rendered more glorious by the magnanimity of pardoning enemies and restoring kingdoms to the conquered than by the multitude of victories and triumphs. Their example deserves the more to be followed by him who, not proposing to himself, for his sole end, glory – although a very great reward – principally desires to discharge the true and proper office that belongs to every Christian prince.

But to come closer to the point, in order to convince those who esti-mate human affairs by human ends, let us consider what resolution is looked upon to be the most serviceable to those very ends. I verily think that of all Your Majesty's greatness there is no part more marvellous and more worthy than the glory you have attained of being hitherto invincible, and of conducting all your enterprises to a most happy end with so much reputation and prosperity. This is without doubt the most precious jewel, the most singular treasure among all your treas-ures. How then can it be better consolidated and secured, how can it be more certainly preserved than by putting an end to the wars with so generous and magnanimous an end, by taking the glory acquired away from the power of fortune, and bringing this ship, laden with wares of inestimable value, out of the wide ocean into a safe harbour? But let us insist farther. Is not that greatness which is preserved by free will more desirable than that which is maintained by violence? None doubts it, because it is more stable, more easy, more pleasing and more honoura-ble. If Caesar obliges the King of France by so signal an act of liberality, by so inestimable a benefit, will not he always be the master of that King and his kingdom? If he gives so manifest an assurance to the Pope[5] and to the other princes that he contents himself with the states that he has in possession and has no thought but how to promote the universal welfare, will they not renounce all fears? And when they have no further grounds for apprehensions or disputes, they will not only love but also adore so great a goodness. Thus, with the will of all will he give laws to all, and have it infinitely more in his power to dispose of Christians by benevolence and authority than by force and imperiousness. Assisted then and followed by all, he will be enabled to turn his arms against the Lutherans and infidels, with more glory and with more opportunities of making greater conquests – which I see no reason why we should not as well desire to be made in Africa, or in Greece, or in the Levant, even though the enlargement of dominion among Christians were attended with so much facility as many, in my opinion, vainly imagine. For the power of Your Majesty is so greatly augmented as to be too fearsome to all; and if they should perceive that it is designed to be carried to a greater height, by necessity they will all unite against you. The Pope, the Venetians, all of Italy dread your power, and if we may judge by frequent signs, the King of England[6] must take umbrage at it.

The French may possibly be for some months amused with hopes and fruitless negotiations, but at last it will be necessary to deliver their King, or they will be thrown into despair, and when desperate they will join with all the others. If the King be set at liberty on conditions of little advantage to Your Majesty, where will be the gain of losing the opportunity of exercising such extraordinary magnanimity, which, if not exerted at this beginning, when you would afterwards seek to display it, will carry with it neither praise, nor glory, nor the like grace? And if you set him free on conditions advantageous to you, he will not observe them; for no security he may have given can be of such importance to him but that he will be much more concerned to prevent his enemy from becoming so great as afterwards to have it in his power to oppress him. Thus we shall have either a useless peace or a dangerous war, the consequences of which are uncertain. Whoever has enjoyed a long state of felicity has the greater reason to dread a change of fortune, and he who once had it in his power to settle all his affairs on a good foundation feels the bitterest regret when things take a turn for the worse.

I trust, Caesar, that I have satisfied your command, if not with prudence, yet at least with affection and fidelity. And now nothing remains on my part but to pray God to give you a mind and ability to take such a resolution as may be most agreeable to His will, most conducive to the advancement of your own glory, and finally best suited for promoting the good of the Christian Commonwealth, of which, on account of the supreme dignity in which you are placed, and because it is manifestly the will of God, it is fit you should be father and protector. —

Caesar heard this counsel with great attention, and without showing any sign of displeasure or approbation. But, after being silent for a long while, he made a sign for others to speak; on which, Fadrique, Duke of Alba,[7] a person of great authority in Caesar's court, made the following speech:

— I shall hope to be excused, most invincible Emperor, if I should confess that I have no judgement different from the common judgement, nor capacity of carrying my understanding to a higher pitch than that to which the understanding of other men has arrived. In fact, I shall perhaps be more commended if I should advise you to proceed by the same methods by which your fathers and grandfathers always proceeded. For new and strange counsels may perhaps at first sight appear more glorious and magnanimous, but are sure to prove more dangerous and more fallacious than those that have at all times, and with all men, been approved by reason and experience. The will of God first, and the valour of your generals and soldiers second, have given you a greater victory than has been gained by any Christian prince for these many ages; but all the fruits of success in battle consist of making a right use of the victory, and not to do this is the more disgraceful than not to win, as it is a greater fault to be cheated by those things that are in the power of him who makes a wrong assessment of the situation than by those that depend on fortune. The more then are we to beware of taking a resolution that must in the end give you shame before others and repentance before yourself; and the more important the affair is of which we treat, the more circumspectly are we to proceed, and to take with maturity those resolutions that, once found erroneous, can never afterwards be rectified. You are to consider with yourself that if the King is set at liberty, he is immediately out of your reach, but while he is a prisoner it is always in your power to release him; and he ought not to wonder at your slowness since, if I mistake not, he is conscious to himself in what manner he would act if Caesar were his prisoner.

The capture of the King of France was certainly an affair of the greatest moment. But whoever well considers the case will find his dismission to be incomparably greater; nor will it ever be considered prudent to take a resolution of such importance without very long consultations and revolving the case infinite times in the mind. I would not perhaps be of this opinion could I persuade myself that the King, if he were at present set at liberty, would acknowledge so great a benefit with due gratitude; and that the Pope and the other Italian powers would lay aside covetousness and ambition along with their fears. But who knows not how dangerous it is to found so important a resolution on so fallacious and uncertain supposition? In fact, whoever well considers the condition and manners of men will sooner judge the contrary, for nothing is in its own nature more transitory, nothing of a shorter date, than the memory of benefits – and the greater they are, the greater measure of ingratitude (according to the proverb) is required to pay them, for he who is either unable or unwilling to cancel them by recompensation, often tries to cancel them either by forgetfulness or by persuading himself that they were not so considerable;[8] and he who is ashamed of having been reduced to a state that had need of benefits, is also galled at the thought of having received them, so that the hatred arising from the memory of the necessity under which he had fallen operates more strongly in him than the obligation presented from the consideration of the kindness that has been showed him.

Besides, what nation is there to whom insolence is more natural and levity more proper than the French? Where there is insolence, there is blindness; where there is levity, there is no knowledge of virtue, no judgement to discern the actions of others, and no gravity to estimate what is fit and proper for oneself.[9] What then is to be expected from a King of France, puffed up with as much pride as can be conceived in any French king, but that he burns with rage and indignation at being a prisoner to Caesar, at a time when he thought himself sure of triumphing over him? The memory of his disgrace will always be fresh in his mind, and after he is at liberty, he will be so far from believing that the way to obliterate it is by gratitude that he will be always striving to get superiority over you. He will persuade himself that he has been dismissed on account of the difficulties of retaining him, not out of goodness or magnanimity. Such is almost always the nature of all men, such is always the nature of the French, in whom whoever expects gravity or magnanimity must expect new orders and regulations in human affairs. Thus, in the room of peace and re-establishment of order and harmony in the world, new wars will arise, greater and more dangerous than the past. For your reputation will be lost, and your army, which expects the due fruits of so great a victory, deceived in its hopes, will no longer have the same valour and vigour; nor will your affairs be attended with the same fortune, which hardly stays with those who retain it, much less with such as drive it away. Nor will the goodness of the Pope and the Venetians prove of any other kind, but, on the contrary, repenting of having suffered you to obtain the past victory, they will do their utmost to prevent you from obtaining any more, and the fear that they now have of you will prompt them to use all their endeavours to prevent their falling again under new fears; and thus, when it is in your power to hold all bound with the chains of terror and amazement, you yourself, out of excessive goodness, will make them unchained and bold.

What may be the will of God I do not know; nor do I believe it known to others, because we are usually taught that his judgements are a deep secret and unsearchable.[10] But if we may venture to guess from such clear appearances, I imagine he is favourable to your greatness, and cannot suppose that he dispenses his blessings to you in such an abundance only to have you waste them, but in order to render you as superior to others in fact and reality as you are in right and title. To lose therefore so fair an opportunity, which God has put into your hands, is nothing but to tempt him, and render yourself unworthy of his favours.

Experience and reason have always demonstrated that success never attends an affair that depends on many hands.[11] I much question therefore whether he who imagines that the heretics can be oppressed or the infidels subdued by the union of many princes, forms to himself just notions of the nature of the world. These are enterprises that require a prince of such power as to dictate and give directions to the others, without which all efforts will meet with the same success for the future as they have had in times past. For this end, I believe, God has opened you a way to [the universal] monarchy, by which only one can answer these holy intentions; and it is best to delay the commencement of such

undertaking in order to proceed on better and more certain foundations. Nor suffer yourself to be diverted from this resolution by the fear
of so many alliances one threatens to create, for the opportunity is too
great that you have in your power: for if matters will be rightly negotiated, the King's mother,[12] out of natural love and from a necessity of
recovering her son, will never give up the hope of getting him out of
your hands by an agreement; nor will the princes of Italy ever unite with
the Regency of France, knowing that it is always in your power to break
such a union by delivering the King, and even to make it turn against
them. They must remain in suspense and amazement, and at last strive
who shall be the foremost in receiving laws from you, for whom it will
then be glorious to exercise clemency and magnanimity, when affairs
are reduced to such a situation that they cannot help acknowledging
you for their superior. In such cases did Alexander and Caesar exercise
these virtues, liberally pardoning injuries; but they were not so inconsiderate as to involve themselves afresh, with their own hands, in those
difficulties and dangers that they had overcome.[13] He who acts in this
manner deserves praise because he has but few examples, but he who
does a thing for which there is no example is perhaps imprudent.

Therefore, Caesar, my opinion is that the greatest profit be made of
this victory that is possible, and that with this view the King, always
treated with the honours suitable to kings, be conducted, if it cannot
be into Spain, at least to Naples, and that in answer to his letter you
send him a messenger with the most kind missive, who shall propose
the conditions of his liberty, which may be such as, when they come to
be examined in detail, carry with them a reward worthy of such a victory. These foundations and ends of your proceedings thus settled, time
and the accidents that will arise will either hasten or retard the King's
deliverance and determine whether we are to have peace or war with the
Italians, to whom at present we should give good hopes. Let us augment
as much as possible the favour and reputation of our arms by art and
industry, that we must not every day tempt fortune anew; and let us be
prepared for an accommodation with this or that power, or with all
together, or with none, as opportunity shall suggest.

These are the methods that were always pursued by wise princes,
and particularly by those who were the founders of so much greatness;
they never rejected the means that offered themselves for their promo-
tion, nor slackened sail before a prosperous gale of fortune. You must
do the same, for what in some of them might have appeared ambition,
belongs to you by justice. Remember, Caesar, that you are a prince,
and that it is your duty to proceed in the way of princes; and that no
reason, divine or human, suggests that you omit the opportunity of

reviving the usurped and oppressed authority of the Empire, but only obliges you to have a mind and intention to avail yourself honestly of it. And remember above all how easy it is to lose great opportunities, and how difficult to acquire them, and therefore that it is necessary to strive with all diligence to keep fast hold of them, and not lay our stress on the goodness or prudence of the vanquished, since the world is full of imprudence and malignity. And considering that the Christian religion can rely on no other means of defence but from your power, be not wanting to augment it as much as you can, not so much for the interest of your own authority and glory, as for the service of God, and out of zeal for the universal good. —

Notes

1. Charles V of Habsburg, King of Spain from 1516 to 1556 and Holy Roman Emperor from 1519 to 1556.
2. García de Loaysa y Mendoza (1478–1546). He would become cardinal in 1530.
3. Louis II Jagiellon, King of Hungary from 1516 to 1526, married Mary of Austria, sister of Charles. After taking Belgrade in 1521, the Ottomans were now about to inflict on Louis a disastrous defeat (Battle of Mohács, 1526), which would cost him his life and lead to the occupation of much of his kingdom.
4. According to tradition, Luther posted his ninety-five theses in October 1517. This is conventionally considered the beginning of the Protestant Reformation. Luther was excommunicated in January 1521 and the Edict of Worms banned his writings the following May. By then, what had begun as a theological dispute had acquired a serious political dimension. Several German princes were sympathetic to Luther, and he came to be seen as a sort of national hero, whose anti-Roman sentiments were shared by many.
5. Giulio de' Medici, pope as Clement VII from 1523 to 1534.
6. Henry VIII, King of England from 1509 to 1547.
7. Fadrique Álvarez de Toledo y Enríquez (c. 1460–1531), Grandee of Spain.
8. Cf. *Maxims and Reflections (Ricordi)*, Engl. transl. by M. Domandi, Philadelphia: University of Pennsylvania Press, 1965, C 24.
9. Cf. ibid., C 167.
10. Cf. ibid., C 92.
11. Cf. ibid., C 97.
12. Louise of Savoy (1476–1531) played a crucial role as Regentess during her son's captivity, as she managed to provide the kingdom with the necessary political stability and continuity, and set up relevant diplomatic alignments against Charles V with England, the Ottoman Empire, the Pope and Venice.
13. Cf. *Maxims and Reflections*, op. cit., C 73.

Chapter 9
On Whether or Not the Venetians Should Make an Agreement with the Emperor or Risk War against Him*

Although the Venetian Republic had reluctantly shifted sides and signed a defensive alliance with Charles V in July 1523 (see the penultimate debate above), when the French passed into Italy again its assistance to the Imperials was lukewarm at best. In particular, as the Imperials evacuated Milan upon the arrival of Francis I, in the autumn of 1524 (see the introduction to the previous debate),

> *being required [. . .] to send to their army the troops they had engaged for in the articles of the league, the Venetians, though they did not absolutely refuse, yet gave cool answers, with an intention to regulate their counsels according to the turn of affairs, either because some of them called to mind their ancient confederacy with Francis or because they believed that the King of France being in Italy with so powerful an army, and his enemy in so weak a condition, he must be victorious; or that they more than ever suspected the ambitious designs of Caesar, for to the surprise, and almost with the complaints, of all Italy, he had not yet given to Francesco Sforza the investiture of the Duchy of Milan.* (The History of Italy, XV, x)

It is not surprising, then, that upon the justifications that the Venetian ambassador made to Charles after his decisive victory at Pavia (24 February 1525), the Emperor 'said to the attendants that his excuses were not true, however he would accept of them as such' (ibid.).

More than any other Italian state, Venice could not possibly like the implications of the imperial success in Lombardy. The shaky position of Francesco Sforza entailed the possibility that Charles reserved the right to seize the Duchy of Milan, in which case the Republic would have

* 'Sulla proposta di alleanza fatta da Carlo V ai Veneziani' and 'Sullo stesso argomento. In contrario', in Francesco Guicciardini, *Opere*, vol. VIII: *Scritti politici e Ricordi*, ed. by R. Palmarocchi, Bari: Laterza, 1933, pp. 136–44 and 145–52, respectively.

found itself squeezed in between Habsburg and imperial dominions on all sides. In addition, the French eclipse from Italian affairs meant the disappearance of the only credible counterweight to Charles's power. At the same time, the Venetians could not challenge the Emperor on their own. The year was thus spent in negotiations with Charles, on the one hand, and with all those who had reason to oppose his triumph, on the other – especially Pope Clement VII and the French regency.

Due to his chronic financial weakness, the Emperor was above all interested in the money that an agreement with the Venetians would bring. In fact, the Imperials asked them, among other things, for 100,000 ducats by way of satisfaction for non-observance of the past alliance, in order to renew their confederacy. Being willing to give 80,000 ducats only, the Venetians then engaged in a long dispute about the 20,000 ducats difference, until they received notice that the King of England was now moving closer to France (the alliance would be made on 30 August) and that a number of German troops, after payment of their arrears, were being dismissed from the imperial army. Thus, the Venetian Senate resolved to wait and see.

Affairs were precipitated in the autumn. On 14 October 1525, Girolamo Morone, Sforza's chancellor, was imprisoned by the Marquis of Pescara, the commander of the imperial army in Italy, on the charge of having designed a scheme involving Milan, Venice, the Pope and other Italian states, and supported by France, that would lead to the expulsion of Charles not only from Northern Italy but also from the Kingdom of Naples (see the introduction to the next debate). Accordingly, the imperial troops occupied Milan (and several fortresses in the Duchy), while Sforza locked himself up in the citadel. Many thought, at that point, that Charles had found the pretext he was looking for to seize Milan.

It is at this time that the debate below was written. The two speeches come from miscellaneous papers and were not included in The History of Italy. *However, Guicciardini does write about this delicate moment in the* History (XVI, x). *The Venetians were once more close to an agreement with Charles,*

> *but this new event which happened at Milan threw the Senate into very great perplexity, being on one hand vastly concerned to find themselves the only power left in Italy to make resistance against Caesar, with the danger, already threatened by the Marquis of Pescara, of having the war transferred into their own dominions (for which purpose there appeared already some preparations), and no less embarrassed, on the other hand, as knowing how mightily an agreement with themselves would facilitate to Caesar the acquisition*

*of the Milanese, which added to so many states, and to so many
other advantages, was the ready way to bring themselves, with all the
rest of Italy, under the yoke. This reflection was enforced by the continual persuasions of the Bishop of Bayeux, whom Madame the
Regentess had appointed to treat of a union between herself and
the Italians against Caesar. In this exigency their consultations were
frequent, but dubious, and full of various opinions; and, though it
were most conformable to their custom to accept of an agreement,
because it removed the present danger, whence they might have
hopes to trust their affairs to length of time, and to opportunities
that republics, which, in comparison to princes, are immortal, have
reason to expect, yet it appeared also to them a matter of too much
importance that Caesar should establish himself in the state of Milan
and that the French should be excluded from all hopes of having
any friend or ally in Italy. Wherefore, being determined at last to
enter into no obligation, they answered the Protonotary Caracciolo
[Charles's ambassador to Venice] that their past conduct was sufficient evidence to every one (and he himself, who had been present
at the conclusion of the [1523] confederacy, was a good witness),
how much they always coveted the friendship of Caesar with whom
they had confederated at a time when their joining with the French
would have been, as everyone knew, of mighty importance, and
that they had always persevered, and now more than ever, in the
same disposition. But that they were of necessity held in suspense by
observing a change of so great importance newly made in Lombardy,
and especially when they reflected that both their confederacy with
Caesar and so many other movements which had been set on foot
of late years in Italy were made for no other end than with a design
that the Duchy of Milan should be settled on Francesco Sforza, as
the principal foundation of the liberty of Italy and the security of all.
Wherefore they entreated His Majesty, that acting in this case suit-
ably to his own temper and known goodness, he would remove this
innovation, and establish the repose of Italy as it was in his power to
do, since he should always find them most readily disposed, both by
their authority and forces, to follow this holy inclination; nor would
they ever give him any cause to charge them with being wanting in
any good office that concerned either the universal good, or his own
particular interests. Although this answer gave no hopes of coming
to an agreement, it did not however produce a rupture and hostilities
because both the increasing by the day of the disorder of the Marquis
of Pescara and Caesar's desire of first making himself master of
the whole state of Milan and to establish that acquisition on a firm*

bottom, and of dispatching so many other affairs which lay upon his hands, gave him no leisure to set about an enterprise of such great moment.

After the King of France had been captured and taken to Spain,[1] the Venetian Senate debated whether they should make an agreement with Caesar,[2] which his ambassador urgently solicited. He who advised against the agreement spoke like this:

— The present consultation, honourable senators, is hard, unusual and almost hopeless, for wherever we turn we run into enormous dangers and difficulties, which are so tangled that one should have qualities that are less human than divine in order to unravel them, for human reason is not enough to see clearly the future in such a snarled situation. Nevertheless, it is our duty, as much as we can, not to put prudence aside or leave our decisions to chance, and therefore not to lose heart but to arm ourselves with fortitude to endure all that might occur. In fact, the greater and the more terrifying the dangers, the more we must help ourselves by prudence and courage, by which, adding the grace of God, this republic has come out of extremely serious situations at other times; and we must not despair that the same will happen now, provided that by helping ourselves we give God cause to help us.

We all believe, from what I have understood in our discussions every day, that Caesar is ill-disposed towards us, and that, out of his aspiration to become master of Italy and the ancient disputes and hatred that he and the House of Austria have against us, he will harm us any time he can, whether we come to terms with him or not; for those motives are more potent in princes than faith and treaties are, especially considering that those who are ill-disposed and stronger never want justifications. Thus, our coming to terms with him secures us neither for ever nor for a long time, but it only entails this effect: while if we do not make an agreement he will perhaps wage war on us at present, if we do he will defer war to another time and occasion. Nor will this delay occur in order to do us benefit and give us advantage – for, given that he intends to oppress us, one must believe that any offer and any friendship of his is insidious – but because the agreement with us conveniently enables him to pursue his other plans with no obstacle from our side, and then to resume oppressing us with more advantage when it will suit him.

We must therefore consider which is greater for us, the benefit of delaying the war against him or the cost of giving him the opportunity to establish his other affairs with no consideration of, and no opposition from, us. I cannot see what benefit delay entails other than postponing dangers and troubles, under the hope that time might bring about some unhoped-for accidents that will free us from this perilous situation; in fact, one of the remedies that the wise usually suggest in adversity is that man should do his best to defer evil as long as he can because once you have time it occasionally so happens that chance frees you from those evils from which your own industry and forces have not been enough to liberate you. And yet this remedy is very fallacious, for it has no foundation other than a fortuitous event; as such, it is good when delay, on the contrary, does not increase the danger and the evil. But when deferring makes danger or evil grow, he who adopts this rule is, in my opinion, like a debtor who, in order to have more time to pay back, accepts huge interests that increase his loss without comparison, or a master of a ship who, cornered by the storm, delays so long in throwing part of his goods overboard to save the rest – in the hope that the tempest might mitigate – that in the end either he does not have the time to save himself or he must throw overboard many more goods than would have been necessary at the beginning.

We find ourselves, if I mistake not, in a similar situation: should we reject the agreement, if we have war now, our enemy will be less able to injure us, and we will have some more hope to be able to help ourselves, than it will be the case later when, having made the agreement now, and having thus enabled him to colour his designs, he will resume making war against us when it suits him. This, did I not see any other reason for it, is sufficiently shown by the fact that Caesar urges us, in every way and with threats, to make the agreement, which he would not do if it did not suit him. And everything that is convenient to him is unfavourable to us, who are afraid of his power; and the man who always wishes, as a rule, the opposite of what his enemy seeks can almost never go wrong. But when things are manifest, there is no need to make conjectures. The affairs of Caesar are in such a condition, and his power is so frightening to everyone, that he must fear that the Pope,[3] the Duke of Milan,[4] the Florentines and we will in the end make an alliance, which is encouraged by the King of England[5] and the French, to break his designs. And he knows that the Italians would be willing to do it if they were sure that the French, out of the hope they are given to have the King back by agreement, did not fail them. Not only would this alliance be sufficient not to let him grow further, but also to beat him in Italy. To which, provided he does not really intend to set the King at liberty, as hitherto indicated by no sign, he has no better remedy than keeping the French in these hopes as much as he can.

But since he cannot reasonably go on for much longer with this artfulness (for either the agreement between them takes place or the French will soon lose all hopes), he must, while keeping the French in suspense, take some step in Italy that will assure him from the danger, or that at least will make him better able to withstand a flood that might hit him. To this purpose, he has no better way than making an agreement with us. Once we have agreed, he will rid himself of the Duke of Milan at once – something that he has already begun to do; once he has rid himself of the Duke, he will do whatever he pleases with the Pope and the Florentines, who will have no escape; and then, when he will want to make war against us, not only will he have deprived us of their company, but he will also avail himself of the money and forces of those states. More importantly, the French, although they will despair of the agreement and will be determined to pass into Italy with great fervour, and will be called on by us, will get much colder as soon as they see that the forces of their enemy have grown much while the foundations of which they would have hoped to avail themselves have failed them. On the contrary, if we do not make this agreement, Caesar will hesitate much more to use force against the Duke, the Pope, the Florentines and the others; and even if he did use force, they, hoping that we will join them, will perhaps think to defend themselves, which they will not be able to think once they have given up hope on us. And if Caesar adds these other foundations to the power he has in Italy, we are left with no way to defend ourselves.

The agreement with us, therefore, gives him the opportunity to secure and establish his affairs; on the contrary, if we do not make the agreement, we keep him more in suspense and in the air; nor do we deprive ourselves of the hope not to be alone at some time. And if one said that, in any case, even if we do not make the agreement, these others will always be spectators, for one cannot hope for an alliance among the Italians unless the Pope decides to head it, and that we have seen so much evidence of his timidity and irresolution that it is clear to us by now that one cannot rely on him,[6] I would reply that once the Duke of Milan, the Pope and the Florentines have been oppressed, we are left with the utmost certainty that we can no longer have them with us. But as long as they are alive, some accidents might occur that would assist us, that is, in case the French, despairing of the negotiations in Spain, decided to pass into Italy; for under these circumstances I believe that the Pope too, who we know for sure dislikes Caesar's power, would seem to see the game so safe that he would take up arms. And even if he did not, the hope of making him declare himself in their favour would make the French and all the others undertake this enterprise more vigorously, while the Imperials, fearing to be attacked by that group too, would have much less courage and reputation. On the contrary, if they are already lost, neither would our enemies have reason to fear them nor our friends to hope for them. Therefore, since our not making the agreement is a means by which we can likely save these others, we must do anything we can to save them, not to their benefit – for if the Pope is not willing to help himself he does not deserve to be helped by others – but for our own safety, and, should the negotiations in Spain ever come to the point that the French, realising they have been deceived, wish to pass into Italy – as I hope will happen soon – to make sure that things are not compromised in such a way that they must desist from this thought.

We may be diverted from such a decision by the fear that Caesar might make a deal with the King of France in which they both agree that we become the prey. Such a deal can come from two causes, the first, that Caesar is inclined to it, as he has always said, the second, that he may be induced to it out of the resentment that he will have against us because we have not wanted to make an agreement with him and the fear of these alliances as soon as the French will be thrown into despair. Thus, our principal danger being the union of these kings, we increase it by our refusal to come to terms with him. To which I reply that I believe that the agreement between the two kings will not take effect, for I cannot see any security in it, especially now that the French, not being concerned about war in France on account of the alliance they made with the King of England,[7] have no need to rush into it out of fear. Thus I think that the French will not accept any agreement in which they must trust that the liberation of the King will be at the discretion of the Emperor, especially now that things have gone on for so long that they have by now been made sensible that Caesar is not induced to set the King at liberty by generosity, desire of peace, or love, but that the agreement will be made either out of necessity or in order to deceive them. For his part, Caesar cannot trust them; nor can he ever have security enough to make him believe that the King of France, once set at liberty, will execute a treaty that will make Caesar the lord of the world and him and the other princes his slaves.

And that this is true is demonstrated by the urgency with which Caesar solicits us to make the agreement, which he would not do if he wanted to settle with the French, because it would be of no use to him. In fact, if he designed to ruin us by the power of that union, it would be more honourable and justifiable to him if he did not make an agreement with us one day only to fail us the next. And should the settlement between the two kings be so disposed as to have to follow because both are inclined to it, it would not follow, neither more nor less, from our decision to make or not to make the agreement with him; therefore, it is pointless to discuss this. Being there no such inclination, as I believe there is not, and being there distrust, as there is by necessity, neither resentment nor fear will make Caesar rush into this agreement. Neither resentment, for he is not of such a nature as to anger if this entails a loss for himself; nor fear, for he will have ways to make sure, by offering some deal to the Italians, that the Pope, the Duke of Milan, we and the others are safe from the fear we have of him – which he could do with more ease and less danger than setting free a King of France who he believes, once liberated, will have reason to be his enemy, in conjunction with all of us.

No doubt, if I mistake not, setting the King of France at liberty out of the fear of the union of many puts Caesar in greater danger than securing himself of us by arranging things in such a way as to make everyone lay aside the suspicion that he wants to make himself lord of Italy, which can be done easily. In addition, even if this agreement between the two kings came into existence, the less we must fear it the better the situation in which the French will find themselves when they make it, and the more the difficulties that will trouble Caesar; for the French will have little reason to put themselves at his discretion, and the more he will be guided by necessity, the less he will be able to lay down the law to them – and under such circumstances, the liberation of the King will likely be the first thing. I ask you: when will the affairs of the French be taken into more consideration, if we make the agreement with Caesar or if we do not? To be sure, for the reasons mentioned above, the affairs of the French will be taken into much less consideration by Caesar if we make the agreement, for they will lose the hope to trouble him in Italy. Therefore, should the two kings come to terms, our settling with Caesar benefits him and enables him to arrange things better to his advantage and, accordingly, our detriment.

In conclusion, either the union between these two kings will take place as a matter of course, in which case it does not matter whether or not we make an agreement with Caesar, or it will not, out of the difficulties it presents, unless resentment or necessity induces him to it, in which case, in my view, our not coming to terms with him will prevent it, for he will have better ways to secure himself of us; and should that union take place, the greater the disadvantage of the French when they make it, the more it will harm us. I admit that this case is so difficult and uncertain that I might very well be wrong, for one might find ways that I do not see to bring security between the two kings, and it might also be that Caesar, considering how things have been going for the past months, has fallen into so great a suspicion of us and the other Italians that trusting the King of France seems less dangerous to him, although this is not likely. Thus, relying on the opinion that it is improbable that Caesar and the King will come to terms is most dangerous and to be avoided, were there another path that we might take more safely. But it seems to me that if we make an agreement with Caesar in order to escape the danger of this union, we head, as I said earlier, towards our certain ruin, and we will find ourselves in such a situation that we can be assisted by nothing but unlikely accidents and events, on which alone it would be folly to rely. Conversely, if we do not make the agreement, we can have the same hope of unexpected future circumstances and there is also some reason to hope to save ourselves.

Thus, if we are certain that this path will lead us to our ruin, it is necessary to take this other path, in which there is much danger, but which is not without hope, which may seem greater to some, lesser to others, but it cannot be denied that there is some. Nor do I take it for granted that if we reject the agreement war will be waged against us at once for, on account of our fortified towns and the ways by which we can defend ourselves, it is not so easy an enterprise that they can hope to take it; and things are conditioned in such a way – and will be all the more so if the two kings do not come to a settlement soon – that our despairing entails for them the danger that we rush to make such generous offers to the French that we create in them a greater desire to pass into Italy than they would normally have had. In addition, the Imperials do not have so much money that they must want to spend it around our extremely well-provided cities only to find themselves worn out in case some huge flood hits them. But even if I were sure that they would make war against us, I would not change my opinion, because it is better for us to have war now when, as I said, our enemies are less fit to injure us than they will be at another time, out of the opportunity they will have to grow most powerful and deprive us of all hopes of assistance by our deal with them. In this, you must show your old prudence and courage, and the fear of present evils must not affect you to the point that, in order to defer them, you end up entering into much greater evils and dangers.

It is the duty of those who govern cities to avoid war as much as one can, but it also becomes their wisdom to anticipate a burdensome and dangerous war in order to avoid a more burdensome and more dangerous one. This may be difficult for others, but it must not be for our republic, which, in addition to her power and the opportunity to defend herself, has had many years of war against these same enemies, and at a time that we had lost so much of our territory that we were left, on land, with nothing but Padua and Treviso, we had lost our army around Vicenza,[8] and we were worn out by enormous expenses;

and yet, in the heat of war, although King Louis [XII],[9] our ally, had been beaten by the English in France[10] and all of Italy and the Swiss had joined with these others,[11] we were courageous enough to reject a deal that under those circumstances was fairly tolerable, for all that we hold now, except for Verona, would have been restored to us. Therefore, since we know these evils only too well, returning to the troubles to which necessity leads us must look less difficult to us; and we must consider that in sustaining war now we lack nothing of that which we are going to have if they make war against us at another time, but that we now enjoy many advantages that will all turn against us at a later moment.

For all these reasons, I advise that we do not make the agreement. I do recommend that we apply every diligence to keep the negotiations open, if this can be done, until we see how the talks that are being held in Spain will affect the relations between the two kings, for our decisions might vary greatly depending on such talks. But if this cannot be done, I advise that we take on a burdensome and dangerous war now rather than deferring it to another time only to have a war entailing a burden and a danger that will be without comparison much greater. —

On the Same Issue. The Opposite View.

— I will leave preambles aside, honourable senators, for we are in such a situation that we need to come to a final decision more than we need speeches, and everyone knows the importance of this deliberation so well that any reference to it would be superfluous. The Emperor is asking us to accept an agreement whose terms are, if not good and appropriate to the dignity of this republic, at least quite tolerable under present circumstances; in fact, the conditions he submits are such that if they contained no other evil than the provisions that he puts in front of us, no one would find it difficult to accept them. He puts in front of us war, in case we reject the agreement, and none of us doubts that this would be a most pernicious war, which we would have to sustain alone against such a powerful and fortunate prince, against an army made of good soldiers and good captains who are held in great esteem because of their cunning, their valour and their repeated victories. Conversely, we are worn out by long and continuous expenses, and we have neither an army equal to that of the enemy – for we have mercenaries whom we gathered hectically where we could find them – nor the number of good captains necessary for the way we intend to adopt to defend our towns; the war must be fought on our territory, which besides being most dangerous on account of the innumerable cases of rebellion and other accidents that may occur, will deprive us at once of all the public and private revenues from our land dominions.

In fact, no development could be worse for us than having this war now; thus, according to the rules that the wise give, it is our duty to delay it for as long as we can, and do anything in order to defer the start of this evil, which we fear, for as long as one can, given that human affairs are so subject to change that infinite cases of death and other accidents we cannot think of may occur over time, which would free us from this trouble; and, as the proverb has it, he who has time, has life. But one cannot defer war if not by making this agreement, which is, in the end, the lesser evil among the bad choices. To which the person who spoke before me has replied that temporising would be good if it did not increase the evil, but that the longer you defer, the greater the evil becomes, for our agreement would enable our enemy to appropriate himself completely of the state of Milan, and arrange things with the Pope and the Florentines as it suits him, so that should it ever come the time that the French despaired of the settlement between the two kings and intended to pass into Italy, either they would not dare to do it, because they would see that their enemies had grown so much in power and reputation or, if they did, we would be weaker on account of the fact that the Imperials would avail themselves of the money and the dominions of those who would perhaps have joined us, had they preserved themselves. Therefore, we should do anything we can so that it is not so easy for the Imperials to arrange the rest of Italy to their advantage and the French do not want the courage to pass; and all the more so, since the talks in Spain have reached such a point that, predictably, either an agreement will follow soon or the French will despair of having peace and will perhaps turn to war.

On this, I am of a different opinion, for it does not seem to me that if war were deferred to another time it must bring greater difficulties and dangers than it must bring now; in fact, it appears to me that it will have the same features then as it has now – if you examine the case well. First of all, the Duchy of Milan finds itself in such a situation that, whether or not we make the agreement, it has no remedy, because the Imperials hold all its territory, except for the city, which neither is supported by anybody nor does it have any forces or assistance at all, and since they captured [Girolamo] Morone all the vigour that was there has been removed; the Duke is of no use on account of his serious illness and because he normally is neither wise nor courageous, so that there is the danger, in my view, that not only the city but also the castle will capitulate. As for the rest of Italy, there is no need to talk about it, for it all depends on the Pope, who is so timid and irresolute that he abandons himself to certain death rather than wanting to run the danger of dying, and in effect he will not move unless under most safe conditions, that is, unless the French and the rest of the world move. Thus, the preservation of the Pope and the Florentines is of little or no moment to us, because one cannot expect any resoluteness from them and they are so utterly disarmed that, without being forced otherwise, they will provide the Imperials with money and all that they are demanded as soon as they receive the minimum request from them. I do not see, therefore, how their preservation is so useful to us that we have to make war on its account, especially because, in my opinion, what we can hope for from the King of France at another time is no different from what we have seen in the past months, for the same reasons will always be there, and perhaps some more.

If the two kings make peace – which I do not believe on account of the difficulties that have been wisely mentioned – this is bad news for us; but it will be even worse if we will not have made the agreement, for in this case, with no regard and no further justification, our enemies will immediately wage war on us. Conversely, if we will have settled, this prince, who rightly or wrongly professes faith and goodness, will perhaps be ashamed to break the agreement before the ink of the treaty is dry. Nor do I expect that the peace between them can be such that the King of France must not observe it, for security will be greater on the side of the Emperor, who has the game in hand; and even if the two kings were equally strong, the Spanish are so much more astute that they will always fool the French.

If these two kings do not make peace, I do not expect better, for the Spanish will not lack the artfulness to drag the talks out so that they will easily keep the simple-mindedness of the French in hope for longer, especially because Madame [the Regentess],[12] who holds power, is a woman and a mother who will unwillingly abandon such hopes. And even if the French despaired of the agreement, I do not hope that they will undertake this enterprise in Italy, because now that they have made an alliance with the King of England they no longer fear war in France. Thus, they are not affected by the necessity to secure themselves, especially because it becomes their natural inclination not to take future dangers into consideration and not rate highly the things that are not yet present. Both the noblemen and the people are tired and naturally abhor the enterprise of Italy, where they have lost so much of their nobility; they have been beaten so many times that they have in horror the very name of this country; the hope to recover their King by a war in Italy will not make them move, for it is too distant a thing; the government, in addition to the King's mother, is in the hands of several princes, not all of whom, perhaps, desire the liberation of the King; they are of various opinions, jealous of one another and, as Frenchmen, full of frivolousness and vanity, debased by so many blows, from whom we cannot expect a prudent or manly enterprise.

We will thus draw upon ourselves a war at this time under hopes that, in my view, will fail us, and we will lose those benefits that time occasionally brings. Conversely, if we make the agreement, war is delayed, and in the mean time some assistance, which we do not yet see, may come to our affairs; nor do we prevent the French from coming into Italy by this agreement, in case they were inclined to do it and it seemed to us that the conduct of Caesar were such that it would be convenient for us to bring them. For, having the Swiss and us with them, even if the Imperials have occupied the state of Milan and beaten the rest of the Italians, the French can vigorously attempt this enterprise; of which we have seen evidence, for they have done it at other times, with less opportunity and more obstacles.

In the first enterprise that he undertook in Italy after his crowning,[13] this King who is now held prisoner was opposed by the Emperor,[14] the King of Spain,[15] the Swiss, Pope Leo [X],[16] the Florentines and all of Italy, except for us. And yet, with our help alone, he was bold enough to do it, and he conquered. Therefore, should we be so inclined, he could attempt this enterprise all the more now that he will be encouraged and perhaps assisted by the King of England. He would have on his side the Swiss, who are of greatest moment to the affairs of Milan; the peoples of the Duchy, who out of their desire for just that Duke, would be hostile to the Imperials should they become the lords of that state. As for the rest of the Italians, the more they are oppressed by Caesar, the more they will perhaps react vigorously out of despair on this occasion, or at least he would not take from the Pope and the others the advantage he hoped to if they joined with him voluntarily. Our agreement with Caesar, therefore, would not deprive the French of the way of passing into Italy, if we refused to side with him by not keeping faith and not observing the treaty. But this is no time to discuss such a matter or to compromise the faith of our republic for no reason, for I would always recommend observing agreements, unless they are made from fear and force, because in this case they obligate our word more than our will, and the ambition and the proceedings of those with whom we have settled are such as to teach us what measures we must take.

I furthermore believe that there are three things that we must fear: a war now, that is, at a time when the French are still attached to hopes of peace, for as long as they entertain such a folly, we cannot rely on them, being they blinded by this expectation, nor on the Pope and the other

Italians, who remain irresolute out of the fear that the two kings will make peace; nor can we hope not to bear the consequences of all this. We have to fear, like the others, peace between these two kings, which, should it be signed, will include explicit articles to our disadvantage. Lastly, we have to fear that, if such peace is not made, the Emperor, after either passing into Italy or reinvigorating and establishing his affairs well by other means, will wage war against us.

In all these dangers, if I mistake not, our disadvantage is greater if we do not make the agreement than if we do. Concerning war at present and at a time when the French still hang on the hopes of peace, if we make the agreement we free ourselves from this danger, for our coming to terms will no doubt defer war for so long that the Imperials will become certain [of our good disposition]. If we do not make the agreement, we must fear war at present, as is made manifest to us – of which I will speak below. As for the second case, that the two kings make peace and the Emperor wants to attack us, to have or not have made the agreement neither benefits nor harms us; yet, the shame from violating a treaty barely signed and the want of any semblance of justification might be a bridle on him capable of at least deferring war for some time. Thus in this case the fact of our having made the agreement cannot harm us; rather, it can be useful in providing us with at least some delay, which is of no little benefit to those who are in a difficult situation. In the third case, that the French despair of having peace, I do not see how our agreement with Caesar can harm us, for if he will want to injure us we will be able to avail ourselves of the French – should they intend to pass into Italy – the same as if we had not made the agreement; above all, their and our forces, and those of the Swiss, will be enough for any enterprise. And the benefit for which we will be able to hope from the Pope and the other Italians is in this case neither so great nor certain as to make us relinquish the benefit of time, from which we can hope for much more. And if the Emperor, although ill-disposed towards us, is inclined to make war in France first rather than to injure us, this enterprise might carry so many difficulties and accidents that such a very long delay would be our preservation.

Therefore, in any of these three cases on which our dangers depend, the fact of our having made the agreement brings us some fruit or does not harm us to the point that it is not much more useful to enjoy, as the wise say, the benefit of time. And since the most important danger is the peace between the two kings – for in this case we might be crushed between the forces of one and the other, nor could we hope for assistance from anybody – it is not to be doubted that our rejection of the agreement with Caesar is one of the major reasons that may dispose him to such peace, for he will be certain that we are ready to call the French into Italy and make some alliance that will be dangerous to his power, which he cannot prevent more safely than by making peace with the King of France, provided he finds a means that enables him to secure himself of the King at least for some time, which he does not lack. And this will be more useful to him than seeking to assure Italy against his power, for he cannot do this unless he leaves the state of Milan free to the Duke, withdraws all his troops to the Kingdom of Naples, and gives up thoughts of passing into Italy with his person. Not only can he not reassure us without compromising his own position, but also he would lose all the opportunities and hopes to acquire new dominions that the capture of the King of France has given him; nor would he gain from this victory anything but the person of the King held in prison, which would be of no use. Thus it is to be believed that he will seek to gain dominance of Italy by setting the King at liberty rather than gaining nothing by keeping him prisoner.

If we do not make the agreement with Caesar, therefore, we facilitate the peace with the King, which is most pernicious to us. And since all our dangers are very great, but these two are the greatest, that is, the peace between the kings and war now, if we do not make the agreement we almost make it necessary for the Emperor to make the peace; and once this is done, we are no doubt left abandoned by all and at his discretion. Further, if we do not make the agreement, we draw upon ourselves the war, which I believe they would wage on us, for although they are forced anyway to keep their army as it is as long as the talks in Spain remain in suspense, they are not increasing their expenses: they will feed their troops off our territory, from which they plan to draw revenues and advantages, and lighten the burden on theirs. By being at war, they maintain the reputation of their arms; and their captains, above all the Marquis of Pescara,[17] wish to have the opportunity to obtain some good results useful to Caesar. They will not be subject to the danger of losing anything, and should they manage to seize one of our cities they would pierce us with a sword that we will not remove at our leisure. Nor will they take into consideration the danger of inciting us to make generous offers to the French, for after seeing that we have rejected the agreement, they will be certain that, without being otherwise incited, this is our design anyway; in fact, they will be of the opinion that making us spend money is an appropriate way to thwart our intentions.

In sum, I believe that if we do not make the agreement we will have war at present – and a war so troublesome and dangerous that we must do anything to escape it, or at least defer it for as long as one can, especially because delay can bring us immense benefits and the liberation from all these evils; nor can it do us any harm of great moment, in my view. It is our duty to remember that human affairs are so uncertain and subject to so numerous and various accidents that even the wise cannot assess the future, and only rarely does anything occur that has been conjectured by them. Therefore, they often deceive themselves who at present deprive themselves of a good or undergo an evil out of fear of what is to come, for many times what they have feared does not come to pass and they end up suffering at present for no purpose on account of a vain and uncertain fear. I do recommend that, as he who has spoken before me wisely said, we attempt everything one can to keep the negotiations going without breaking them, although things are so constrained that we can have little hope of this; but should it be necessary either to make the agreement at present or make war, I judge that making the agreement is without comparison the lesser evil. And may our Lord God enlighten your mind by His grace as you address such decisions. —

Notes

1. Francis I of Valois, King of France from 1515 to 1547, fell into the hands of the Imperials at the battle of Pavia in February 1525 and was taken to Spain in June.
2. Charles V of Habsburg, King of Spain from 1516 to 1556 and Holy Roman Emperor from 1519 to 1556.
3. Giulio de' Medici, pope as Clement VII from 1523 to 1535.
4. Francesco II Sforza, Duke of Milan from 1521 to 1535.
5. Henry VIII Tudor, King of England from 1509 to 1547.
6. On the 'timidity' and 'irresolution' of the Pope, see the next debate.
7. On 30 August 1525.
8. Battle of La Motta, 7 October 1513.
9. Louis XII of Orléans, King of France from 1498 to 1515.
10. Battle of Guinegate, 16 August 1513.
11. The Holy League of 1511.
12. Louise of Savoy (1476–1531), King Francis's mother.
13. In 1515.
14. Maximilian I of Habsburg, Holy Roman Emperor from 1493 to 1519.
15. Ferdinand II of Aragon, King of Aragon from 1479 to 1516 and Regent of Castile from 1506 to 1516.
16. Giovanni de' Medici, pope as Leo X from 1513 to 1521.
17. Fernando Francisco de Ávalos Aquino y Cardona (1490–1525), commander of the imperial forces in Italy.

Chapter 10

On Whether the Pope Should Make an Agreement with the Emperor or Wage War against Him*

When Cardinal Giulio de' Medici was elected pope as Clement VII, on 19 November 1523, many expected that he would be an important ally to Charles V, Holy Roman Emperor, in his struggle against Francis I, King of France. After all, the Cardinal had been the leader of the philo-imperial movement at the Roman Curia for quite some time, for he believed that a concerted effort with the Emperor was necessary not only to oppose the spread of Lutheranism but also to rid the Church of the French presence in Lombardy, as Francis's seizure of the Duchy of Milan, in 1515, had resulted in a serious constraint on any further expansion of the papal dominions in the Po Valley. In the last period of the pontificate of Leo X – the previous Medici pope – the Cardinal supported the creation of an anti-French alliance with Charles (May 1521). The military operations, in which he participated in person as Pontifical Legate, led to the expulsion of the French from Milan – where Francesco Sforza was proclaimed duke – and the papal occupation of Piacenza and Parma, in the autumn of 1521. Similarly, during the brief pontificate of Adrian VI (1522–3), the Cardinal played an active role in convincing the Pope to sign another anti-French alliance with the Emperor in August 1523. More generally, as Guicciardini writes in The History of Italy *(XVI, i),*

> *during the reign of Leo [X] and after his own promotion to the cardinalship, he took a world of pains for advancing the grandeur of Caesar, and [. . .] Leo and he, with excessive cost and danger, opened the way to so great a power in Italy.*

---

* 'Ragioni che consigliano a Clemente VII di accordare con Carlo V' and 'Sullo stesso argomento. In contrario', in Francesco Guicciardini, *Opere*, vol. VIII: *Scritti politici e Ricordi*, ed. by R. Palmarocchi, Bari: Laterza, 1933, pp. 162–77 and 178–97, respectively.

In light of all this, it is not surprising that Charles looked at Cardinal de' Medici as a most reliable friend and supported his election with all his influence (and quite a lot of money).

Yet, after his assumption to the Pontificate,

> *either on considering that it belonged to his office to act as a father and common pastor between Christian princes, and to be rather a peacemaker than a fomenter of wars, or beginning, though late, to be alarmed at so much power, (ibid.)*

Clement's attitude vis-à-vis the Emperor became more reserved. One of the ostensible causes of concern was that Francesco Sforza had not received the imperial investiture for Milan, which led many to suspect that Charles intended somehow to annex the Duchy. More generally, Clement seemed to resume the traditional policy of the popes, who had always been alarmed at the possibility that too vast a concentration of power in the hands of a single ruler – any Italian state or, possibly even worse, a Holy Roman Emperor – would be detrimental to the authority and independence of the Church. Although Clement observed the terms of the 1523 alliance, he notified the Emperor that he would not renew it the following year; in fact, he launched a series of peace initiatives, always underlining his impartial and neutral stand. And when Charles decided to continue his war against Francis by invading Provence in the summer of 1524, Clement flatly refused to help him financially, arguing that the existing alliance had only a defensive nature. Relations between the Emperor and the Pope thus began to deteriorate.

In the autumn of the same year, Francis passed into Italy again, occupied Milan and lay siege to Pavia. As he seemed about to defeat the Imperials, Clement, while still putting forward peace proposals that both sides rejected, made a secret agreement with him, by which he pledged not to assist Charles, in return for a French guarantee to the dominions of the Church and the Medici government in Florence (12 December 1524). Shortly afterwards, Francis asked Clement to grant passage across his territory to the Duke of Albany, who, at the head of a French contingent, was to engage in a diversionary attack upon the Kingdom of Naples for the sake of distracting the Imperials from the war in Lombardy. The Pope did his best to make the King change his mind:

> *Clement was no ways uneasy at the King's getting possession of the Duchy Milan, because he imagined that whilst Charles and Francis had both a footing in Italy, the Apostolic See, and his Pontificate,*

would be secure from the power of both; and for this very reason
he could not be pleased at the King's making himself master of the
Kingdom of Naples, dreading that a prince, already so powerful,
should be master at the same time of that Kingdom and the Duchy.
(ibid., XV, xiii)

But this was to no avail. At this point, deeply embarrassed, he was
forced to inform Charles of his deal with the French king, to which the
Emperor reacted with an angry letter.

    Understandably, after the French disaster at Pavia (24 February
1525) and Francis's imprisonment at the hands of the Imperials, Clement
thought that his fate was sealed. However, the dire financial conditions
in which the victorious army found itself, and the Emperor's need to
establish his affairs firmly before taking any further step, were conducive to an agreement (1 April 1525) between the Pope and the Viceroy
of Naples, the representative of Charles in Italy: in return for large sums
of money to be paid by him and the Florentines, Clement obtained a
guarantee of his dominions, the promise that the cities of which he had
been bereaved by the Duke of Ferrara would be restored to him, as
well as other concessions. In addition, both the Emperor and the Pope
pledged to defend the Duchy of Milan, which, for the time being was
assigned to Francesco Sforza under the Emperor's protection. Shortly
afterwards, the Pope received vast offers from the Regentess of France,
who promised to finance the war effort, in case he – and the Venetians –
took up arms against the Emperor. Clement decided to observe scrupu-
lously the treaty just signed but, much to his disappointment, he came
soon to realise that the Imperials were not doing the same:

For they would not accept, in part of the money promised, the
twenty-five thousand ducats paid by the Florentines according to
his orders while the agreement was under negotiation, the Viceroy
having the conscience to pretend that if it had been stipulated other-
wise it had been done without his commission. The soldiers also had
not evacuated the dominions of the Church, but, on the contrary,
the Piacentine was full of garrisons. These hardships inflicted by
the Caesareans [. . .] perhaps might in some measure be excused by
their want of money and quarters [. . .]. But what above all things
gave him most uneasiness was the Viceroy's hearkening to the Duke
of Ferrara and giving him hopes that he would not compel him to
evacuate Reggio and Rubiera and to prevail with Caesar to take his
state under his protection, though he had every day promised the
Pontiff that as soon as the Florentines had finished their payments

he would put him in possession of those towns [. . .]. This being a point not excusable by a want of money, for there would be a larger sum coming to him [from Clement] on account of the restitution of those towns, it gave room for probable conjectures that it proceeded either from a desire to humble the Pope, or to gain over the Duke of Ferrara, or from a design, which they constantly had in view, to oppress the liberties of Italy. (ibid., XVI, vii)

To make matters even worse, Charles did not ratify the April agreement in its entirety, and this led to further suspicion and concern, and to endless negotiations.

During the summer, Clement moved closer and closer to the Venetians and the French, both of whom had been steadily calling on him to participate in an anti-imperial coalition. Although reluctant at first – he, just like the Venetians, feared that the Regentess was simply interested in exerting pressure on Charles in order to induce him to revise the immoderate terms he had imposed for Francis's liberation – the Pope seemed finally to make up his mind when he heard that the Emperor intended to pass into Italy to be crowned: this 'created him vast uneasiness, both from the condition of the present times, and from the inveterate disposition of the Roman pontiffs, to whom nothing used to be more dreadful than the coming of Roman emperors armed into Italy' (ibid., XVI, viii). By then, Clement was also involved in a parallel design orchestrated by the Duke of Milan's chancellor, Girolamo Morone. The scheme, which bordered on the fantastic, was as follows. It was well known that the Marquis of Pescara, the commander of the imperial army in Italy, born to a Spanish family in Naples, was dissatisfied with the manner in which Charles had rewarded him after his exploit at Pavia. A proposal was to be put to the Marquis that he would betray the Emperor, and, at the head of an army made of his own available troops and papal–Venetian forces, and with the support of France, and possibly England, attack and take Naples, of which he would be crowned king by Clement. In this way, not only would Charles be prevented from seizing the Duchy of Milan, but he would be expelled from Naples too, and all of Italy finally liberated from his threat. When the Marquis was approached by Morone, he hesitated for a while; then, probably realising that the plan could not possibly succeed, he informed Charles, who ordered him to play along, for the sake of gaining time and compromising the Italians more and more. Finally, Morone was imprisoned on 14 October; he 'gave an ample detail of the whole proceeding of the conspiracy, accusing the Duke of Milan as privy to everything, which was the chief point in view' (ibid., XVI, x). As a result, Milan was immedi-

ately occupied by the imperial army, and all Italy, at this point, seemed to be at Charles's discretion. Even more importantly, for our present purposes, this was the second time, in less than one year, that the Pope had double-crossed the Emperor. Negotiations were still under way, on the basis of the April agreement and its subsequent modifications. What should the Pope do, at this point? Should he come to terms with Charles or should he go ahead with the alliance against him? The two speeches below deal with Clement's predicament at this juncture.

Unlike all the other situations addressed by the debates of the present collection, in this case Guicciardini was personally involved. Besides being a top official of the State of the Church, he knew Clement very well, not only because they were both Florentine patricians, but also because they had interacted on a regular basis for years, by correspondence, and in person, at the time of the 1521 campaign against the French, in which they both took part. When Clement became pope, he appointed Guicciardini to the Presidency of Romagna. It is from there that, after hearing of the French catastrophe at Pavia, he began to send letters to Rome, warning against the imperial threat. The speeches were written some time in the autumn. To be more precise, the second speaker makes an explicit reference to the desperate health condition of the Marquis of Pescara – and the Marquis will die on 3 December. Although the debate was not included in The History of Italy, *the reader can find a concise summary of the two opposite views in XVI, xii, leading, in the following chapter, to a magisterial psychological portrait of the Pope and the presentation of his two main advisers.*

Of the ministry those who had a mighty interest with him were [Archbishop] Nikolaus [von] Schoenberg, a German, and [Bishop] Gian Matteo Giberti, a Genoese, the former reverenced, and in a manner feared by the Pontiff, the latter very acceptable, and greatly beloved by him [. . .]. Nikolaus, on account of a national tie, or for some other respect, being devoted to the interest of Caesar, and by nature obstinately attached to his own opinions, which often differenced from those of others, so immoderately favoured the cause of Caesar, that he was often suspected by the Pontiff as one who had more concern for the interests of others than for those of his master. The other in truth knew no other patron, or object of his affection, than the Pontiff; but, being naturally eager and vehement in the management of his affairs, though in the time of Leo [X] he had been a most bitter enemy to the French and a favourer of Caesar's cause, yet since his death he was become quite the contrary. Hence those two ministers, who bore the greatest sway with the Pontiff, being at

*open variance, and not proceeding with maturity, or with any regard
to the honour of their master, but exposing his coldness and irresolution to all the Court, rendered him contemptible and in a manner
ridiculous to the generality of mankind. As he was then by nature
irresolute, and those whose duty it was to assist him in coming to a
determination on so difficult and perplexed an affair helped only to
increase his doubts and confusion, he knew not which way to turn
himself.*

*It is quite evident that Guicciardini must have had these two men in
mind when he wrote the speeches. Among other things, the first speaker
says that he is not Italian, knows that he is suspected of being too
close to the Emperor, and is referred to, by the second speaker, as 'the
Archbishop' – all of which makes it easy to identify him as Schoenberg.
Since Giberti was, as has been said, the other main advisor to the Pope,
it is plausible to attribute the second speech to him. We should keep in
mind, in addition, that Giberti and Guicciardini held exactly the same
views on the issue under discussion.*

*Guicciardini was called to Rome to join the group of the Pope's
advisers in January 1526 and immediately became one of the promot-
ers of an anti-Imperial alliance. As the French King, once set at liberty
(March 1526), made it clear that he had no intention of observing the
terms of the agreement he had just signed, the alliance of Venice, Milan,
the Church and France finally materialised (League of Cognac, 22 May
1526). Following his appointment as Lieutenant General of the papal
army, however, Guicciardini was to be an impotent witness to the hes-
itations of the military commanders and the allied governments that
would allow the Landsknechts to storm and sack Rome in May 1527.*

After the arrival of the [papal] delegate[1] at the court of Caesar[2] and the
departure of Madame d'Alençon,[3] which entailed the rupture of the
peace negotiations between the French and the Emperor, it was being
debated before Pope Clement [VII][4] whether His Holiness should make
a new confederacy with Caesar, as he was offered under honest and
reasonable conditions, or temporise to see the resolutions of the French.
About which, he who recommended that His Holiness should make a
viable agreement with the Emperor spoke as follows:

— I shall speak more out of obedience to Your Holiness than in a spon-
taneous manner, since I have seen not so much that my counsels have
not been accepted – of which a servant cannot complain – but that I
have become suspect as being too affectionate towards Caesar's inter-

ests. And yet, had I been believed, you and the other Italian states would not be in the troubles in which you are now. For, had you continued, after assuming the papacy, to favour that side that was obliged, and in a manner a slave, to you on account of your bringing about its greatness, and not begun to promise your neutrality to the King[5] by sending your ambassador all the way to France, he would have been likely not to pass into Italy, and Caesar's power would not have grown so much as to be fearsome to Your Beatitude. In fact, feeling obliged to you, and having the need to preserve your friendship, Caesar would have always been a most obedient son to you. And had you decided to be neutral, either in order to escape expenses, or because this seemed to you a safer way, or a course of conduct more appropriate to a pontiff, and always kept a strict neutrality – as I also recommended – and had not given umbrage to the Imperials by making a treaty with the King of France at the peak of the war, and affronted them by permitting the ammunition to pass [through your dominions][6] and by granting passage to the Duke of Albany[7] [on his way to the Kingdom of Naples], and availed yourself, with no need whatsoever, of his troops for the affairs concerning Siena, only to make their complaints and suspicions arouse more[8] – had you, I say, kept a strict neutrality, Caesar's victory at Pavia would not frighten you so much that in order to escape ruin you are now forced to make a new agreement with him and lose much of your dignity.

And, after so many troubles, had you trusted more what I was saying about Caesar's good disposition and his devotion to the Apostolic Seat, and had you not allowed those who wish to have it overturned to persuade you of the contrary, and not attributed to him that which proceeded from some of his officers in Italy, in part out of their malice, in part out of the condition of the times, you would not have become involved in any negotiation against Caesar; and having considered how powerful he was, and how established his victory, you would have relied more on temporising with him, conciliating his affections and not giving him any just cause for complaint and suspicion than on the levity of those who claimed that what could not possibly succeed was in fact easy.

Now that the disease is almost incurable, and that one has made the Emperor sensible that not only would one willingly hinder his actions but has also attempted to bereave him of the Kingdom of Naples, and that the greater the sores, the more requisite an attentive doctor and a proved medicine should be, one attempts to remedy the past errors by new errors, more pernicious than the former, to make hasty decisions on most important matters on the grounds of a necessity that your bad counsellors themselves have created by their perverse advice, citing

as evidence and justification not reason but despair, and calling courage and fortitude that which proceeds from the utmost cowardice and
timidity. I, Your Holiness, since you wish me to speak, do not see how,
if you take up arms, you can entertain any likely hope of victory; nor do
I despair that, once you have truly broken all the negotiations that you
are holding against Caesar, a good concord with him – if you want to
have it – can be obtained as conveniently as the condition of the times
allows. And I will strive to demonstrate both things.

I believe that he who wishes to form a judgement about whom shall
win a war will first consider the armies, and which is better, that is, on
which side the better captains and troops are – which, in this case, could
not be more manifest. The imperial captains, by now, are old, crafty,
experienced, very reputed, and no evidence of their valour is necessary
other than the deeds they have accomplished and the many victories
they have won by courage and industry, so that their quality cannot
be put in doubt. Their troops too are excellent, their sinews being the
Spanish and the Germans, both of whom are vigorous and resolute
peoples; the former, moreover, are most agile and industrious, and the
latter, confident in their discipline and organisation, are soldiers who
have exercised themselves in these Italian wars and are accustomed to
conquer: their captains know who they are, and they know their captains. They love military honour and glory, which they hold in the highest regard, are devoted to their prince, and consider that satisfying him
is no little gain and that, conversely, failing him is no little loss. They
hope that victory will make Italy their prey, [and fear] that defeat would
not only make them lose what they possess and the high rank they know
they have in this country but also endanger their life. Everyone knows
with what respect they are held and how feared they are; their very
name, and the fact that it terrifies all of Italy, will always be of great
moment for victory in any war.

Let us now compare all this with the conditions of these others, and
we shall see of what means you can avail yourself to conquer. First,
concerning the generals, if they must be Italian, the heads are to be the
Duke of Ferrara,[9] if he will join the league, and the Duke of Urbino;[10] if
French, the best one they have is Lautrec, who has been defeated by the
same enemies in the past, as he was in Milan;[11] therefore, not to mention
his other qualities, which are in any case well known, you can imagine
what reputation he will carry with him or with what courage he will
move against them. The Duke of Ferrara has little experience of war,
and when he has waged it he has not done much more than the managing of artillery.[12] Those who are informed about his last enterprise
aimed at the recovery of Modena have always affirmed that this under-

taking was managed with little courage and in a disorderly manner.[13] I admit that he has a greater reputation than anyone else in Italy, and that, out of his greatness, the other lords will conform with his views with no difficulty; but this is not sufficient against enemies who are to be chased away with the sword, and not with cries. And seeing a duke march out in the field will not much scare those who have defeated and captured a king of France along with all the nobility of such a kingdom. One relies, as far as I understand, on the Duke of Urbino, which I do not deplore; yet, in his case too, we have not witnessed any such experience on his part as to lay the stress of so great an enterprise entirely upon his shoulders.

To command six or eight thousand men is one thing; but to be the general of such an army is a different business, especially against vigorous, crafty and experienced enemies, and in an enterprise in which one can find oneself under the necessity of managing all sorts of military arts: marching out in the open field, defending and taking towns, inviting the enemies to come to battle, attempting to temporise without fighting, now relying on force, now knowing how to put the advantages at one's disposal to effective use. Therefore, if you tell me that, in this army, nobody can be trusted upon more than these men, I will easily concede as much; but if you tell me that they are such as to be sufficient for so great an enterprise, I shall hush out of respect but, having not witnessed any other experience, I would not be inclined to affirm so.

Nor do I intend to omit that I know Your Holiness has no greater enemy in Italy, and perhaps the entire world, than these two dukes. One has been bereaved of his dominions, part of which is still occupied, and the other has been made to suffer as many persecutions as anybody knows, which have continued under any circumstance and at any time until yesterday, until this morning;[14] nor have any means, entreaties, humiliations, offers ever been able to mitigate these harsh treatments, in either case; and any promise, blandishment, offer of reconciliation made to them has been an instance of simulation, a plot; so that they can be certain that they would find themselves in the same situation under any new circumstance. Thus I do not know how you can be willing to rely on them, entrust your state to them, believe that they will labour for your greatness, which they will always fear. I have never been in favour of persecuting them, not seeing what we could gain from it, if not many imputations and much loss; but I am not disposed either to encourage you light-heartedly to entrust yourself to them so fearlessly.[15] I wish to God that those who advise you so to do will have, to speak modestly, better fortune in this course than they had in advising you to injure them.

It remains to compare the quality of the troops, which is too manifest a thing. The sinews of your infantry will be the Swiss, on whose usual temper and the difficulties one has in managing them I do not intend to comment; but they have been beaten so many times by these enemies, and are so dispirited – as everyone admits – that I believe they cannot tolerate the sight of them any more, let alone sustain them. You will have no Landsknechts, or only a few; nor could you trust a large number of them in a war against Caesar.[16] It will thus be requisite to rely upon a very great body of Italians, of whom I shall speak mannerly, because I come from another nation; but an endless number of experiences have shown what little stress can be laid on them and that they cannot be compared to foreign infantries. Nor do I mean that this results from want of valour in the men, as rather perhaps from the condition of the times and circumstances of Italy, and the ways and places in which they have been put to use. They have not exercised themselves in ordered lines of battle, like the Germans; they do not have a prince whom they wish to satisfy, like the Spanish. Wars, in Italy, have been made in the name and company of foreigners for a long time now, so that the men cannot be influenced by the desire to satisfy a prince of theirs; nor have they had the opportunity to take the glory of their nation as an aim. If they were in service out of Italy, perhaps they would be more united among themselves, more firm in the face of danger, more obedient, less mutinous, and would better tolerate the delay of their pay; nor would they leave as soon as they receive the money. Be that as it may, they have all these defects.

Should you have to avail yourself of only five or six thousand Italian foot, I would believe that you could perhaps find as many of such a quality as to face any danger; but since you need a larger number, you will find yourself disappointed. What do you expect from an army hastily drawn from this muddle of men, very many of whom have never seen war, an army of so many pieces, of so many bishoprics? Will you put it to use safely against the Spanish, among whom many foot perform the office of captain and many captains are skilled enough to be generals? So good a disposition of all the members of their army has procured much honour for the generals, for before the dangers come one can rely on many men to whose opinion it is useful to listen, and in the midst of dangers not only do they observe and execute well the orders of their captains, but they also, in case of need, know how to make use of themselves, which is of great advantage to the captains who are in some trouble, as one reads about [Julius] Caesar. And truly, the good qualities of their chiefs make the valour of the foot useful, and not only is the valour of the foot so great as to perform their offices well, but it also allows the captains to produce better effects.

I ask you: considering these disadvantages, on what is the hope to win founded? It is requisite either that you rely on being so much more numerous than they are as to prevent them from marching out and on defeating them in the towns; or that, should they be as powerful as to march out, since I do not believe that you design to fight them, your temporising will occasion disorder among them on account of a lack of money; or that, while the game is being kept in suspense in Lombardy, one lights another fire in the Kingdom of Naples, where one makes such progress as, by conquering down there, to strengthen your reputation and forces and weaken the enemies, so that victory in Lombardy will become easier. Now I pray you to listen patiently to all the fallacies that you take upon yourself.

In the first place, I do not believe that the Spanish will shut themselves up in the towns, for if they add eight or ten thousand Landsknechts to the forces they have now – which they can do most easily – they will be able to face any army of yours, because they will always have additional men, even if your army were greater. And when armies are so large it matters little that the enemies exceed you by four or five thousand men, for not all of them fight anyway. And even if they did not march out at present, I ask you whether you count on storming the towns or taking them with the benefit of time. If you rely on force, you deceive yourself, for even if the Imperials designed to abandon Milan and Cremona, Lodi, Pavia and Alessandria are fortified towns and will be guarded in such a manner that one will not be able to reduce them by force but with the greatest difficulty. So that, after making you wander around those towns for two or three months – as they did with the French at the siege of Pavia – they will march out, larger in number, and it will be as if war had just begun, except that your army, having lodged already in the open air for a long time, in the heart of winter, will be less rested and more disordered than theirs, for they will have always lodged in the towns with leisure. Thus, it is requisite to be prepared to see them march out, at the beginning or shortly after. And if you intend to come to battle, it will be too disadvantageous for you; nor could you ever make a more imprudent resolution, or one that you will regret more. And if you decide not to have a battle but to temporise, look how weak your position is already, for you undertake an enterprise to conquer a state, and you do it well resolved not to fight against your enemies because you judge them to be more powerful than you are.

But let us insist further. If they approach your army, as they will certainly do, since they know their advantage and your timidity, what will you do? Do you not know that when two armies are in close proximity a number of occurrences may happen so that one has to fight out of necessity, especially when one of the parties so wishes? Not to mention that, by attempting to hinder you from procuring your provisions or by other arts, they will be able to force you either to fight or to retreat, of which one would be against your resolution, and the other would be done with great danger and considerable loss of reputation when the enemies are near.

But let us presume that you can maintain your interests without coming to an engagement: what will you gain out of temporising? Do you think that they will lack the money to sustain themselves? You have seen how vain this design has been in the campaigns against the French, for the Imperials had money for longer than expected, and when they wanted it their troops, their foot, remained in service for several months without pay. Now the same will happen, and much more so, for Caesar, as I shall say below, has more money now than he had then, and his troops will bear the delay more patiently, having seen that they received payment in the end, the other time; and as soon as they are one or two months in arrears, which is likely to happen, their desire not to lose what is due to them for their service will be like a pledge, for it will make them stand still.

But tell me: will this temporising benefit you? One of your foundations is the Swiss, whose impatience is known to all. Do you not know that your party will be made of so many bishoprics and will be dependent on so many heads and wills that if only one of them varies it will ruin everything?

There are two reasons why the enterprises that are undertaken by many against one fail, although the former are more powerful than the latter. The first is that the provisions do not always concur all at the same time, for when one has concluded the necessary preparations, the other has just begun, the other still is not ready at all, so that, since only rarely do things turn out according to the plan, the results one has imagined while sitting at one's desk do not become real. The second is that, since motion depends on many, if one fails to do his duty everything falls into disorder, and when many are involved and time is given, it is likely that one fails because he changes his mind, or dies, or out of other impediments that occur every day to one out of many more frequently than to just one. This is the reason why the wise recommend that he who participates in enterprises whose success depends on many should labour to achieve his purposes soon, for such undertakings fall into disorder in the long run. And I leave you to consider how seriously you are observing this piece of advice, since you rely on temporising.

But let us concede that gaining time will do not harm to you: what benefit will you have from it? None, unless you upset the Kingdom of

Naples as the affairs of Lombardy are in an impasse. Yet, this will not be as easy as it would have been at the time of the Duke of Albany, for the King of France was then in Italy with his person, held Milan, and the affairs of Caesar appeared to be on the decline. Everything has changed now: the King is prisoner, and Caesar's reputation is as high as the sky. Thus, movements will not be so easy, and everyone shall willingly wait for the events of Lombardy, where all the rest will be settled; and even if one made innovations in the Kingdom of Naples, the Imperials will at least keep the fortresses – Ischia, Gaeta and Taranto – which are the bridle on that kingdom, so that as long as Caesar does not lose the forts, he cannot be said to have lost his dominion. All this presupposes that he will lie still, as if he were dead; nor will he rescue the affairs of Italy. Those who believe this deceive themselves grossly, for he is not accustomed to want for men, provided he does not want for money; and he will not want for money on account of the affinity contracted with the King of Portugal,[17] which, combining together the dowry and the contribution of money from the people, will put more than one and a half million ducats in his purse, and this will enable him to make war against all the Christian princes.

You will soon hear that one is fitting out fleets in Spain to come to Italy, calling diets and taking up arms in Germany, and all this will frighten Your Holiness, but it will be so late that there will be no remedy left. If the King of France and the King of England[18] concurred in distressing Caesar beyond the Alps so that he were necessitated to make use of his troops and money against them, I would call your enterprise safe. But if, being free from any such concern, he can attend to Italian affairs with all his forces – as will be the case, for nobody talks about war beyond the Alps – it is folly to believe that Caesar will not vigorously come to the succour of Italy; and the reputation of the King of England will be of little value to you if you can avail yourself of it but in name; nor will the boasts of the French, unless they undertake this enterprise with all the forces of their kingdom.

On what is this hope to conquer founded, then, if your enemies have an army that is more powerful than yours, hold extremely well-fortified towns, and you cannot expect them to fall out of want for money? I see no hope, unless you count on Caesar's ill fortune. Yet fortune has continually favoured him in such an extraordinary manner and has worked, so to speak, so many miracles for him, that even if all the other reasons were so disposed as to be the opposite of what they actually are, this one alone would frighten me. All books are full with the power of fortune in war and how much one fears a fortunate prince, and a multitude of experiences are witness to this. Fortune has blinded princes into procuring his greatness, to which they had to be enemy, and has driven infinite men out of their minds in order to make him great; fortune has delivered victories to him when he was expecting defeats, and has ensured that mercenary soldiers who have never seen or met him have served him without pay in a more affectionate and warm manner than that with which any prince was ever served who participated in war with his person; fortune not only has made him conquer dominions, but has also given him the opportunity to take them in a justifiable manner, as is the case of Milan now, for everyone knows that the Duke [of Milan][19] and [Girolamo] Morone[20] have provided him with a most just occasion to punish them; fortune has him encounter obstacles not to make him succumb but to make him more powerful by humbling those who oppose him, and necessitates him, in order to make him greater, to undertake one enterprise after the other, which perhaps he would not do by his own natural inclination; fortune, I fear, not content with having made him king of so many kingdoms and emperor and opening a way for him to the temporal monarchy of the Christians, wishes also to make him pope or master of the State of the Church, for it ensures that a pontiff precipitates himself to take up arms against him so that, as he will come away as conqueror, not only will he be able, but almost necessitated, to reform the Church and the pontifical authority as he pleases. Will not Germany be pungently stimulated to this? Will Italy blame him? Will not Spain follow him? Are not all the lay persons enemy to the ecclesiastical persons?

Remember, Your Holiness, that the power of the Church lies in its spiritual arms and that its temporal arms have always been of little value. You know the Italian proverb that derides the armies of the Church; as for those of the Venetians, I will not mention them, for they never conquered if not by keeping their swords in the sheath. Shall we then believe that the Pope and the Venetians will be sufficient to expel from Italy so great a power, so victorious an army? Fear deceives us, passion blinds us, the fortune of Caesar leads us to hasty measures. But let us insist further. If the war is found to be burdensome to Caesar, has not he in his hands the peace with the French? Will not he make them lay down their arms any time that he shows the owl to them,[21] as the Florentine proverb says? The King's mother,[22] out of natural love, the greatest noblemen, not to oppose the liberation of the King, the whole kingdom, which will take the affairs of Italy into little consideration having seen that France has not been mutilated, will leave you to be Caesar's prey every day for the sake of recovering their king; nor will they ever, provided they have him back, refuse an agreement by which not only will they leave you at Caesar's discretion but they will also turn against you, to your loss and damage.

You know what sort of negotiations the French have held: you know that in past months, after inviting and persuading you to adhere to their designs, when hope was at its highest, being induced by a few good words of Caesar's, they ridded themselves of you and sent Madame d'Alençon to Spain, with the intention of selling you a hundred times a day. This they will always do, for the same reasons will be there; nor will Caesar, if he comes to an agreement with them, want for means to secure himself; so that at least the first executions will be carried into effect, and especially those against Italy. Thus you are to lose anyway, either because you will be forced by enemies or because you will be abandoned by friends; and since the Venetians have well-fortified towns, the first ruin will fall upon the Pope and the Florentines, whose towns are weak and unprovided for, whose dominions lie in between the Duchy of Milan and the Kingdom of Naples, and who have reason to beware of Siena, always friendly to the Empire, located as it is in the very bowels of the Church and Florence.

Therefore, no reason can justify this enterprise, if not necessity. Yet necessity does not justify it either, provided one does not want to be more afraid than necessary and wishes to consider that the remedy for the dangers and evils does not consist in entering greater dangers and evils but in attempting to diminish them as much as one can and, if one cannot rid oneself of them completely because such is the posture of affairs, in accommodating oneself to the condition of the times and taking the lesser evil one can have for good. The fear one has of Caesar proceeds from two foundations. The first, one is afraid that he, considering himself offended by the negotiations that have been held in the past months, or being at least apprehensive of them, intends to humble Your Holiness in order to revenge, or at least secure, himself. And if he ventures on this, he will not be contented with inflicting a little loss upon you, but he will attempt to harm you as much as he can and, since you are at his discretion, he will be able to do all that he designs to do. And considering that he has the intention of ruining the French and the Venetians – great enterprises that might draw along with them many difficulties and dangers – he will reasonably wish, before venturing on this, to put in order the other affairs of Italy and secure himself of a Pope who appears suspect and an enemy to him, so that if, by chance, his affairs were reduced to some straits, Your Holiness, whom he can no longer trust, could not join together with the others to ruin him.

The other reason that makes one afraid is the natural ambition of all princes, who always seek to expand their power and dominions; and this one seems to aspire to the [universal] monarchy. The State of the Church is vast and fine, not to be contemned by he who is attempting to take the whole. It is to be expected that he will bereave it of its temporal power and reduce the pontiffs to the condition in which they used to be as their elections and their entire conduct depended on the emperors; by which not only will he satisfy his ambition but he will also believe not to offend conscience, having restored to the empire the rights that were held by his ancestors and left the spirituals to the Pope, *et quae sunt Dei Deo*, and the temporals *et quae sunt Caesaris Caesari*.[23] I believe that those who say so are not certain that this is to happen; nor can I be certain that the opposite is to be the case. But I am convinced that my opinion persuades reason to a far greater extent than theirs.

Coming to the count of ambition first, I say that this prince has always demonstrated his good disposition in all his deeds, and has made profession of conscience, of his devotion to the Church, of his not wishing to disturb the affairs of others, or has at least desired to be believed that he proceeds justly and rightly. I could quote abundant evidence of all this, but since these testimonies are well known to Your Holiness – and you have admitted this to me on many occasions – I shall not repeat it. Now, if this is truly his disposition, we are not to fear these dangers: since the ruin of the Church is not the greatest reward that there is, as I shall say below, we have no reason to believe that a prince who is good, devoted to, and most observant of, the Apostolic Seat suddenly turns out to be a robber, an assassin, and that he will so shamefully and impudently deprive the Church of those things that it has received from nobody but his ancestors and has owned for centuries, so that they no longer belong to Caesar, but to God and his vicars. If this is dissimulation, I say that it is more important and valuable to him, having still to wage very great wars and take care of very serious affairs, to retain the fame he has acquired and the profession he has made, than to bereave the Apostolic Seat of its dominions, especially because as the Church is powerful in Italy, he knows that you will gratify him and accommodate him with all that you can, so that he will benefit, both in Italy and out of Italy, from having you as a friend and an ally much more than he would from despoiling you. Moreover, he would make himself known to the entire world as a wicked man, and lose that reputation which he clearly values much.

We have therefore no reason to believe that, out of ambition, he will come to a resolution that will neither make him greater nor increase his advantage, but which will obscure his glory and honour. Nor will he out of revenge, in my opinion. The injuries that he can claim Your Holiness has inflicted upon him amount to negotiations that have had no effect; he knows, moreover, that you have been under the influence in part of fear, in part of the oppressions and disappointments that you have suffered from the Viceroy[24] and his captains, of which he has complained and excused himself with you several times. Besides all this, it is not to be believed that indignation will induce him to do things that are not useful but shameful to him, and even if it could, it is more likely that he would defer revenge until another time, that is, after he has carried out the most important enterprises, for his interest and honour so require. And this draws along with it so great a delay that new circumstances can easily be expected of such a sort as to deliver Your Holiness from this danger; or the space of time, together with the good manners that you will have kept with him, would likely mitigate his indignation.

Coming to his apprehension, I do not think that it is so great as to have him harm you so much, for affection and benevolence have naturally existed between him and Your Holiness; nor does the Church aspire to subject France or Italy, but only to preserve that which the emperors have granted to it in the past; thus, as long as he does not molest it, his acquisitions are not to be distasteful to you, and he has no reason to fear that his power displeases Your Holiness, as long as you are sure that he does not mean to oppress you. Such a security depends on him, for each time you see him in Italy with his person, and he honours you, observes his promises, and holds you in the respect that becomes a pontiff, you will continue to be most secure that you have nothing to fear from him, and your security will secure Caesar, for he will have no reason to fear Your Beatitude, and this will be an easier, juster and more glorious means to secure himself of you than attempting to oppress and ruin you. All the more, if you break off the negotiations that are being proposed to you and establish the agreements you have made with him, this will be a care of yours that will begin to persuade him that you intend to live in good understanding with him; and he will confirm himself in his friendly disposition toward you more each day, as he sees that you cut any such conversation in the future and no longer lend your ears to anything that is proposed against him.

Those who wish that you take up arms against Caesar will say, Holy Father, that even if one presumes that he is not an enemy to you, nevertheless his greatness harms you, for he is so powerful in Italy that your reputation diminishes because it totally depends on his will. And, I will admit, if things could be reduced to such terms that in Italy no prince could give laws to the others, this would be the best condition that one could have; but I shall say that as it pleased God – or the ordinary cycle of human affairs is of this kind – that the power of Caesar is so great, one can desire but cannot hope for this; so that he who wants to kick against him will kick against the goad. It is therefore the office of prudence not to act in such a way as to put one's affairs in a worse situation by despair and take precipitate measures altogether, but to accommodate oneself to this necessity and seek to obtain the least infelicitous arrangement that one can; and if one cannot live with the qualities and the authority that one wishes, one should not choose to die because of this. For besides life being better than death, times and events may return of such a sort that they will be utterly useless to he who has died, but would restore dignity to he who is still alive.

I, Most Blissed Father, do not mean that it would better become a pontiff to neglect this lordship and the temporals and keep the spiritual authority only, to be, in effect, pontiff and not prince. Although I do hold this opinion to be true, I acknowledge that these words of mine may sound too unusual to those who allow themselves to be deceived by bad habits. But, accommodating myself to the general manner and corruptness, I say that if I saw any hope that one could moderate the power of Caesar by taking up arms, I would encourage this, even if this were dangerous. But, seeing nothing but desperate and utterly groundless resolutions – and he who takes them will not only accelerate his ultimate ruin but will also be accounted an imprudent and improvident man – I could never recommend that, out of fear of Caesar's will, you should come to a resolution to which no reason gives hope of success, as no one can deny that there are many convincing reasons why he will be benevolent; nor could I ever advise that you, out of fear that Caesar's power might make your authority look lesser, should make a decision by which not only will your authority be diminished, but it will be utterly destroyed in both temporals and spirituals.

Remember, Your Holiness, that he, who out of fear of some uncertain evil, embraces the ultimate evils out of despair, is not accounted courageous but timid and most cowardly; that to take precipitate measures is not great-heartedness but extreme folly; and that it becomes your degree, dignity, prudence and experience of affairs neither to ruin the Apostolic Seat nor to take remedies that are rash and appropriate for the youth, but to proceed, in a resolution of so great a moment, in a considered manner and with such maturity that, should the results be unsuccessful a thousand times, at least one could not say that the advice was not good or thoughtful, and that your resolution wanted prudence more than good fortune.

I shall pray God that he may enlighten you in your decision; but whatever resolution you make, whatever its fortune, I offer myself to you, as a loyal and affectionate servant, as I am obliged to be and have always been in the past. —

On the Same Issue. The Opposite View.

— To talk about things past is superfluous, Most Blissed Father, because it is out of time. And even if we had reason to do it, Your Holiness would not deserve to be blamed for not having resolved for neutrality, but rather for not having openly strived with all diligence to make the French seize Milan. And he who encouraged you to do this, so that Italian affairs would be counterpoised, should be judged a partisan less than he who advised you to favour Caesar's greatness, which carries with it the subjection of all the others. But leaving this aside, because it is too late, I say that if you have not seen in the past events that which needed to be seen, or if, as I do believe and could easily justify, your decision has wanted less wisdom than fortune, and if, on account of all this, Caesar's affairs have grown to such a reputation and been raised up to the sky, you have no reason to lose heart or to be frightened for having taken an erroneous resolution or not having been assisted by fortune, for desponding would serve no other purpose than, by occasioning yourself to be accused of eternal shame, to increase your evils and dangers, which, the greater they are, the more vigorously and great-heartedly they need to be faced.

You are not the first prince who, having to handle difficult resolutions, has not chosen well. In fact, this often happens to all, for men are not gods, and the future is most uncertain. You are not the first prince who, in the midst of trouble, has managed to restore his affairs by the assistance of God and his own endeavours, and to whom fortune, which was an enemy at the beginning, has returned, as fair and prosperous as ever. In fact, it is proper for the ship of Saint Peter to sail against winds and waves only to have, in the end, the sea not only pacified but also most obedient. Therefore, do strive against the difficulties in which you find yourself with a good and vigorous disposition, and bravely embrace the available remedies, choosing the safe ones, if you can have them, and, if you cannot, insisting on whatever you have resolved upon, no matter how uncertain and dangerous this may be, for making difficult provisions that are attended with danger is an evil lesser than letting oneself certainly perish.

The Archbishop has rightly said that nobody can take for granted how Caesar would behave with you if he passed into Italy with his person or established his affairs here in another way, for this being a matter that depends on his own will only, one can have no certainty at all of what he intends, or will intend, to do. Yet it seems to me that the reasons for fear are without comparison more numerous and more powerful than those for hope. It is natural for princes, as it is for private individuals in their mode of being, always to seek to increase their greatness, and the greater they are, the more they will want to reach the highest posts and believe this to be proper for themselves, and being usually inclined to this, they will take any other thing into little consideration and lay low all the other regards.

Thus, if I fear that Caesar – who, as I see it, pretends to the domination of Italy, in fact perhaps the monarchy of the Christians, and who, not being satisfied in Italy with the Kingdom of Naples, has now taken the state of Milan – wishes to make himself lord of Florence, master of Rome and all the dominions held by the Church, and give laws to all with absolute authority, I believe that I dread him more reasonably than do those who assure themselves of the contrary, for my fear is founded upon his own proceedings and the common desires of all princes.

I do not know what foundation this confidence of theirs can have other than his will; and this reason alone, even if there were no other causes for concern, which I shall mention below, is sufficient to make Your Holiness distrust him utterly. But there are other reasons. We have seen how disappointed Caesar's officers were as you moved away from contributing to the imperial cause to neutrality, and the insolent words of the Viceroy as you refused to assist them in their enterprise in Provence, for they already thought that it was due to them that you had to be not an ally but a servant of theirs, and that you should support them in the undertakings that would increase their power only to a no lesser extent than you had done in those that tended to a common benefit. You also know how displeased they were with the agreement that you made with the King of France, as he was at the siege of Pavia, although it carried no obligation other than neutrality: for any time you have refused to spend money and take up war on their behalf, they have taken it as an affront, as if they had already presumed that the Church would dutifully serve the Emperor.[25]

Therefore, if they took offence at neutrality before they had conquered and thought that the whole world was reasonably theirs, what do you think their disposition to you is now that they know of the negotiations you have held to expel them from Italy after they took the King of France to Spain? Although such talks can be excused as being born out of the way they have mistreated you, this would be sufficient before a just judge; but no reason is allowed before him who finds it reasonable that everyone should do as he pleases and patiently bear that their money and dominions be at his disposal, as he thinks fit; in fact, those who are not thankful for being flogged are just as gravely offensive to him as those who, although unprovoked, oppose him.

Caesar has established his ends and, be those just or unjust, he has reason to hold as an enemy, and desire to ruin, everyone who seeks to disturb his designs. Given you have done this, and in the manner in which you have, anyone who presupposes that he is not a deadly enemy to you is greatly mistaken. And although he might find it convenient to hide or dismiss such an enmity, as I shall discuss below, suspicion is left there, which cannot allow him to put to use this prudence or goodness of his, whatever it may be. He is certain by now that you are displeased with his power and that you have sought to beat him, so that he has been made sensible that any time you should see the opportunity you would be against him. Nor can one find any means to secure him against this, for jealousy is only too natural for states;[26] nor will the security that his ways of proceeding can give you give him security, as the Archbishop said; in fact, he will know that his suspicion keeps you in suspicion by necessity, and your suspicion multiplies his suspicion. And such suspicions cannot be cured but by the one who will be in such a position that the other will not have the means to injure him.[27] Thus, even if his ambition ceased and he were not indignant, suspicion forces him to secure himself, and he cannot secure himself unless he abases you. By abasing you, he will make a most bitter enemy of you; hence, as he begins, he will be necessitated either to ruin you utterly, or to lower you so much as to leave you little less than ruined.

Even those who have not seen any other sign should understand these reasons; all the more, those who have undergone all that you have do not need any other grounds to believe what I am saying. The agreement that you made with Caesar after the battle of Pavia,[28] although it was greatly beneficial to him, for it rendered that victory secure to him and served as a means for conducting the King of France to Spain, although you observed it in the most scrupulous manner and added to the obligations of the treaty all the proofs that Caesar and his officers managed to desire, although you uttered no word and undertook no action that might have displeased him – this agreement, I say, has nevertheless been scorned in all its parts; not only have they failed to carry it into effect, but they have also adopted an attitude full of contempt and disappointment. When you paid them that grand sum of money, they seized thirty thousand ducats from you, against all honesty; the dominions of the Church, which they promised to evacuate, have been burdened with soldiers; after much derision, they had the legate go to Pizzighettone, with the hope of restoring Reggio and Rubiera to you – to which they were obliged – only to dismiss him with manifest ridicule;[29] in the mean time, they have promised the Duke of Ferrara to restore these two towns to him, and showed desire to enter into an agreement with him and take him under their protection. A thousand other negotiations with you have taken place, all full of contempt, fraud and deceit, as you know, on account of nothing but their being displeased at your power and authority and their design to keep these wounds of yours open, so that you be weak, nerveless and at their discretion. For they intend to bereave you of your state, or they hate you, or fear you.

Nor can anyone tell me that these manners have come from Caesar's officers against his will, for if it were a momentary affair that did not rely on any deliberation or approval from Spain, this could be believed. But when it comes to an affair that has been going on for many months and that is of such moment, to say that his men have acted against his will is too ridiculous an excuse, especially because those who are not blind have been able to see that although the words that have come from his court have been different, the effects and the way of proceeding have been the same, both in the case of the hopes they gave to the Duke of Ferrara and in any other instance. Thus Your Holiness can be certain of the intentions of the master by the motions of the officers, and expect from him, should he pass into Italy or resolve otherwise, the same disposition, although the effects will be the worse the more he will be able to injure you.

Nor should Your Holiness feel reassured by what the Archbishop said about Caesar's good nature, the profession he makes of proceeding in a justifiable manner, the little gain he would make out of ruining you. I do not want to talk about his goodness, for it would not be proper to talk about such a prince in any way other than the utmost reverence, nor do I intend to say that power cannot be reconciled with conscience, and that every prince can more easily be a good prince than a good man. But you are accustomed to handle important state matters, and have seen many things present and read and heard about many things past: you know how difficult it is to restrain his desire to grow in power and how many arguments could be used against those who wish to deny this. For the heart of man is occult, and simulations are often deep, so that he who founds his judgement on words and outward appearance easily deceives himself. With regard to this, all the other Christian nations are overcome by the Spanish, who are nothing but artifice and simulation; I do not say that a prince who is among them has taken part of their customs, for in truth I do not know, but it would not come as a great surprise.[30] Nor is it to be argued that until now he has made a profession of proceeding in a justifiable manner, for even if this were true – which I do not wish to discuss for the same reason I mentioned above – those who do so out of deception usually lay such an artifice aside as soon as a great opportunity presents itself to be seized, and take off their mask; for having achieved one of the ends on account of which they have availed themselves of deceit, they find it less difficult to discard it. And, in this regard, securing oneself of a pontiff at this time is so great a prize that it would not come as a surprise if Caesar changed his usual attitude in order to accomplish this.

I do not believe that he will act so much under the influence of a covetous desire to seize the dominions of the Church – although this would be no little gain – but rather to be secure that a pontiff's power cannot injure him, in fact to have a pope of such a sort as he can trust and of whom he can avail himself. Which he might do not so much in a just manner, but rather in such a way as he would not want some appearance of justification, under the title of a council for the reformation of the Church, in which he might make so large a part of Christendom participate that it could almost be called a universal council. Such things, when they begin in this manner, result in the deposition of pontiffs or, in the case that an emperor is very powerful, in abasing the authority of the popes to such an extent that they are no longer to be feared. In doing so, he shall satisfy his interest and the hatred he might feel towards you; and he will have a semblance of justification, and perhaps, since men easily deceive their own conscience, especially in that which is advantageous to them, it shall seem to him that he is doing nothing that is not lawful and commendable.

Caesar will not be the first to be tempted by this ambition or design, for those who have been powerful have always desired to unite spiritual authority with temporal power. In Rome, the emperor was also Pontifex Maximus; the kings of Jerusalem likewise; in our time, Maximilian [I],[31] Caesar's grandfather, after becoming a widower, entertained among his other chimeras the notion of becoming pope; the ancient Christian emperors, when they were powerful, on account of the fact that, according to our laws, they could not be pontiffs, claimed that the pope could be elected but with their participation and at their will. Shall it come as a surprise to us if a similar project will now be born in the mind of Caesar, as we see that, by following the footprints of the other powerful rulers, he tends to the [universal] monarchy?

Human affairs are subject to this condition or, let us say, circle: that which is, is always similar to the past, and that which shall be will always be similar to that which has been. Present and future things are different from things past in superficial terms and appearance, but similar in essence and substance. Thus, if one measures the former by the standard of the latter one cannot err. And if we see, every day, that the popes desire temporal lordships, does it come as a surprise that an emperor has an inclination for spiritual authority? And if he has this intention, reason wants that he will not defer until he has accomplished the enterprises against the Venetians and France, for, as the Archbishop said, such undertakings will take time and might carry with them many accidents, so that leaving behind a powerful and most suspect pope would not be safe for him. Thus, it is convenient for him, before embarking on deeper seas, to dispose first of Italian affairs in a dexterous manner rather than, not having digested them yet, put further food in the stomach. These people are not like the French, who proceed cravingly and furiously; they are best suited for the preservation of their dominions, for they know how to establish and secure them well; thus, considering both reason and their customs, we have to believe that if they run into no opposition as soon as Caesar passes into Italy, or, should he not pass, as soon as they take the castle of Milan, they will begin to secure themselves of Your Holiness, in whole or in part, according to the circumstances.

But let us concede, without allowing this presupposition to alter the truth, that Caesar's good nature ensures you that he will observe the agreement and behave well towards you. Will you not be left, in any case, if he prevails over Italy, with none of the reputation, authority, dignity and majesty that become a prince? Your predecessors have given laws to the emperors and motion to all the worldly affairs; when you were a cardinal, you were in a manner adored by most powerful kings, who contended who should gain your favour; now, as a pontiff, you will be at the discretion of the Emperor, and seek not only to satisfy him, but also to be agreeable to his men; everyone will know that you depend on him, thus you will be left with no reputation or credit. If the secular princes were good and moderate, I would confess that a pontiff would have less reason to care for temporals, for his jurisdictions would be very great, provided they were left untouched. But who knows not how much a pope who is not armed and feared is exposed to injuries, in what little consideration his censures and other weapons that do not cut are taken, and how much spirituals and ecclesiastics are anyone's prey unless the power of the pope defends them? You cannot therefore preserve the pope's authority unless you preserve the prince's; and the prince's authority is annihilated as soon as it is forced to acknowledge that it depends on the discretion, on the nods, of somebody who is more powerful. To rule is the substance of the prince, the essence of princedom. Thus, as soon as you are to obey, although you have the name of prince and the robes and insignia of princedom, you are, in effect, any other thing but a prince.

We read that the ancient wise – and if I remember well an admonition given [also] to Jupiter – recommended that one should avoid reducing oneself in such a condition as to be forced to rely on others as much as one should avoid death. Therefore you can see what good is promised, what room is left for you among princes, what hope is given that Caesar will be friendly towards you by those who encourage you to put your head in his lap, which means nothing but to renounce being a prince and to reduce yourself, out of the fear of some evil, to a plight in which nothing would be lighter than death to any manly and great-hearted man. This is not gaining time, but ruining oneself, not preserving one's life, but dying with eternal shame; for a prince lives so long as he preserves his majesty and the dignity of prince, and once he has lost this, he is more than dead, more than buried. Thus I will dare to say that you have to undertake the enterprise to preserve your princedom not only if it were attended with many dangers but also if it were almost desperate – of which I shall speak below, after examining first how dangerous making this league would be and how much hope of success one could entertain.

I shall not deny that the army that Caesar already has in Italy – and the larger one that he will be able to have thanks to the Landsknechts – is strong in captains and good foot and that its reputation is great on account of so many victories and so much good fortune, and that now, out of that affinity with the King of Portugal, Caesar can avail himself of money, which he used to want for in the past, and that considering all this and the fortified towns they hold in Lombardy, the enterprise of expelling them from the Duchy of Milan is dubious, difficult and dangerous. But I shall never consent that such an undertaking is a desperate one and that the Imperials are not to run into many difficulties and dangers in sustaining themselves.

Do leave aside the general reasons, which are that the effects of war are dubious; that the party that looked weaker often achieves victory; that a little accident, a little event, often occasions changes and effects that are of greatest moment; that no one holds fortune in his power, and he who has enjoyed a propitious and fair fortune for a long time not only cannot expect that it will continue to be on his side, but also has reason to fear its mutations to a greater extent than the others, and all the more so the more exceedingly benevolent it has been, for its way has always been, is and will be, to be uncertain, capricious and unstable. Leave aside – I say – these general reasons and other similar ones that can be mentioned: I admit that the enemies have good captains and good soldiers, but not such that they are to be feared so much as to leave the domination of the world to them with no opposition. They are only men; and if you consider their conduct over time in a diligent manner you will be sensible that they have conquered out of the ill fortune and imprudence of their enemies perhaps more than out of their own valour;

and if they have conquered thanks to their valour, nevertheless the latter has not been so rare and admirable that the others have reason to despair of being able to do as well. Their trials have been made in Italy against nobody else but the French, whose imprudence, disorder and impatience are so well known that any reference to them is superfluous; nor does it come as a surprise that the French have been defeated, for it all consists in sustaining that furious and rash attack of theirs, at the beginning of which they are no more than men, but after which they are perhaps less than women.

The French have lost their most recent enterprise in Italy for no reason other than the poor manner in which they managed their affairs: not only did they waste much time and opportunity around Pavia with great indolence [. . .] but, although their forces were decreased and their infantry less numerous than that of their enemies, once the Imperials marched out, they decided to wait for them in a most dangerous post. You know whether the previous victory at Milan, of which you were at the head,[32] resulted more from fortune than valour, and whether, although it was an easy enterprise at the beginning, it turned into such a difficult and dangerous undertaking, due to the coldness of the Imperials, that the French often found themselves in an advantageous position. I do not intend to examine the battle of Ravenna[33] and the events that occasioned the French defeat at the Garigliano river in detail;[34] but my conclusion is that he who places the Imperials above the other men and calls them invincible is under the influence of some common opinion more than reason.

The sinews of their army will be the Landsknechts, against whom we will avail ourselves of the Swiss who, for disposition, order of battle, courage, and experience in war, are one and the same thing as them; nor are they accustomed to flee them. And if the Swiss behaved badly in the battle of Pavia, more for the disposition of Heaven or the disorder of the French than any other reason, this makes me more hopeful that they will behave well now, as they have done in so many battles in Italy, not only because their own state will be at stake in the field – Caesar's power being their ruin – but also out of the desire to make amends for this latest ignominy and recover their old reputation. It is most true, in fact, that our Swiss are at least as valorous as the Landsknechts; the Spanish, who are so feared, are no more than three or four thousand foot at most; and if they grow in number, they will by inexperienced soldiers who will not have the qualities that are so frightening. An Italian infantry made of four or six thousand choice men, well provided with common guns and harquebuses and under the command of a Giovanni de' Medici,[35] will fight valiantly against them, and finding itself having to compete against the Spanish, it will have neither less desire to conquer nor less consideration of military glory and the honour of its nation than they will have; and the Italian foot will be men in every sense no less than the Spanish will be. When private Italians have fought against the Spanish, and have fought for the glory of the nation, they have given demonstration of this. And wherever choice men, that is, soldiers who esteem the honour of their office, are under a good command, they will do the same.

As for men-at-arms, they will not have an advantage over us, nor, in my view, will they as for the captains, whom in fact I trust much, for every one of those who have been named by the Archbishop, besides being incited by the reputation and the glory of the arms, will risk his own state. This is why Your Holiness can rely on them, for they have the same interest, in fact the same necessity. And the fact that the Spanish are by now notorious in Italy for their deceit and perfidy is the greatest bridle that one can have on any Italian ally who might be tempted to make a separate agreement with them for the sake of improving his condition. Among the imperial captains who are acquainted with Italy, if [the Marquis of] Pescara[36] – whose state of health, we are told, is desperate – will fail them, none is held in even mediocre esteem by their army, except for Alarcón,[37] who nevertheless wants for many of the qualities that are usually noted in great commanders. Thus, if we resolve to be afraid of substance and effects only, and not of names and vain opinions, I do not know why our alliance should despair to produce an army that can be put in the field against them.

I do not know yet whether war will have to be waged with impetuosity or delay, whether we will have to avoid coming to a battle, or look, or wait, for it, for these decisions are to be made in the moment. And if the enemies abandon the field, our army will be able to besiege their towns in perhaps a more valorous manner than the French did; and if they retire into Lodi, Pavia and Alessandria, it will not be of little moment to begin by pulling them out of Milan and Cremona. If they want to hold all these places, the burden will be too heavy for them, especially because the peoples [of the occupied dominions] have already turned into bitter enemies to them, as everyone knows. It was the friendship of those peoples that, in the first enterprise, frightened the French so much that they shamefully let Milan be wrested from them, and that has afterwards been the main means by which the Imperials have defended that duchy so many times. The passage of the Landsknechts was easy then, because the Venetians were friendly or neutral and the Imperials could avail themselves of the Marquis of Mantua as they saw fit; but now, since the Venetians are enemies, if the Imperials evacuate

Cremona and Milan the assistance provided by the Landsknechts could be rendered difficult.

If they march out in the field, our army – provided it is as good as I said – will be able to come to battle, should this be of service; should this not, being under the shelter of strong towns and having the means to fortify its quarters, it will easily be able to avoid battle without danger, for by now everyone has learnt Prospero [Colonna]'s art.[38] And although Caesar has the money that the affinity with the King of Portugal carries with it, our league will, without comparison, have more money, and its temporising will last for longer. All the more, if we set fire in the Kingdom of Naples, as we planned, and Caesar does not make the appropriate provisions, we will be able to produce such a blaze that his affairs will suffer to the utmost extent, and the ruin on one side will carry with it the ruin on the other. The people of the Kingdom of Naples cannot be more discontented: the barons turbulent and passionately desirous of novelties, for many reasons; the kingdom with neither arms nor government. And although the person of the King of France will not be there, the French name, the hope for a king of their own who will reside there – which they all desire very much – the reputation of the Pope, of the Venetians, of all Italy, will. Such foundations are likely to occasion great movements in a kingdom that is apt to be embroiled by a light wind.

If Caesar wishes to obviate these troubles, he will not be able to do it without taking time, entering into difficulties, and incurring infinite expenses, and he will hardly be able to resist in Naples without desisting from, or slackening much, the preparations in Lombardy. War offers many opportunities by the day, and makes manifest to those who are attacked vigorously numerous impediments that cannot be estimated at the beginning. And although one cannot be certain of such difficulties, one cannot be certain either of many dangers that have been, conversely, taken into consideration, for it would be too timid and partisan a thing to hold them to be true. Those who, not being aware of difficulties and dangers, judge a hard enterprise to be easy, are imprudent; nor are they called courageous but feral, for courageous is he who sees the dangers but does not fear them more than one needs to. And the difference between two wise men, one of whom is courageous and the other timid, is this: they both foresee the risks, but the latter takes the dubious dangers for certain and seems to see that all which may happen is happening already; the former is cognisant of the same risks but, knowing that all which there is danger of occurring does not always come to pass (for many perils are repulsed by force, many others are avoided by human industry and prudence, and of some we are at times rid by chance and circumstance itself), in making decisions, he does not presume all dangers to be certain but in fact drops those that he believes can be dropped with some hope.

If you measure the foundations of our undertaking by such a standard, I am most certain that you will find this enterprise to be neither so desperate nor so imprudent; in fact, given the peoples are friendly, having more money and means to assemble and maintain more forces, and a juster cause (provided this matters), that is the liberty of the Church and the others, I am persuaded that anyone who is wise and not a partisan will judge that the hopes of our league are more numerous and vast than those of Caesar, as long as the French do not change their mind.

The thing that has encouraged the Emperor, and still does, gives vigour to those who express the opposite view, and is, in truth, a very important reason, is the fear that the French will come to an agreement with him at the peak of the war, out of the desire to recover their king. And since we have seen that they intended to settle with Caesar by restoring to him all of Burgundy, or part of it, they will make much larger concessions on the affairs of Italy. The thing is of so great a moment that, could this danger be removed, our enterprise would be undertaken under the utmost advantage in any other respect. And this alone, it cannot be denied, makes it dubious, difficult and extremely dangerous, especially because the French are as imprudent as they are and their kingdom is held by women[39] who will regulate their motions more with affection than reason. Nevertheless, if we could walk another road that were safe or less thorny than this, it would be a folly to undergo this danger. But since any other path is attended with greater dangers or, better still, ruins, it seems to me that necessity forces us to take this one, in which, if you consider all the cases, accidents can easily occur that would alleviate this danger.

Things are disposed in such a way that, with or without an agreement, nothing but a most deadly hatred can subsist between these two kings, for Francis, instead of the good promises that he had been made and the humanity and great-heartedness that he presumed he would find in Caesar as he was conducted to him in Spain, has encountered disappointment and all the opposite of what he had hoped for: he was prevented from seeing Caesar until he was close to death, while [the Constable of] Bourbon,[40] a most bitter enemy to him, was held in the utmost favour and honour. Thus, he is most certain that Caesar will not be inclined to make an agreement out of affection, or royal soul, or desire for peace, but that the Emperor will propose to himself vast advantages from his imprisonment or deliverance.

Therefore, the whole point is that his liberation should take place in such a way that, once he is free, he will not be so constrained as to carry into effect, out of necessity, those articles detrimental to Italy on which he will have agreed in the settlement. And this we can hope for, in my view, as long as the first steps that our league takes will result in some good progress, so that Caesar will be induced to peace out of necessity and fear. All the more that, the league being in arms and assisted by the Swiss (who, I presume, will remain with us even should the French make the agreement with Caesar, for it is in their interest), the executions to be carried into effect against Italy would take a long time, which would give to the King of France the time to consider his affairs well. And it is reasonable that he will be more influenced by the fear that the Emperor, who is a most deadly enemy to him and who manifestly aspires to the [universal] monarchy, will subject Italy, by means of which he could beat him in France, than any consideration of whatever bridle, sons given as hostages, or any other thing he might have put in Caesar's hands for the sake of freeing himself.

I will add that even if I were certain that, once war has broken out, the French should come to a settlement and that their king, once delivered, should carry out those first executions to the detriment of Italy, that is, let it fall into Caesar's hands, I would not perhaps change my mind. It seems to me that this is a lesser danger than letting Caesar's affairs go, for in this case you might retire into France,[41] where the King, being already free of his bonds – on account of having observed the first articles of the agreement – and seeing the danger closer – due to the impetuous growth of Caesar's power – would have reason to conciliate your affections and enter into a strict alliance with you; and it is to be believed that the King of England would do the same. But the other case is much worse, for if it is fated that Italian affairs are to go to ruin, it is far better that Caesar should be forced to deliver the King – which will leave us with some hope – than he should make himself master of Italy while keeping the King prisoner, for in this case either he will beat France without difficulty, or at the very least you will find no safe refuge with the French, for you will have reason to fear that they will sell you again for the sake of recovering their king. These are extreme resolutions, I admit, but the situation in which you find yourself is no less extreme; the same means have been embraced by other princes in dire straits, especially many Roman pontiffs, who have taken risky deliberations rather than putting themselves in the hands, and at the discretion, of the emperors. And a pope can do this with greater facility than any other prince, for the latter cannot carry his state with him, but the former always carries with him at least part of the pontificate and the reverence and majesty that he has in Rome.

In sum, all things considered, it is not to be doubted that if Your Holiness, together with the others, does not take up arms against Caesar, he will soon seize the entire Duchy of Milan, pass into Italy at his leisure this summer or increase his forces there as much as it suits him. He aspires, as it is plain for all to see, to ruin the Venetians and beat France; it is not safe for him to attempt these enterprises unless he establishes the rest of Italy well, and this he cannot do unless he abases Your Holiness. Therefore, every reason makes one believe, in fact hold for certain, that he will begin with you at once, and reduce you to a petty pontiff, and perhaps see to it that somebody else, who depends on him entirely, will be placed in this Seat. And not even those who hope for the better will deny that, since he is most powerful, you will be left his servant and chaplain, and in such a way that seeing yourself deprived, with regard to the effects, of your majesty and dignity, you will suffer death a hundred times a day.

These evils are most certain and immediate, and if somebody's death, or similar accident, may by chance relieve you, the same may happen if you take up arms, which nobody can deny that are attended with some hope to rid you of these dangers and with mighty expectations to succeed if the French do not change their mind; and if they do, there is still more hope of salvation under the shelter of the arms than in the case that Caesar, having grown so powerful in Italy, will become harsher. Therefore, those who are frightened by the dangers of war should look upon the evils of peace with the same eye with which one will look upon them as soon as opportunities to make war have disappeared. Such evils are more certain, no less slow to come, and in some cases greater; and should they be lesser, that is, presuming Caesar does not mean to ruin you, one cannot deny that they will none the less be so great that you have reason to judge them a little less onerous than death; and yet, those who hope for this less harsh condition hope, in my view, for that which is not reasonable, is not likely, is not to be expected. I see well that your coming to an agreement with Caesar provides him with larger means to injure you, but I do not see that it makes him change his mind.

Moreover, he who considers which resolution is more glorious, greathearted and worthy of a prince will find that labouring and making every attempt not to go into slavery is a manly thing, and worthy of a man, while the opposite is full of eternal infamy and ignominy. We have seen in our time kings and powerful princes lose their state out of ill fortune, and we read about an infinite number of similar cases in the ancient histories, for it is natural in the motions of the world that empires should rise and decline; but we have not perhaps seen, or heard about, any princedom – I am speaking of the great ones, similar to yours – changing hands with greater facility. Should you lose your state – God forbid – without making opposition, one will not be able to say that you have been bereaved of it, but will have to admit that you have dropped it in a careless manner.[42]

No private individual has ever lived who was so weak and abject that, seeing those who intended to strip him of his cloak approaching, has not attempted to defend himself or flee; and you, who evidently see that those people intend to strip you of your dignity and authority, resolve to stand still, not to move, to let the enemies do as they please? This is not what was expected from Your Beatitude; nor does it become the experiences you had before being elected pope, as you tasted both good and ill fortune. Your knowledge of things, your brightness, your extensive capacity, the diligence and assiduity with which you attend affairs, the confidence that your integrity is to give you, your good disposition and inclination towards the common good: all this does not deserve that, now that a matter of the utmost moment to you is at stake, you make so base, so careless, so idle a resolution.

[Pope] Boniface [VIII],[43] one of your predecessors, having been shut in his Anagni palace by the Colonna, and having no way to defend himself or flee, sat on the pontifical seat wearing the apostolic clothes, and at least, in a great-hearted manner, opposed to his enemies all the authority, splendour and majesty that the vicars of Christ carry with them. And although this was not enough to escape that unhappy condition, at least it made one celebrate his great-heartedness and praise him in his ill fortune as a man who had made all the opposition he could to the ultimate dangers with a brave soul. You, and every prince, cannot but wish that your affairs continue prosperously and that you never have to try dangerous medicines; but, as you fall into adversity, you have to attempt all the remedies one can, with a steady soul, not to lose your state, go into slavery, and obscure your rank and majesty. Should you not succeed, for one cannot always resist fortune, you are left with nothing else to do but to show your virtue, your great-heartedness, in dire straits. If this is done, you may end up in an unhappy condition, but at least you end up honoured, and leave a glorious memory of yourself to posterity and compassion to the present man. But if you perish in an idle manner, your name will be infamous and abominable to both the present and future times; and who is to hold in esteem this glory, this dignity of memory, more than princes? Just as they have been placed in a high degree above the others, so their deeds too are to be higher, more glorious and more splendid than those of the others, and they are to wish, if I mistake not, more for death than life if their dignity and majesty are abased, if only slightly.

You find yourself, therefore, in a condition in which your state, authority, memory and honour are at stake. If you come to an agreement with Caesar, it cannot be denied that this will completely annihilate your authority, your rank of prince, and any hope of honourable memory; moreover, very many reasons make one believe that the same will happen to your state and safety. If you take up arms, there is some hope to preserve all these things, and also to augment your glory and dignity. Remember that those who abandon themselves are abandoned not only by fortune but by God too, who, as the proverb has it, does not help him who does not help himself; and, on the contrary, fortune often favours the bold. History is full of instances of persons who have delivered themselves from dire straits by courage and by dauntlessly entering dangers, which have no reason to frighten those who find themselves under necessity. Nor is it rashness to take up dangers although you see that they are attended with risks, for in most difficult situations there is no security; nor can so serious a disease be cured without hazardous remedies. In fact, too much prudence is imprudence, in difficulties; and the prudent man, in effect, is both he who refers himself, to some extent, to the power of fortune, when the posture of affairs so requires, and he who knows how to choose safe resolutions, when security can be obtained. But, to conclude, to take up war is, I admit, a very dangerous decision; but the other decision carries with it, it seems to me, most certain evils. Should you ruin, ruin will be great in either case; but in the former, the end will be honourable and the attempt great-hearted, in the latter, the proceeding will be most idle and the end most reproachable.

The conclusion, for I do not intend to say more, is this, I believe: if you think that you can tolerate living under the name of prince but stripped of the dignity and majesty of a prince, to bear infinite indignities without living in despair, or better still, without dying a thousand times a day, and if you trust that Caesar, being content with being able to give commands to, and constrain, you, will observe the convention and will not bereave you of the pontificate and the temporal dominion, then you can resolve to make an agreement with him. And in order to form a sound assessment of this, it is requisite to take into consideration not only things as they stand now but also the fact that he will increase the size of his armies, desire to pass into Italy and perhaps come down to Rome, and establish his affairs firmly, according to the success with which these steps will be met, for should you fear all this then, it would be folly not to begin defending yourself now. But if you cannot resolve to live in this low and ignominious condition or, even if you can reduce yourself to such a baseness, you do not trust that Caesar will treat you with humanity and keep his promises, then I say that all advice is superfluous, and that you have no choice, for necessity forces you, even with enormous danger, to take the road of war for the sake of attempting, with some hope, to escape the extreme and most certain evils that attend the road of peace. Should you decide to do so, the sooner the better, for time gives to the Imperials the means of making provisions and is useful to them in many ways, while it can easily occasion many difficulties and impediments to us. However, should you resolve to come to an agreement with Caesar, I would not recommend the same, for the longer you keep him in suspense, the better, for the sake of delaying his actions as much as one can, and because it will never be too late to precipitate yourself into servitude. —

Notes

1. Giovanni Salviati (1490–1553), Cardinal of St Cosmas and Damian, was to negotiate the ratification of the treaty signed by Clement VII and the Viceroy of Naples, Charles de Lannoy, several months earlier (1 April 1525).
2. Charles V of Habsburg, King of Spain from 1516 to 1556 and Holy Roman Emperor from 1519 to 1556.
3. Marguerite de Navarre (1492–1549), also known as Marguerite d'Angoulême or Marguerite d'Alençon, was Francis's sister. In September, she travelled to Spain to discuss the liberation of her brother, and had a fruitless interview with Charles on 4 October.
4. Giulio de' Medici, pope as Clement VII from 1523 to 1535.
5. Francis I of Valois, King of France from 1515 to 1547.
6. During the siege of Pavia, the Duke of Ferrara provided Francis with ammunition, which was forwarded by the assistance of the Pope (*The History of Italy*, XV, xiii and XVI, i).
7. John Stewart (c. 1481–1536), Duke of Albany and former Regent of Scotland, was in the service of Francis I.
8. Clement had asked the Duke of Albany to establish a friendly government in Siena only to slow down his advance towards the Kingdom of Naples, for, as already noted, he was uncomfortable with the idea that Francis might seize both Milan and Naples. Yet, upon seeing the Duke engaged in this affair, the Imperials suspected that the agreement between the Pope and the French King entailed much more than the former's neutrality (*The History of Italy*, XVI, i).
9. Alfonso d'Este, Duke of Ferrara from 1505 to 1534.
10. Francesco Maria Della Rovere, Duke of Urbino from 1508 to 1516 and from 1522 to 1538.
11. Odet de Foix, Viscount of Lautrec (1485–1528), Governor of Milan, defeated at the battle of Bicocca (27 April 1522).

12. It should be noted, however, that Alfonso's artillery was unanimously held in great esteem. Notably, it had played a decisive role, on the French side, at the battle of Ravenna (11 April 1512).

13. Among 'those who are informed', Guicciardini himself deserves to be mentioned, for he was then Governor of Modena and succeeded in preventing Alfonso from attacking the city, in September 1523. Guicciardini's own version of this episode (*The History of Italy*, XV, iv), however, is less dismissive of Alfonso's attempt than are the words he puts in the speaker's mouth.

14. The Duke of Urbino lost his state in 1516, as Pope Leo X assigned that duchy to his nephew, Lorenzo de' Medici. It was only after Leo's death (1521) that the Duke managed to get most – but not all – of his dominion back. As for the Duke of Ferrara, he had lost Modena and Reggio to Pope Julius II, in 1510 and 1512, respectively. Since then, endless talks with the popes and the French – Alfonso's allies – had led nowhere. Although the Duke took Reggio back in 1523, his dominions, contended as they were by Rome, became an important bargaining chip in several negotiations involving France, the Emperor, the Pope and Alfonso himself. According to the agreement signed by Clement and the Viceroy of Naples on 1 April 1525, Reggio and Rubiera were to be restored to the Church, and the issue was still part of the papal–imperial treaty under discussion at the time of this debate.

15. Not only will the Duke of Ferrara not adhere to the alliance, but he will even assist the Imperials on their way to Rome. The Duke of Urbino, for his part, will participate in the campaign against Charles as commander of the Venetian army. His leadership, however, will be highly controversial, and will make some – including Guicciardini – suspect that his conduct reflected some desire to take revenge on the Pope.

16. Meaning that, the Landsknechts being German, they had a natural affinity for a Habsburg emperor.

17. Charles will marry, in March 1526, Isabella of Portugal (1503–39), the sister of John III, King of Portugal from 1521 to 1557.

18. Henry VIII Tudor, King of England from 1509 to 1547.

19. Francesco II Sforza, Duke of Milan from 1521 to 1535.

20. Girolamo Morone (1470–1529), Sforza's chancellor.

21. The owl was considered the most effective animal lure for fowling purposes.

22. Louise of Savoy (1476–1531) was the Regentess of France.

23. '*Reddite quae sunt Caesaris Caesari et quae sunt Dei Deo*' ('Render to Caesar the things that are Caesar's, and to God the things that are God's') are, of course, the well-known words attributed to Jesus in the gospels (Matthew 22: 21, Mark 12: 17 and Luke 20: 25).

24. Charles de Lennoy, appointed Viceroy of the Kingdom of Naples by Charles in 1522, negotiated the agreement of 1 April 1525 with Clement VII.

25. For a reconstruction of these events, see *The History of Italy*, XVI, i.
26. Cf. above, p. 84: 'Nothing is, by nature, more apprehensive than states.'
27. Cf. *Maxims and Reflections (Ricordi)*, Engl. transl. by M. Domandi, Philadelphia: University of Pennsylvania Press, 1965, C 27.
28. The agreement of 1 April 1525. See, for more details, *The History of Italy*, XVI, ii.
29. 'The Pontiff, to solicit the accomplishment, and to obtain that the troops should evacuate the State of the Church, sent to him [the Viceroy] Cardinal Salviati, his Legate in Lombardy, and deputed Legate to Caesar. The Viceroy assured the Cardinal that he would make the Duke restore Reggio by force of arms, if he refused to do it voluntarily; but the effects did by no means correspond with his words' (*The History of Italy*, XVI, vii).
30. Charles was born in 1500 in the Flemish city of Ghent and moved to Spain only in 1517.
31. Maximilian I of Habsburg, Holy Roman Emperor from 1493 to 1519.
32. Under the command of Francis I, the French took Milan in 1515 and held the Duchy until they were expelled from it by an imperial–papal army, to which Clement VII, at the time still cardinal, was the Pontifical Legate (and Guicciardini Extraordinary Commissioner) in 1521–2.
33. At the battle of Ravenna, 11 April 1512, the French inflicted a serious defeat upon the papal–Spanish army.
34. The Spanish victory at the battle of Garigliano (29 December 1503) led to the French loss of the Kingdom of Naples.
35. Giovanni de' Medici (1498–1526), the most promising young Italian *condottiero* at the time. He will participate in the coming war against the Imperials and die after being wounded in battle.
36. Fernando Francisco de Ávalos Aquino y Cardona (1490–1525), commander of the imperial forces in Italy.
37. Hernando de Alarcón (1466–1540).
38. Prospero Colonna (c. 1460–1523), a veteran *condottiero* of the Italian wars, ended his career as commander of the imperial–papal army that drove the French out of Milan in 1521–2 and defended the duchy against their comeback in 1523. Colonna was famous for his temporising strategy. This is what Guicciardini writes on him in *The History of Italy* (XV, vi): 'Prospero, by these arts, twice defended the Duchy of Milan much to his honour, he being the only or the chief person who used them both defensively and offensively; for by cutting off his enemy's provisions, and prolonging the war, he consumed them with weariness, length of time, poverty and disorders. In this manner he both defended himself and conquered without fighting, and even without drawing a sword, or breaking a single lance. His example has been since followed, and many wars, that had lasted for several months, have been terminated more by industry and good management, and making a proper use of all advantages, than by battles.'

39. Francis's mother (the Regentess) and sister (Madame d'Alençon).
40. Charles III, Duke of Bourbon (1490–1527), was the last great lord to rebel openly against a French king. Due to his tense relations with Francis I, he plotted against him with Charles and Henry VIII; upon the failure of his design, his lands were confiscated by the King and he joined the imperial side in 1523.
41. Avignon, where the popes resided from 1309 to 1377, was still under the jurisdiction of the Church.
42. Guicciardini expressed himself in very similar terms in the letter to Niccolò Machiavelli of 26 December 1525 (J. B. Atkinson and D. Sices (eds), *Machiavelli and His Friends: Their Personal Correspondence*, DeKalb: Northern Illinois University Press, 1996, p. 373).
43. Benedetto Caetani, pope as Boniface VIII from 1294 to 1303. The episode referred to is the so-called 'slap of Anagni', the last incident of his long struggle against the patrician Colonna family.

Chapter 11

On Whether the Emperor Should Make an Agreement with the Italian States or the King of France*

Although the French defeat at Pavia and the capture of King Francis I (24 February 1525) had placed Charles V in a position of uncontested superiority in Italy, the Emperor was not inclined to proceed now to a direct subjugation of the Italian states. His chronic lack of money made it imperative to find, first of all, the necessary financial resources to pay his troops; in addition, his desire to impose an unconditional surrender on France (see above, Chapter 8.) suggested that this was not the right time to risk an open conflict with the Italians. The latter, for their part, were holding their breath. According to Guicciardini,

> *all the potentates of Italy who, finding themselves in a manner wholly disarmed, were struck with the greatest terror at the thoughts of Caesar having so very powerful an army in the field, without an enemy to oppose him. Nor were their fears so much allayed by what many reported of Caesar's good disposition and inclination to peace, without any desire of usurping the states of others, as they were increased on the consideration of the danger that, moved either by ambition, a passion natural to all princes, or by that insolence which commonly attends victories, and besides instigated by the forward zeal of those who had the management of his affairs in Italy or, lastly, stimulated by his Council and whole Court, he would not neglect so fair an opportunity, of itself sufficient to warm the coldest disposition, to turn his whole thoughts on making himself lord of all Italy, especially as they did not ignore how easy it was for any great prince, and much more for a Roman Emperor, to justify their undertakings under pretences which might have the appearance of reason and honour.* (The History of Italy, XVI, i)

---

* From: *The History of Italy*, XVI, xiv.

Francesco Sforza was given the Duchy of Milan back – although his position was far from solid, for the imperial army was still in Lombardy and he had not received the formal investiture yet. Simultaneously, Charles opened negotiations with Pope Clement VII and the Venetians and accepted a number of minor Italian states under his protection. The element that all these agreements and negotiations had in common was a steady imperial demand for money. All but the Venetians bent.

At the same time, Charles was negotiating with France about the terms upon which peace was to be made and Francis liberated. As we have seen above (cf. the introduction to Chapter 8), the Emperor's conditions were extremely harsh, centred as they were on what amounted to a veritable dismemberment of that kingdom. Burgundy, annexed by the French crown in 1477, was the main, albeit by no means the only, bone of territorial contention, as neither the King nor the Regentess (his mother) was willing to cede it. Francis, for his part, was ready, among other things, to give up all his claims on Naples and Milan, marry Charles's sister, accompany him with his army and fleet when he would go to Italy to be crowned by the Pope, and, above all, pay very large sums of money in exchange for the contested territories and his own liberation. Needless to say, while negotiating with the Emperor in an attempt to convince him to revise his conditions, the Regentess was negotiating with the Italians too – especially the Pope and the Venetians – and incited them to wage war on Charles with French support. Her offers, however, were always rather generic. It was clear to the Italians that she was interested above all in the liberation of her son at the lowest possible cost, and that her Italian diplomacy was mostly meant to scare Charles into making concessions. Trusting her, as long as the French King was in captivity, would entail the risk of being caught completely off guard should Francis and Charles eventually reach an agreement at the expense of Italy.

In this triangular relationship involving the Emperor, France and the Italians, everybody was sitting simultaneously at two tables, trying both to prevent the other two from joining their forces and to extract as many concessions as possible from each of them. It was Charles who had the upper hand in the game. With his usual lucidity, Guicciardini captures the essence of the situation in a few lines:

and nothing [was] more easy to Caesar than by feeding the French with hopes to divert them from the thoughts of taking up arms, and by this artfulness to keep the Italians in suspense, so that they should not venture to take new resolutions. And thus sometimes by slackening, sometimes by straining the reins of his conduct, he held the minds of all in confusion and perplexity. (ibid., XVI, ix)

France improved her bargaining position when, in the summer, the Regentess managed to break out of her isolation thanks to an alliance with England (30 August), 'the first dawning of hope on the Kingdom of France, as it began to take breath after so many afflictions' (ibid., XVI, vi). If nothing else, France was now relieved of the threat of having to face the joint hostility of Charles and Henry VIII. But as long as the French King was in the Emperor's hands, the room for manœuvre remained quite narrow, as Charles was not at all inclined seriously to reconsider his initial demands. And just as the Italians were afraid of an agreement between Charles and Francis, Charles could not rule out that the Italians, if exasperated, would accept the offers of the French. While the Viceroy of Naples had, on the Emperor's behalf, come to an agreement with the Pope (1 April 1525), the Emperor was not ratifying it, thereby inducing fear and suspicion in the Pope (see the introduction to the previous debate); negotiations with Venice were going on, but to no avail (see the penultimate debate). As for the Duchy of Milan, things were even less stable.

It should be kept in mind that the restoration of Francesco Sforza and the liberation of Milan had been the ostensible reasons for the outbreak of war in 1521, when the French still ruled the duchy. Although the mission was accomplished between 1521 and 1522, Milan was still far from being safe and independent. As long as a French comeback could not be ruled out, the Duke and the Emperor were, in a manner, forced to cooperate. But when Francis was defeated and captured at Pavia, Sforza

> apprehended that Caesar, now secure of the King of France, would either seize on his state for himself, or grant it to persons who should wholly depend on him. This suspicion, which arose from the very nature of things, was not a little increased by the insolent speeches thrown out by the Viceroy before he conducted the King of France into Spain, and also by the other generals, and by the marks of disrespect which they showed to the Duke as well as by their openly wishing that Caesar would oppress him. (ibid., XVI, viii)

And when the imperial investiture on the Duchy finally came, the Viceroy imposed additional financial conditions on it, which were so heavy that the Duke had reason to believe that such demands were made for the sake of delaying the whole business. In light of all this, it is not surprising that Sforza eventually lent his ear to Girolamo Morone's treacherous advice (see the introduction to the previous debate).

The public uncovering of the plot – in which both Venice and the Pope were involved – was preceded by a set of diplomatic overtures towards the Italians, in the summer, by which Charles solicited the Pope to conclude their treaty, renewed his efforts with Venice, and took the last steps concerning the investiture of Milan on Francesco Sforza. Sforza accepted, but did not break off his dealings against the Emperor.

> *Various were the opinions whether these dispatches or instructions of Caesar were sincere or artificial; for many believed that it was not his real intention to give peace to Italy; others doubted that, under fear of new movements, he was willing to keep men under suspense with various hopes, and thought of gaining time by granting the investiture, and giving in appearance a commission for calling off the army, which would be highly acceptable to all Italy, but that he had given private orders to his generals not to remove the troops. Nor were there wanting afterwards some who persuaded themselves that Caesar was before well informed by the Marquis of Pescara of the plot carried on with Morone, and had therefore given such orders not that they should be obeyed, but should serve for his justification, and by these hopes to lull the minds of the people in security until a proper time appeared for putting his designs in execution.*

Yet, Guicciardini concludes, 'considering the steps taken afterwards by Caesar in many affairs, it is without doubt less fabulous to adopt for truth the better and more favourable interpretation'. (ibid.). Be that as it may, Morone's design provided the Emperor with the perfect excuse to take Milan:

> *hence was Caesar, even if he had entertained no thoughts of making any farther seizures in Italy, furnished with a just cause, and in a manner necessitated to form new schemes; and even supposing that he had ambitious ends, he had the opportunity of covering them with the most honourable circumstances and most justifiable colourings that his heart could have wished. (ibid.)*

After Morone's imprisonment and the occupation of Milan (October), the formation of the anti-imperial league seemed imminent; yet, Charles's diplomacy managed to postpone it, by convincing the Pope to suspend his negotiations with the other powers for two more months in order to work out the appropriate way to deal with Sforza (who had locked himself up in the citadel), for the Italians insisted that he should not be removed from his duchy. By January 1526, however, it was time to make a decision, as Charles and his advisors had come to the conclusion that it would be too dangerous to have a war against

so many enemies, and it was thus necessary either to come to terms
with the Italians, by pledging to restore Milan to Sforza, or to make an
agreement with the King of France. This is the issue under discussion in
the debate below.

According to Guicciardini, although many members of the Council
believed that an accommodation with Francis would entail too many
risks, many others, particularly the Flemings,

> *were possessed with such a longing desire of recovering Burgundy as*
> *it was the ancient patrimony and title of their princes, that it would*
> *not suffer them to discern the truth. It was reported also that the*
> *large gifts and promises of the French had a considerable influence*
> *on many. And above all Caesar, either because such was his first*
> *inclination, or because the authority of the Viceroy [. . .] was of*
> *very great moment, or else because he thought it too much beneath*
> *his dignity to be constrained to pardon Francesco Sforza, willingly*
> *hearkened to those who advised an agreement with the King of*
> *France. (ibid., XVI, xv)*

As the Great Chancellor had predicted, however, the exorbitant and
humiliating peace terms imposed on Francis (Treaty of Madrid, 14
January 1526) would induce him, upon his liberation, not only to reject
the arrangement but also to join the Italians in the anti-imperial League
of Cognac (22 May 1526).

[Being summoned one day the] Council, and Caesar[1] being present, in
order to put a final determination to an affair that had been under debate
so many months, the Great Chancellor [Mercurino da Gattinara][2] spoke
thus:

— I have always been under apprehensions, most invincible Caesar,
that our excessive desires and imprudent goals would be the cause that
in the end we should reap neither honour nor profit from so great and
bright a victory;[3] but I did not however imagine that winning would
endanger your reputation and your state, which I now plainly see is
likely to be the result. For we have now under debate the making of an
agreement by which all Italy will be thrown into despair, and the King
of France[4] set at liberty, but on such burdensome conditions that, if not
by will, yet at least out of necessity, he will become a greater enemy to
us than he was before. I too wish, as heartily as others, that at the same
time Burgundy might be recovered and the foundations laid for the sub-
jecting Italy; but I know that he who is thus hasty in grasping so much

is in danger of holding fast nothing, and that no reason requires that the King of France, after he is set at liberty, should fulfil his engagements to you in such important articles.

Does he not know that if he restores to you Burgundy he opens you a gate of France, and that it will be in your power to make incursions as far as Paris? And that when you have the means of annoying France on so many quarters, it will be impossible for him to resist you? Does he not know, and everyone else, that his consenting that you should go to Rome armed, that you should put a bridle on Italy, and that you should reduce the spiritual and temporal state of the Church to your will would be the cause of doubling your power? And that you never can want for money nor arms to molest him, and that he must be necessitated to accept all the laws you shall please to impose on him? Who then can believe that he will think himself bound to an agreement by which he will become your slave and you his lord? Shall he want for the complaints and the outcries of the whole Kingdom of France, the persuasions of the King of England,[5] and the stimulations of all Italy? The love perhaps that subsists between the two of you will be the cause that he will repose confidence in you or willingly see the increase of your power? Were there ever two princes between whom there were more grounds for hatred and contention? Here is not only an emulation of power, which uses to put weapons in the hand of brothers against one another, but ancient and very bitter enmities, commenced from the times of the fathers and grandfathers of your grandfathers, so many wars long carried on between these two Houses, so many treaties of peace and agreement not observed, so many injuries and affronts given and received. Do we not believe that he burns with indignation to reflect that he has been for so many months your prisoner, kept always under so strict a guard, without ever having the favour of being conducted into your presence? That in this prison, through grief and inconvenience, he has been at death's door?[6] And that he is not now set at liberty out of magnanimity or love, but from the fear of so formidable an union against you? Can we believe that an affinity contracted by necessity is of more force than so many incentives? And who knows not what value princes set upon these ties? And where is there better evidence of the regard they pay to affinities than among ourselves?

Some perhaps may fancy that passing his word, which he will give us, for his returning to prison, may be sufficient for our security. But what inconsiderate grounds, what imprudent hopes these would be! The extreme grief that affects me, when I find that some are for taking so pernicious and dangerous a resolution, constrains me, Caesar, to speak my mind freely. We all know what value is to be set on the word of honour when state interests are concerned, and what stress is to be laid on the promises of the French who, although frank and open in all other matters, are in this regard perfect masters in the art of deceit, and that their king is by nature as much deficient in deeds as he is abundant in words. We may therefore well conclude that no benevolence between two princes, whose injuries and hatred descend with their blood by ancient inheritance; no memory of benefits, of which there is none; no faith nor promises, which in state matters have but little weight with many, and with the French none at all, will induce that king to make good an agreement that will exalt his enemy to Heaven and bring himself and his kingdom under manifest subjection.

One could answer, I am sensible, that for fear of what I have just suggested, he will be demanded to give two of his sons as hostages, one of them his eldest, the love of whom must occasion him to set a higher value on them than on Burgundy. But I am afraid that this love of his children will rather have a contrary effect when their memory shall present itself to his mind, and he shall consider that by observing the agreement he lays a foundation for making them your slaves. I know not whether this pledge would be sufficient even if he should be deprived of all hopes of recovering them any other way. For it is a matter of too serious concern to endanger his kingdom, which once lost is very difficult to be recovered; but he might well hope to recover his sons with time, or by agreement, or on some other occasion, and the delay will be less troublesome on account of their tender age. But having found means to bring almost all the Christian princes to unite with him against you, who doubts but he will enter into close confederacy with them, and seek to moderate the agreement by force of arms, and that the fruits we shall reap from the victory will be a very vigorous and dangerous war, excited by hatred, necessity and desperation, from the King of England, King of France, and all Italy? From all which we should be able to defend ourselves, would it please God not to slacken his hand in working for us every day those miracles that he has so often wrought for us until the present time, and if fortune should change her nature in our behalf, and her inconstancy and mutability should become towards us an example of stability and constancy, contrary to all the examples of past events.

We have in all our counsels, for so many months together, concluded that we are to use our utmost endeavours that the Italians might not join with the government of France; and now we precipitate ourselves into a resolution that removes all the difficulties that have hitherto kept them in suspense, that multiplies our dangers and the forces of the enemies. For who knows not how much more potent a league will be which shall have for its head the King of France, than one made with the government of France while the King remains your prisoner? Who knows not that no cause has hitherto held the Pope from confederating against you, but the fear that you may separate the French from your enemies by offering them their king? Which the Pope and the others will fear less, when we shall have his children and not him. Thus the remedy that we provide for avoiding the danger will, without comparison, increase it, and instead of breaking that union, we shall ourselves be the instruments of rendering it more firm and powerful.

It will be said to me: what is then your opinion? Is it your advice that we reap no profit from so great a victory? Are we to remain continually is this state of perplexity? I confirm what I have often said, that it is very pernicious to take in more food at one time than the stomach is able to digest, and that it is necessary for us to regain the friendship of Italy, which demands nothing but its security, and to endeavour to obtain of the French king Burgundy, with whatever else shall be possible for us; or otherwise to make an agreement with him by which Italy shall be left at our discretion, but so mild and moderate with regard to his interests that he may have reason to observe it. And in making a choice between these two ways it is requisite, Caesar, that your prudence and goodness should prefer what is stable and juster to that which at first sight may perhaps appear more profitable and grand. The state of Milan, I confess, is richer, and more convenient on many accounts than that of Burgundy, and there is no friendship to be contracted with the Italians but by leaving Milan in the hands of Francesco Sforza[7] or of some other who shall content the Pope.[8] And yet I much prefer taking this course to an agreement with the French, because Burgundy is more yours in justice than Milan, and easier to keep than the other, where you have not a single person that is well affected to you. To attempt the restoration of Burgundy, your ancient inheritance, is highly commendable; to aspire after Milan, for either yourself or one who shall wholly depend on you, somehow exposes you to the public accusation of ambition. The first is required of you by the memory of so many glorious progenitors of yours, whose bones interred in captivity cry for nothing but to be delivered and restored by you – and their so just, pious and holy prayers are perhaps the cause of rendering God the more propitious to you. It is a more prudent as well as more feasible resolution to seek to establish a friendship with one who unwillingly becomes an enemy than with him who cannot possibly at any time be your friend. For the King of France will never harbour any other than hatred and the desire to oppose your designs; but the Pope and the other powers of Italy, as soon as [your] army is removed from Lombardy, being secured from their apprehensions, will have no occasion to contend with you from either fear or emulation, but remaining friends with you, you will now and always enjoy the convenience and profit of their good correspondence.

You are invited therefore to choose that friendship by honour, utility and security, and, if I deceive not myself, no less by necessity. For, even supposing that you should make an agreement with the King on no other obligation than of assisting you in your enterprise on Italy, it does not appear to me probable that he will fulfil it, because he will imagine that his leaving Italy to be your prey will too much endanger his own kingdom. And, on the other hand, he will appear to himself to have vast opportunities and hopes, by means of so potent an union, to create you much trouble and uneasiness, and to reduce you to an agreement on less burdensome conditions. Thus of a king prisoner we shall make him free, and our enemy, and shall give a head to the Kingdom of France, so that, in conjunction with so many others, he may make war upon you with more forces and more authority. How much better is it to agree with the Italians, to enter into a firm and sincere alliance with the Pontiff, who has continually desired it, and to deprive the French of all hopes of a conjunction with them! For in such a case, not necessity, nor the fear of new leagues, but your own will and the quality of the conditions will draw you to an agreement with the French; then you will see that want and despair will force them not only to restore Burgundy and to make you greater offers, but also to put into your hands such security as shall leave no room to fear for the performance of their engagements. Since the children are not sufficient to secure you while the French can feed themselves with hopes of so considerable a conjunction, and if they were to make an addition of Bayonne, Narbonne and their fleet, it would hardly be enough to warrant their observance. In this manner, you will reap great, honourable, just and secure fruits from your victory; otherwise, either I have no understanding at all in any affair, or this agreement will so endanger your state that I know not what will secure it if the imprudence of the King of France proves no greater than ours. —

The Great Chancellor by this vehement and accurate speech, and by the reputation of his wisdom, had persuaded and drawn to his side a great part of the council, when the Viceroy,[9] who was the author of the contrary opinion, spoke, as it is said, in the following manner:

— The man who, most glorious Caesar, out of a desire of having too much, aims at grasping more than he can hold is by no means to be commended; but then he is no less to be blamed who, from an excessive suspicion and distrust, voluntarily deprives himself of vast opportunities, acquired with a multitude of difficulties and dangers. Both errors are indeed very considerable; but a fault that proceeds from a timidity and meanness of spirit is more inexcusable in so great a prince than that which arises from a certain generosity and greatness of mind; and it is more laudable to seek with danger the acquisition of too much than, for the sake of avoiding danger, to let slip and vanish the rarest opportunities that a man is blessed with.

Now this is in effect the counsel of the Great Chancellor, who doubting that this agreement will not procure both Burgundy and Milan (for we are by no means to suspect that he is under the influence of a love of Italy, his country, or the benevolence he bears to the Duke of Milan) proposes a way by which, according to him, you gain Burgundy and lose Milan, a state without comparison of the greater importance, but, according to me, by which you lose Milan without gaining Burgundy. And thus, where this victory has most gloriously opened you a way to the lordship of all Christendom, there will remain nothing for us, if we follow his advice, but loss and disgrace. And indeed I see no security at all in his counsel, but rather very great danger attended with very small advantage – which besides may easily slip out of our hands – full of infamy and shame. But, on the contrary, an agreement with the King of France appears to me attended with very great glory, very great advantage and sufficient security.

For I would ask you, Chancellor, what reason have you, what assurance, what promise, that the Italians, after we shall have evacuated the Duchy of Milan, will take care not to violate the agreement, nor intermeddle between the King of France and us? And not rather that, after they shall have debased our reputation, after they shall have made us disband the army, which is a bridle on their malice, after they shall be secured from the coming of new bodies of Germans into Italy – because there will be no place in Lombardy to receive them, nor where they can shelter themselves – what security, I say, have you that the Italians, at such time, continuing their designs, by threatening the Kingdom of Naples,[10] which will remain in a manner at their discretion, will not try and force us to set the King of France free? Have you any trust, Chancellor, in the gratitude of Francesco Sforza, who, after so many benefits, has requited you, Caesar, with such base treachery? What will he not do now, when he has been made sensible that you desire to punish so heinous a piece of iniquity with justice, now that he fears your punishment and expects safety from your enemies? Have you any confidence, Chancellor, in the friendship of the Venetians, who are born enemies to the Empire and the House of Austria, and tremble, Caesar, at remembering that as it were but yesterday your grandfather Maximilian [I] bereaved them of many of those towns that they now possess?[11] Have you any faith, Chancellor, in the goodness of [Pope] Clement [VII], or in his inclination to the Emperor? The motive of [Pope] Leo [X]'s alliance with Caesar, after attempting many things against us, was a desire for taking revenge on the French and securing himself from them as well as his ambition to seize Ferrara.[12] After Leo's death, this man, Cardinal, hated by half the world, remained our friend out of necessity; but after he was made pope, immediately returning to the natural inclination of the pontiffs, which is to fear and hate the emperors, he has nothing in more detestation than the name of Caesar.[13]

All these parties excuse themselves by pretending that their machinations proceeded not from hatred or any other passion, but only from the fear of your power, which ceasing, all their designs will cease too. Either this is not true, or, although it might perhaps have been true in the beginning, it is necessary that it must have since taken other roots and become a different attitude. For it is natural for fear to be followed by hatred, for hatred to be followed by injuries, for injuries to be followed by a conjunction and intimacy with the enemies of the injured, together with both designs not only of being secured from him but also of profiting by his ruin, and the memory of injuries, which is greater without doubt, and more implacable, in him who does, than in him who receives, them. Therefore, even if we presume that in the beginning fear alone was that which incited them, the same fear must have occasioned them to become your enemies, to divert their inclinations and place their hopes on the French side, and then to begin, in all the conventions that they have negotiated, to divide the Kingdom of Naples among themselves. And now, whatever security we give them, or whatever agreement we make with them, hatred and fear will always remain kindled in their breasts; and far from relying in what they imagine extorted from you by necessity, but thinking they may with the greater facility bend us to a compliance with their will, apprehensive also that at last there might be an agreement between us and the King of France like to that made at Cambrai,[14] and desirous – to use their own words – of freeing Italy from the barbarians, they will have the boldness to think of prescribing laws to you, to demand the deliverance of the King of France. If you should deny their demand, Caesar, how will you defend the Kingdom of Naples against them? If you should grant it, once you will have lost all the fruits of the victory, you will remain the most dishonoured, the most debased prince that ever was.

But let us assume that Italy were disposed to observe the agreement and that you were under the necessity either of relinquishing Milan, or of not recovering Burgundy: what comparison is there between one side and the other? Burgundy is a little province, of small revenues, and besides not of such great convenience as many persuade themselves. The Duchy of Milan, for the riches and beauty of so many cities, for the number and quality of its subjects, for the greatness of its revenues, for its capacity of subsisting all the armies in the world, is superior to many kingdoms. But, although it be so large and so powerful, yet the opportunities that arise from its acquisition are more to be valued than the country in itself considered: for while Milan and Naples are at your devotion, the pontiffs must of necessity, as they used formerly, depend on the emperors; all Tuscany, the Duke of Ferrara[15] and the Marquis of Mantua[16] will be subjected to you; the Venetians, surrounded from Lombardy and Germany, will be necessitated to accept your laws. Thus, I do not say with arms or with armies, but with the reputation of your name, with a herald alone, with the imperial ensigns you will command all Italy. And who knows not what is Italy? For the commodiousness of its location, for the temperateness of the air, for the multitude and ingenuity of its inhabitants, who are extremely well suited for all honourable undertakings, for the abundance of all things convenient for human life, for the largeness and beauty of so many most noble cities, for riches, for the seat of religion, for the ancient glory of the Empire, and for infinite other respects, Italy is the queen of all countries, which if you command, all other princes will tremble before you. To compass this design becomes more your greatness and your glory, and is more grateful to the bones of your ancestors, since they too must be called into council; and they, on account of their goodness and devotion, must be supposed to desire nothing but what is most convenient for you, and most glorious to your name.

If we follow then the counsel of the Chancellor, we shall lose a very large acquisition for a small and very uncertain one, of which we ought to take warning by what was about to happen some months past. Do we not remember when the King of France was in such great danger of death, in what an uneasy situation we were, as knowing that by his death we should lose all the fruits expected from the victory? Who can secure us that the same accident may not possibly intervene at present? And more easily, because the remnants of the disease have remained upon him, and because, the hopes that have hitherto supported him being cut off, his griefs, which were the cause of his disorder, will return upon him with greater violence; and especially when, in debating on inextricable conditions and assurances, the new negotiations must be spun out to some length, which will be subject to the same accident, and perhaps to others as great and no less unlikely. Do we not know that nothing has so much conduced to keep the government of France in due order and steadiness as the expectation of a speedy releasement of the King? By which, the greatest French noblemen have been kept in quietness and obedience to his mother;[17] as soon as this hope should fail, that Kingdom would easily be sensible of it and the government would be altered. And once the nobles have got the bridle in hand, they will take no care of the King's liberty, but will rather be pleased with his captivity, for the sake of maintaining themselves independent and absolute lords. Thus instead of Burgundy and of such a multitude of acquisitions, we shall no longer have anything to expect from either his imprisonment or releasement.

But I would ask you farther, Chancellor: is Caesar in this resolution to have any regard to his dignity and majesty? Now, what greater disgrace can he incur, what more remarkable diminution of his honour, than to be constrained to pardon Francesco Sforza? Than that a man who has one foot in the grave, your rebel, a singular example of ingratitude, not by humbling himself and seeking refuge in your mercy, but by throwing himself into the arms of your enemies, should force you to yield to him, to restore the state so justly taken from him, and to receive laws from him? It is better, Caesar, and more suitable to the dignity of the Empire and to your own greatness, to trust once more to fortune, and again to hazard everything than, forgetting your rank, the authority of a prince supreme above all other princes, and the Caesarean name, so many times victorious over a most potent king, to accept, from priests and merchants, conditions of such a nature that more grievous and more unworthy could not have been imposed had you been conquered.

Therefore, on considering all these reasons, and how small the advantage is that can possibly result from an agreement with the Italians, and by how many accidents it may easily slip out of our hands, and how unsafe it is to repose confidence in them, and how full of indignity to abandon the state of Milan, and that it is necessary for us to come to a resolution and to have for once some consideration of our purposes, and that the imprisonment of the King is of no advantage to us but only on account of the gains that may be drawn from his freedom, I have advised, and do advise, that an agreement be made with him rather than the Italians; which none can deny to be more glorious, more reasonable and more useful, provided we can secure ourselves of his observance (and of this I have some grounds for hope) and gratitude, for the benefit he will receive from you, and of the tie of affinity and the virtues of your sister[18] – a fit instrument for maintaining this friendship – but much more of the pledge of the two sons, one of them the first born, than which neither greater nor more valuable to him a pledge we can possibly receive.

And since necessity constrains us to come to some resolution, we ought surely to put more confidence in a king of France, with so great a pledge, than in the Italians, with no pledge at all, in the faith and the word of so great a king than in the immoderate covetousness of priests or the suspicious baseness of merchants; and we may with more ease contract, as our ancestors have often done, an alliance for some time with the French than with the Italians, our natural and eternal enemies. Nor do I only see in this way of proceeding greater hopes that faith will be kept with us, but also less danger, in case of any infringement. For, even if the King should not yield you up Burgundy, he will not dare, while his children remain as hostages, to inflict any further injuries on you, but will seek to moderate the agreement by negotiations and entreaties.[19] Not to mention that, as he was in a manner but yesterday overcome, and today let out of prison, he will stand in awe of your arms, and never have the boldness to make another trial of your fortune. And if he does not take up arms against you, Caesar, it is certain that all the rest will stand still, so that you will acquire the castle of Milan and establish yourself in that state in such a manner that you shall no longer have anything to fear from the malice of any person whatsoever. But as for the Italians, if you should now make an agreement with them, and they should have a mind to break it, there will be no bridle capable of restraining them; and as their power of doing you injuries increases, their will to do them will be free, and increase in proportion. Therefore, in my opinion, it would be the highest timidity and imprudence to lose, out of excessive suspicion, an opportunity of making an agreement attended with so much glory, with so much greatness, and with sufficient security, and in its stead to take a resolution most dangerous, if I mistake not, and most pernicious. —

Notes

1. Charles V of Habsburg, King of Spain from 1516 to 1556 and Holy Roman Emperor from 1519 to 1556.
2. Mercurino Arborio, Marquis of Gattinara (1465–1530). Guicciardini introduces him as 'a man who, though born of low parentage in Piedmont, was yet of great credit and experience, and had for several years the management of the important business of that Court'.
3. At the Battle of Pavia, of course.
4. Francis I of Valois, King of France from 1515 to 1547.
5. Henry VIII Tudor, King of England from 1509 to 1547.
6. 'For the King of France, extremely mortified at Caesar's refusing to afford him his presence when he requested it, took it so much to heart that he fell into a disorder while he was in the castle of Madrid, which reduced him

to such extremity, that the physicians appointed to attend him signified to Caesar that there were no hopes of his recovery if he himself did not come in person to comfort him, and give him hopes of his liberty [. . .]. The visitation was but short, because the most Christian King lay, in a manner, at the point of death, but full of kind words, and certain assurances of releasement immediately upon recovery. And, whatever was the cause, whether the consolation which he received, or that youth was of itself superior to the nature of the disorder, he began after this visit to find such relief, that in a few days he was out of danger, though he was but slow in recovering his former health' (*The History of Italy*, XVI, ix).

7. Francesco II Sforza, Duke of Milan from 1521 to 1535.

8. Giulio de' Medici, pope as Clement VII from 1523 to 1535.

9. Charles de Lannoy, Viceroy of Naples (c. 1487–1527): 'The Viceroy, who had conducted the most Christian King into Spain, and had given him such great hopes, and so ardently solicited his deliverance, more earnestly insisted on it than ever; and his authority, with regard at least to his fidelity and good will, had great weight with Caesar.'

10. Taken by Ferdinand II of Aragon in 1504, the Kingdom of Naples was a dominion of the Spanish crown. The scheme set up by Girolamo Morone contemplated that the Italians – supported by the French – would expel Charles not only from Milan but also from Naples (see the introduction to the previous debate).

11. Maximilian I, Holy Roman Emperor from 1493 to 1519, was a member of the League of Cambrai, which defeated the Venetians in 1509.

12. Giovanni de' Medici, pope as Leo X from 1513 to 1521, made an anti-French alliance with the Emperor in May 1521.

13. For more details, see the introduction to the previous debate.

14. League of Cambrai, 10 December 1508.

15. Alfonso I d'Este, Duke of Ferrara from 1505 to 1534.

16. Federico II Gonzaga, Marquis (and then Duke) of Mantua from 1519 to 1540.

17. Louise of Savoy (1476–1531) was then the Regentess of France.

18. Eleanor of Austria (1498–1558). She would marry Francis I in 1530.

19. As it turned out, the two children remained in Charles's hands for four years, until 1530. This did not prevent Francis from adhering to the League of Cognac and taking up arms against the Emperor again, especially after the 1527 sack of Rome.

Name index

Pontiffs are listed under their papal name, monarchs and female figures under their first name.

Subject index

EU representative:
Easy Access System Europe
Mustamäe tee 50, 10621 Tallinn, Estonia
Gpsr.requests@easproject.com